THE CONTENDERS

THE CONTENDERS

WHO WILL LEAD INDIA TOMORROW?

Priya Sahgal

**SIMON &
SCHUSTER**

London · New York · Sydney · Toronto · New Delhi

A CBS COMPANY

First published in India by Simon & Schuster India, 2018
A CBS company

Copyright © Priya Sahgal, 2018

1 3 5 7 9 10 8 6 4 2

Simon & Schuster India
818, Indraprakash Building,
21, Barakhamba Road,
New Delhi 110001

www.simonandschuster.co.in

Paperback ISBN: 978-93-86797-24-7
eBook ISBN: 978-93-86797-25-4

Illustrations by Deepak Suryavanshi

Typeset in India by SÜRYA, New Delhi

Printed and bound in India by Replika Press Pvt. Ltd.

Simon & Schuster India is committed to sourcing paper that is
made from wood grown in sustainable forests and
support the Forest Stewardship Council, the leading
international forest certification organisation.
Our books displaying the FSC logo are
printed on FSC certified paper.

For Samir Singh, who has no contender

CONTENTS

FOREWORD

Youth is a relative concept in Indian politics. Many of today's 'young' politicians are actually older than, say, David Cameron was when he stepped down as prime minister of UK. And yet we regard them as the generation of tomorrow, as India's future leaders.

Perhaps it has something to do with the circumstances that prevailed when India won independence in 1947. The leaders of the newly free nation were people who had led the struggle for liberation from the British. Because it had been a long, hard battle, they were already quite old or at the very least, middle-aged, by the time they took office in the first government of free India.

Take Jawaharlal Nehru, for example. He returned to India after a British education (Harrow and Cambridge) and soon abandoned his life of privilege to throw himself into the freedom struggle. By the time the British left, Nehru was no longer a young man. When he became prime minister in 1947, he was already nearly 58 years old. And by the time he died in 1964, he was 75.

The Nehru generation and the one that came immediately after it, were around for so long that Indians came to expect leaders to be elderly people who could brag about their experiences. For instance, when Charan Singh finally became prime minister in 1979, he was already 77 years old. His predecessor Morarji Desai had been 81 when he assumed office.

In any other country, the age of prime ministers and potential prime ministers would be an issue. When Ronald Reagan became president of the US in 1981, he was nearly 70 and people wondered if he was too old. When he ran for a second term at the age of 74, his age became one of the campaign's more significant issues to the extent that Reagan had to use a Presidency debate to deflect the controversy.

Even now, Donald Trump, the oldest man to become American president since Ronald Reagan (Trump was already 70 when he assumed office), faces suggestions that perhaps dementia has set in. In contrast, Bill Clinton was 46 years old when he became president; Obama was 47.

There is nothing necessarily wrong with politicians of a certain age (at 68, Narendra Modi is regarded as the youthful leader of a new generation of BJP politicians), but few can deny that there is a mismatch between the age-driven perspective of India's elderly politicians and those they govern.

Put bluntly, India is a country of the young, ruled by the old and the very old.

Something like 50 per cent of India's population is in its twenties. And 65 per cent of the population is under 35. Yet, you will search in vain for a single minister who is under 35 in most Indian cabinets.

Could this be changing?

There are signs that it already is. Till now, Indians have taken the line that older people are necessarily wiser. But bitter experience may have taught the new generation that electing older politicians only leads to a repeat of the mistakes of the past.

Certainly, there is a new generation of politicians out there who are now ready to take control of India's destiny. Most, if not all, entered politics when they were in their twenties and now have a fairly good idea of what they want to achieve and how to go about it.

It helps—at least in the sense that they understand the political system—that many were born into political families and know how to pull the levers of power. As the profiles in this book show, many of them have clearly developed goals and objectives. They know what they want to do and are impatient for a chance to transform Indian politics.

There is, of course, the one overwhelming objection to this generation. Too many of them are dynasts. And some of them are politicians who are ready to inherit their parents' constituencies and support bases.

It is a valid objection, though, if you read the profiles closely, you will see that the proportion who had their careers already mapped out for them is smaller than we realize. Many entered politics without any guarantees of success and have had to struggle at every election.

I suspect that Indian politics in this generation is less about dynasty and more about the emergence of a political class, something like modern Kshatriyas. Most Indians are intimidated by what they perceive as the filth of our political system and frustrated by the barriers to entry. Only those who have grown up within the system are comfortable with politics as a career.

At some stage—sooner, I think, rather than later—this generation will take charge. I don't see how these younger politicians could do a worse job than the generation that preceded them.

So that's not the concern. The real test will be whether they can create a more open system, break the hold of the political caste they come from and allow those who are not born into politics to enter the system.

Priya Sahgal is one of India's most experienced political journalists. Over the last decade she has followed the careers of the next generation of India's political leaders.

This well-researched, insightful and engaging book offers us the best guide possible to the India of the future and to the men and women who will guide the fortunes of this country.

At least one of the people profiled in this book will be prime minister one day.

VIR SANGHVI

where I'd left off a few years ago, I went to meet the sapling that had since branched out on his own, walking away with his father's party from under the older Yadav's rather prominent nose. I travelled to Lucknow from Delhi by car and took the famous Agra-Lucknow toll road. An environmental engineering graduate, Akhilesh had supervised this 326 km long expressway from conception to completion. When I congratulated him on the state-of-the-art project, he beamed proudly and said '*Yeh expressway ke saath-saath growth ka rasta hai*' (This is not only an expressway but also the road to growth). He then asked, 'Did you notice that the toll booths are shaped like A and Y?' Then added with a slight smile, 'It had stood for Akhilesh Yadav then and guess now it works for Adityanath Yogi too.' But he said this without any rancor, accepting the toll of politics with a shrug.

The norms they follow are more public school than old school. Rahul Gandhi makes it a point to end every speech with a 'Thank you for listening to me'. And while Mulayam Singh Yadav takes a 'boys will be boys' attitude to the 1995 Guest House incident where Mayawati was threatened by SP goons, his son is quick to set the record straight on any allegations of foul play. When accused by the Yogi government of having wrecked his official accommodation, a visibly hurt Akhilesh, who sees himself as a creator rather than a destroyer, spent over an hour explaining to the media how an act like this went against his very ethos. Similarly, Lalu's son Tejashwi Yadav is very wound up about being named along with his father in a corruption case, telling me rather earnestly that had he the propensity to be corrupt, he had enough opportunity as deputy CM, but there is not one allegation against him. Omar Abdullah resigned as CM at the whiff of a scandal and had to be placated by his father to be more pragmatic and less sensitive. Harsimrat Badal, the firebrand from Punjab, has often questioned the way politicians are portrayed saying, 'Our children hate politicians. They only read about the terrible things politicians do. But there are good and there are bad politicians. We have to pass an exam every five years, but our good work never gets much publicity.'

Public perception was not something the older generation spent too much time worrying about but it does worry the new age netas, which is a good sign. In fact, when I reached out to them for this book, most agreed to meet me for a conversation that would cut through the noise of television debates. The intent of this project is simple: within these pages, there is a future prime minister, a couple of chief ministers, several cabinet ministers, at least two or three backroom strategists, and one not-so-reluctant fundamentalist. Whether in government or opposition, they will be a part of the leadership structure in tomorrow's India; so the idea is to get to know them, their individual quirks and beliefs that go beyond party stands. Also, to take a look as to how they pitch their modern, mostly international, education within the caste and religion dominated vote banks of India.

Interestingly, they are all taking centre-stage at a time of great churn in political India. In the last five years the axis of politics has shifted from the Congress to the BJP. More than the party, it is one individual that holds sway. Today's Turks have to challenge the 68-year-old prime minister, Narendra Modi, if they want to consolidate their fiefdoms. Logically, as the only other pan-India party, the pivot of Opposition unity should be the Congress. But, with Rahul Gandhi having wasted over a decade in apprenticeship, he doesn't inspire much confidence in other 'secular' allies, as yet. So, once again we see the rise of regional forces as a national alternative. The first time this happened was ironically in reaction to the one-party domination of the Congress, when the Janata Party came to power, with the Bharatiya Jan Sangh—which later became the BJP—support (1977–1979). Over time we have seen the National Front (1989–1991) and the United Front (1996–1998) governments that enjoyed a brief sojourn of power. The NDA and UPA governments that followed have also had regional players in the coalition, but these have been led either by the BJP or the Congress. However, currently the Congress is in no position to take the lead against the Modi-led BJP. This leaves the space wide open for a regional player to step in.

Between the last Lok Sabha and now, there has been a generational change of guard in most political parties. In the last few years, from the north to the south, a baton has been passed on as Rajiv and Sonia Gandhi's son Rahul, Mulayam Singh Yadav's son Akhilesh, Lalu Yadav's son Tejashwi, Farooq Abdullah's son Omar, Parkash Singh Badal's son and daughter-in-law Sukhbir and Harsimrat, Chaudhary Charan Singh's grandson Jayant, M. Karunanidhi's son Stalin and daughter Kanimozhi, all take charge of their legacy. Even Nitish Kumar has appointed a GenNext though a non-dynast, 41-year-old election strategist Prashant Kishor, as his heir apparent. Their coming of age has coincided with the 2019 general elections, and how they play their cards right now will define their future politics. Will their youth appeal to an aspirational India with about 64.4 per cent of its total population between the ages of 15 and 59 years (Sample Registration Survey of India, 2015)? India has the largest youth population in the world and this will be the first time that most outfits, except the BJP, will reflect this demographic in their leadership.

With Modi as the all-too-towering figure on India's political landscape it is but inevitable that the narrative of the day is centred around him; either you are with or against this weapon of mass disruption, who has disrupted politics as usual from its comfort zone. Those who are with him, find it difficult not to be subsumed by his politics. Barely a handful, some of whom are featured in these pages, have managed to retain their USP in a Modi-fied India.

Sometimes it's not institutional legacy but individual chutzpah that plays a role. From the other camp, it is Akhilesh who has taken the first pragmatic step in building an anti-Modi platform. Overriding his legacy of antagonism with the BSP chief, he reached out to his father's bête noire, Mayawati for an alliance that gave the BJP its first poll shock in the run up to the 2019 elections, in the Gorakhpur and Phulpur by-polls (March 2018). Two months later, he repeated this with a tie-up with another of his father's former colleagues, Ajit Singh's son, Jayant Chaudhary, to wrest two more seats from the BJP. It should have been Rahul and not Akhilesh who spearheaded this initiative in forming an alliance against the BJP. However, of late, I do sense a certain wariness in Akhilesh's dealings with Rahul that was not there a year ago when the two UP Ke Ladke tied up to take on the BJP, with disastrous results. There's something more to it than the numbers not adding up. Perhaps it's the Big Brother attitude of the Congress that rankles. Akhilesh, told me once in the middle of the 2017 UP state elections' campaign: 'I know Rahul is a national leader, but in UP I am the bigger party so I am the big brother in the alliance.' And perhaps, it's more than that. For his part, Rahul has not encouraged the SP's overtures of seat sharing outside Uttar Pradesh, thereby curbing Akhilesh's plans to take his party national. I am sure deep down the two sense that the last big fight will not be against Mayawati or Modi but against each other—and not just for the cow belt, but for the entire country.

Others such as Omar and Jayant—maybe it's because they have lesser stakes—are more indulgent towards Rahul's leadership credentials. As Omar says, 'If anyone is going to take the fight to the BJP it has to be the Congress. It's the only one with a pan-India presence. The rest of us will fight the BJP in our own small corner. We will not go beyond that.' But it's a corner they all guard zealously. Even the baby of the pack, chubby-cheeked Tejashwi Yadav, is no pushover. With an endearing enthusiasm he calls everyone else 'Boss' and has even cajoled the reticent Rahul to take him out for lunch at a South Delhi café, but when it comes to seat sharing he is more resolute than Akhilesh. 'The seats will be divided between us and the Congress on winnability,' he says firmly. (Akhilesh had given Congress as many as 105 seats in the 2017 polls, way above the party's winnability quotient.)

To be fair to Rahul, the Opposition is not keen to project any leader against Modi for it has realized that to do so would be to fall into the BJP's trap. Despite all their potential and promise, no young or seasoned leader from the Opposition can match the BJP's star performer. 'It's better to fight him on issues,' says Tejashwi, while Jayant agrees saying, 'This is how we will cut them down to size. We will not talk personalities. It's not one personality taking them on; in UP you have me, Akhilesh and Mayawati. If all of us come together and say the same thing, then it's a strategy of encirclement.'

Interestingly, Kanimozhi, Omar and Jayant have done business with the BJP before—their respective dads have been in alliances with Vajpayee. But all are firm about one thing—that they will never be a part of Modi's BJP. Omar, because of the 2002 riots (to date his greatest regret is that he didn't push his resignation firmly enough when he was a minister in Vajpayee's cabinet at the time). Jayant, because he doesn't like the way the BJP exploited the Muslim vs Jaat riots in Muzaffarnagar in 2013. 'There is a lot of difference between the BJP led by Modi and Vajpayee's BJP,' says Kanimozhi, significantly.

Most featured here have inherited the leadership of their party. Some like Akhilesh, and to a much lesser extent Omar, have had to compete with their fathers for it. But, like it or not, 'This is the way India runs', as Rahul Gandhi said recently when asked to comment about India's dynastic democracy. Indian political dynasties also have a patriarchal tinge where the sons are given an edge over the daughters, from the RJD, DMK, TRS to the Congress, where Priyanka Gandhi Vadra, the charismatic heiress to her grandmother's legacy, operates behind the scenes rather than take centre-stage along with her brother. The background seems too dull a place for someone who is as instinctively political as she is, but the Sister Act depends on the way the brother performs at the electoral box office. This is also the way India runs.

There is a third Gandhi—Sanjay Gandhi's son and their 38-year-old cousin Varun—who decided against joining a Congress presided over by his aunt Sonia Gandhi, and signed up with the BJP. However, Varun has since realized that his very name represents all that Modi is railing against, politics of patronage and privilege. Having been sidelined in the BJP and with his cousin (rightfully) wary of his ambitions to facilitate a return to the Congress, this Gandhi scion finds himself in nowhere land. He is in the process of reinventing himself from a Muslim basher to a SNAG (sensitive new age) leader, addressing college seminars, publishing poems and writing well-crafted editorials; but he's really all dressed up with no party to go to. So, I have left his existential dilemma out of the pages of this book.

Not surprisingly all the non-dynasts in this book are from the BJP. In its early days, with Vajpayee and Advani at the helm, the BJP had promoted a strong second line of leadership. One of its products is the current prime minister of India, Narendra Modi. However, today with the Modi-Amit Shah duo firmly at the helm, the BJP is fast following the Congress model when it comes to stifling a second generation leadership. Despite this, I have zeroed in on a few names. In fact, Amit Shah fits the 'Below 55' age bracket of my book. But unlike the others, at age 52, he has clearly arrived at his destination. He is a leader of today and the boss of those whom I will be profiling in this collection. Then, you may argue, so is Rahul who by virtue of being the Congress president is a notch above the other Congressmen. However, there is a difference between the two. Rahul is still a work in progress, still in the process of building his team and putting his concepts of leadership in place.

Since both the Congress, and now the BJP, follow the same model of a highly centralized leadership, the second rung in both the national parties has less room to manoeuvre than their regional counterparts. The BJP leaders featured here have one thing in common—each has managed to carve his own niche that makes them stand apart from the assembly line of a rootless GenNext that is currently being promoted via the Rajya Sabha route. Uttar Pradesh CM, Yogi Adityanath, got his current job thanks to the Modi-Shah duo, but he is no establishment man and has his own sizeable vote bank. Then has Modi unleashed the genie with Yogi, for there are those who find similarities between the saffron monk and Modi's own growth trajectory? Quite tellingly, it is Ram Madhav, the pragmatic pracharak-turned-politician, who is the better evangelist of the saffron cause, delivering a cleverly crafted sermon in the language of New India, using social media, think tanks and seminar rooms as his podium. But that alone is not his USP. He has managed to craft several audacious state-level wins for the BJP using, 'Whatever means that are democratically possible.' Into this marketplace of democracy, walks in Himanta Biswa Sharma, with the chutzpah and a nuisance value that he could have only learnt from the Shah himself. Only Himanta is an export from the Congress. Soon after joining the BJP he proved himself indispensable in delivering the North East to the saffron fold. He is certainly too ambitious and too savvy a leader, to remain contained in a far corner, away from the mainstream. And while the flamboyant Anurag Thakur, one of the few political dynasts in the BJP, has been temporarily nipped in the bud, I am fairly confident that he lives to fight another day. His comeback will be an interesting one to watch.

One leader whom I have regretfully left out is the 48-year-old Dharmendra Pradhan. Handling the crucial petroleum portfolio in the Modi government, he is the face of its trophy scheme—Ujjwala —which gives subsidized gas cylinders to BPL families. In record time Pradhan has met Modi's target of giving connections to as many as five crore women, and the scheme has already proved a vote-catcher in various state elections. Pradhan's tale is one of earnest hard work, and he is certainly assured a place in any BJP cabinet of the future. When he was given the Petroleum portfolio in 2014 he told me quite candidly, 'I have no hesitation in candidly accepting that in the beginning my understanding of the ministry was *nahin ke barabar* [next to nothing]. However if the PM has had the confidence to entrust me with this, then I had the confidence to take it forward.' He certainly lived up to the said confidence. But what I miss in his story is—something I am sure Pradhan is quite happy to do without—the drama of a rise and fall that's present, in varying degrees, in the others. An interesting side note is that another his men and so limits his interactions to mostly one way video messages on social media. The one-way communication route is a leaf straight out of Modi's book but irony died a long time ago in agitational India. Another reason, told to me by unconfirmed sources but is too juicy not to mention, is that he didn't want to be part of an anthology of politicians. But I could not leave out the country's most argumentative chief minister from this collection. His politics of protest struck a chord with the people of Delhi for he managed to craft the most daring of comebacks in 2015 and seems poised for a hat-trick. It is interesting that while his plans to go national have failed so far, his marathon protests have acquired a national edge, making him a sought after figure within the Third Front.

Having covered the Congress, I have interacted with Rahul on several occasions; the latest being a meeting he had with women journalists on 'gender' issues which included the famous hug he gave Modi on the floor of the house. I have also written over a dozen cover stories on him for *India Today*, each marking his umpteenth makeover and re-launch. His latest coming seems to be the most credible for it has coincided with his taking over as the president of the Congress (December 2017). He still has a long way to go to be truly Gandhian (though he has some of the Mahatama's quotes on his desk), but he's pitting a politics of embrace and empathy, versus, what he claims is the ideology of anger and hate practiced by the RSS and BJP. The newly sainted Rahul is finding some resonance with middle class India that is desperately looking for an alternate narrative to mob lynching, demonetization and joblessness. But, as his own allies will be the first to tell you, it will take more than a hug to convince the voters that Rahul is the solution they are looking for.

Rahul's hug was followed by a wink to his colleagues on the Congress benches. He has been castigated more for the wink than the hug but the way I see it, it's the former that reveals some audacity and a little bit of wickedness that keeps you guessing. And, who knows better than Modi himself, the political dividends of being unpredictable. And as my friend Samir Singh, a keen political observer/armchair political analyst says, 'First it was Rahul and the Congress who made Modi a middle class hero, and now it looks as though Modi is trying to return the compliment.'

I still recall one of my initial one-on-one meetings with Rahul (sometime in 2007). Even back then there was pressure on him to play a more active role. He told me that he worked according to no one's timelines but his own. Rahul has certainly remained consistent to that line of thought. Impatient Congressmen may want him to be more aggressive and hungry for power, but he took his time to sip from the 'poisoned' chalice.

According to his key aides, he has a two-fold strategy in play. The short term plan is for 2019, which is to defeat Modi at whatever cost, even if it means being the lesser partner in state level alliances. His long term goal is for 2024 by when he hopes to establish himself as a credible prime ministerial face. The Congress is currently at its lowest tally ever, but Rahul has shortlisted 12 states, including Rajasthan, Madhya Pradesh, Haryana, Maharashtra and Gujarat which will help increase its numbers in the next Lok Sabha. If the Congress crosses the hundred mark, the short term plan works in giving the Congress a relevant role in any anti-BJP coalition. However, regarding 2024, Rahul may find that there is more than one contender with the same long term ambitions.

Rahul Gandhi's late start had a domino effect on his party's GenNext who have had to adjust their career graphs accordingly so that they don't outshine him. That, and the Gandhi-Nehru hold over the Congress, means that his peers can never aspire to be anything more than a Number 2 in a Rahul-led Congress. Yet, within these confines, both Jyotiraditya Scindia and Sachin Pilot have the potential to emerge as key players in India's governance story, regardless of what the outcome of the Madhya Pradesh and Rajasthan state elections will be. This gives them added heft but also brings in a certain competitive edge in their dealings with one another. Get them both on the same stage and you will know what I am talking about. There are no shared jokes between them as one would expect between two colleagues, each listens very carefully to what the other has to say and then makes his pitch. That's a turf war to watch out for, because even being the Number 2 in the country's oldest political party is a powerful platform. It's also a battle that they've inherited from their fathers, for both Madhavrao Scindia and Rajesh Pilot had an equally cautious outlook towards each other's ambitions. As a totally irrelevant but an interesting aside, let me add that my discerning young producer Richa Kapoor, who finds most political interviews a bit boring, informed me that while she enjoyed meeting both, one was more charming while the other was better looking! Guess being 'young' has its own perks.

Through Milind Deora, the fourth Congress leader, we get a glimpse of the urban middle class concerns that he is always so passionate about, one reason being that this is the dominant nature of his (former) constituency—South Mumbai. But these are concerns which resonate in an increasingly modernized new India. I also see him as a sort of equalizer for whenever the Congress goes on a populist bender—whether it is okaying a legislation to allow the tainted to contest or when reforms are held hostage by freebies—his is the first tweet of caution. But, as he told me one rainy afternoon in South Mumbai, the storm outside reflecting the conflict within, 'There are also some who do this [disagree] deliberately to rock the boat and to show that they are mavericks. However, I have no such qualms. Ninety per cent of the time I agree with my political party. But 10 per cent of the time when one does differ, one has every right to criticize constructively. That's my approach to public life.'

What the electorate expects from these leaders of tomorrow is a break from the cynical, opportunistic, at times pessimistic politics of the past. Most of these new age leaders have graduated from Harvard, Wharton or Cambridge, with degrees varying from environmental engineering, MBAs to development economics and then taken to public life. Yet, they haven't been able to break away from the old rules of engagement. One of the first questions I asked all of them is how they felt about resorting to the old politics of caste and religion despite all their modern qualifications. Initially they all tried a more progressive approach, but it didn't click in an India steeped too deep in its politics of mandir, masjid and Mandal. For instance, Rahul began his political campaign in UP in 2007 with an earnest declaration: 'I must confess, I am blind. Blind to caste and religion.' But later, in 2012, he introduced the technocrat Sam Pitroda to the same voter in eastern UP as a Vishwakarma (not as Sam Pitroda, the man who ushered in the computer age). Similarly, Akhilesh Yadav fought the 2017 campaign on the plank of *Kaam Bolta Hai*. After the loss he told me, 'The public did not hear me talk about development. They instead heard the BJP talk about *kabristan-shamshaanghat* [burial vs cremation grounds]. We did not have the emotional glue to keep our voters together.' He is hoping the right caste-based alliances will prove to be that emotional glue. 'It's not that we won't talk development but we do need the extra edge,' he adds a shade defensively.

Call it their collective failure or a commentary of the

times, but that extra edge is always steeped in religion, caste or populism over reforms. Down south, Kanimozhi remarks that she would never call giving away 1 kg rice for Re 1 a 'freebie' for she says that its only when the stomachs are full will the people be more open to issues such as children's education. Omar sums it up saying, 'Let me put it this way. Development from what I've seen is not really an election campaign on its own but you will be hammered for the absence of development. So, if I don't build roads, I'll take a hammering, but if I have built them, there's very little in terms of public reward for it. *Ban gaya so ban gaya*, people will say—*yeh toh aap ki zimmedaari thi. Aap ne kar lee. Iske baad aap kya karoge*? [Development is your responsibility. What else have you done for us?]'

For those wondering why I chose age 55 as the extended cut-off mark for being 'young', somehow, this seems apt for the Indian context. While a 43-year-old David Cameron became Britain's prime minister, a 47-year-old Barack Obama led America, Justin Trudeau became the PM of Canada at 44 years and Emmanuel Macron, the youngest president of France at 39 years; but the age trajectory seems to be moving backwards here. Jawaharlal Nehru became PM at 57 years, Lal Bahadur Shashtri at 59, Indira Gandhi was 48 years old while her son Rajiv became India's youngest prime minister at 40. After that the prime ministerial age hovered between the 60s and 70s, with I.K. Gujral, A.B. Vajpayee and Manmohan Singh assuming office as septuagenarians, while Narasimha Rao took oath exactly a week before his 70th birthday.

We are a country that honours its old, often at the cost of the young. When compared to global experience there is a Lost Decade in Indian politics where the coming of age is mid to late

40s, rarely earlier. As an aside, let me point out that even the famous band of Young Turks who challenged Indira Gandhi were men in their mid-40s and above. Hence, my shifting of the goalpost to include the chronologically middle-aged as the politically young.

However, it is never easy to chronicle a generation and find a one size label that fits all. Specially in the 21st century where the Romance of a Revolution is reduced to a Snapchat or a hashtag on Twitter. But there hovers on the horizon, a leadership that is just coming into its own and is defining its mettle. Its a mettle that they have to constantly keep redefining, as Rahul discovered during a rally in UP. Addressing a conference of Global Indians in Bahrain (January 2018), Rahul told them how he was once approached by a weeping woman to save her husband who had been arrested by the cops. When Rahul asked the local police to help her he was told that the husband was facing a murder charge. 'Did he murder someone?' asked Rahul. The woman nodded an affirmative. 'Then how can I help you?' he replied in amazement. This is the answer the young leader was given: '*Toh phir tum raj neta honeka kya faida*' (Of what good are you politicians if you can't help?).

Whether they deliver the impossible or uplift the possible, one hopes they'll keep Abraham Lincoln's words as a cornerstone of their leadership paradigm, for he had said once—whatever you are, be a good one.

RAHUL GANDHI

The Chosen One

What do you say about a political leader who is a perpetual work in progress? Rahul Gandhi's family name may come with its very own 'Employment Guarantee Scheme' but it has taken him nearly 14 years to stop living on dole and step up to the job at hand: that of leading the country's oldest political party. But the thing about Rahul is that, just when you are about to write him off, he gives you a 'contender' moment. And sometimes it happens between a hug and a wink.

As a journalist, I have covered every launch and then subsequent, re-launch of Brand Rahul ever since his debut as a first time MP in 2004; and written stories that went from Heir Apparent to Heir Not Apparent; from Rahul Rejuvenated to

Reluctant Rahul and back to Recalibrating Rahul. Hence you will understand my skepticism at his latest re-invention, even though it is by far the most consistent of them all. Perhaps it is because the makeover from a fidgety scion to assertive leader also coincided with his taking over as the Congress president in December 2017.

I still recall an earlier interaction with him. Sometime in 2007 I met him for an interview that did not take place. There was a miscommunication, for when he invited me for a chat I thought it was an on-record interview and arrived at his Tughlaq Lane residence only to be met by a Rahul dressed in track pants and rubber slippers. He explained that if he gave an interview to one publication, then he would either have to give an interview to everyone or antagonize the rest. (This strategy has changed since.) However, we managed a brief conversation where he explained that he was not going to assume any responsibility just because it was expected of him. He stuck to no one's timelines but his own. He would take charge only when he felt he was ready. Some would call this arrogance, others diffidence. In either case, it didn't make the leadership manual.

However, he has certainly come a long way from his Power is Poison moment (when he was made Congress vice president in 2013). He now seems ready to sip from the poisoned cup, stating candidly that should the Congress get the numbers ('depends on how the dice falls') he would be the party's prime ministerial face. Of course, his timing is way off, for just when the Congress Party is at its lowest he decides he wouldn't mind being prime minister after all. When it was offered to him during the UPA years, he not only refused prime ministership but also stayed well out of Dr Manmohan Singh's cabinet. This hesitation cost the party dearly. Rahul did not just lose a valuable opportunity to learn the ropes, but he also ensured that an entire rung of leadership of his peers could not come up either, for fear of propping up potential rivals.

As Rama Lakshmi, editor opinion at *The Print* points out, 'I call it the Lost Decade for the Congress. Ironically, this was the decade when the party was in power, but did not use it to groom the next generation leader. Instead of joining the UPA cabinet, Rahul went on a sort of listening tour. But while he was connecting with the forgotten Kalavatis, an ambitious Narendra Modi was blogging and tweeting the narrative of a vibrant Gujarat model.' As a result, as political scientist Shiv Visvanathan, puts it—'While Rahul has got a pan India image, he doesn't have a pan India impact.'

Given his track record of being an inconsistent leader, Congress allies showed little enthusiasm to the idea of Rahul being the Opposition's PM face against Modi. Realizing this, the Congress now talks about a two-pronged strategy. The short term plan for 2019 is to 'stoop to conquer and do whatever it takes' to defeat Modi. This includes the Congress 'facilitating' an alliance against the BJP, in which it will play the role of a supporting cast. The second goal is a long term one, for 2024, by which time Rahul Gandhi hopes to have established his own credibility to emerge as a viable prime ministerial contender.

The next few months are crucial for Rahul as this is his very last chance of establishing himself as a serious politician, for he's done one make-over too many. His biggest problem has been his lack of reliability, so he will have to use this time not just to redefine himself but also stick to the plan. In his latest coming, he is pitting a hug of inclusiveness and an ideology of love against what he sees as a pushback of fear, hatred and anger from the BJP. As he told the audience at Karan Thapar's book launch in the capital in July 2018, 'We will take on the BJP and fight them, and they will fight us, but we will not hate them.'

It's a view he has been formulating over the years, when he and his sister Priyanka forgave their father's killers. Interacting with some NRIs in Singapore a few months earlier, he had said, 'I remember when I saw Mr Prabhakaran (the chief of the LTTE, the organization which assassinated Rajiv Gandhi) on TV lying dead, I got two feelings—one was why are they humiliating this man in this way, and second was that I felt really bad for him and for his kids. I did that because I understood deeply what it meant to be on the other side of that thing. So to me,' Rahul added, 'when I see violence, regardless of who it is, I know that there is a human being behind that, there is a family behind that, a kid crying behind that.'

It's a strategy that will take some understanding. As a senior Congress functionary explained, Rahul sees the Congress as being a more feminine party than the BJP. He added, 'This is not feminine in the Western meaning of the word, but within a more philosophical context, whereby the Congress comes across as more liberal and sensitive than the masculine, toxic, 56 inches chest thumping BJP.' The Congress functionary added that Rahul believes in the union of Shiv-Shakti where the qualities of both genders work in tandem to create a universe that is sustainable and well-balanced.

These were some of the thoughts that led him across the aisles to hug the prime minister during a no confidence debate in Parliament in July 2018. Given the dominant narrative of mob lynching, trolling on social media and hate crimes, it is easy to see what Rahul is trying to achieve when he sets himself up as the morally correct antithesis to the perceived wrongs in Modi's BJP. 'The basic idea is this that if someone hates you, that is something that they are doing. Hate is their internal emotion, it is their reaction to the world. Responding to their hate with hate is quite foolish. It is not going to solve any problem,' said Rahul at the Bucerius Summer School in Hamburg (23 August 2018). He added, 'Gandhiji said the only way you can counter hate is through love. You can't counter hate with hate because it just increases the hate. When I actually went and showed affection to the prime minister, he was taken aback, he was upset by it. But it works, it really does.'

I do hope he has a better strategy up his sleeve than embarking on the career of a serial hugger. As he joked, 'Whenever I see BJP MPs they take two steps back thinking I may hug them. It is not such a bad thing.' But on a more serious note, he is in politics to win elections, not aspire for sainthood. It's not an NGO that Rahul is running but a political party and for that he needs to show the hunger for power, maybe even a streak of ruthlessness to go for the kill, which is why I prefer the wink he gave to his colleagues on the Congress benches, post the hug. It created the right amount of doubt as to his motives. Moreover, he has already played the part of the nice guy down to being labeled a simpleton; a little bit of strategic cunning will go a long way in establishing the optics of a fighter. Points out Rama Lakshmi, 'Finally Rahul seems to be enjoying his politics; he now appears to understand both the physicality and the morality of India's politics. His act doesn't look forced any longer.' But she adds, 'It shouldn't take a politician a decade to *emerge*. That's how long it takes for a politician to *mature*.'

Initially, after the 2014 Lok Sabha loss when the Congress was reduced to its lowest tally ever—of 44 MPs—Rahul had been missing in action, playing right into the BJP's hands. The right wing trolls had labeled him as a Pathetic Pappu—a sort of village idiot—and unfortunately Rahul did little to dispel this image, especially as the Congress went on to lose every state election it fought against the BJP (except Punjab). What made it worse was that Modi was not unbeatable, as Arvind Kejriwal and Nitish Kumar proved in the Delhi and Bihar assembly polls (2015) respectively. It was only when he was pitted against the Rahul-led Congress, that Modi became invincible. This led the BJP to quip that they had three star campaigners—Modi, Amit Shah and Rahul Gandhi.

Then suddenly something changed. Though it's usually difficult to pin-point the exact moment of transition, with Rahul we do have such a marker. It was in September 2017 when Rahul was at the University of California, Berkeley, in an interaction with some students. He spoke about foreign policy, domestic economy, and even picked up the hot potato of dynasty politics with a silver spoon and an unapologetic shrug, pointing out that 'all of India runs that way'. To everyone's surprise, especially the Congress, his interactions during the US tour got good press both there and back home. Other such engagements followed, with think tanks, university students and business leaders. The one general consensus that came out of these meetings was: He was not quite the *Pappu* he was made out to be. The Rahul who landed in India walked back with a much more confident stride.

Leadership is not political but contextual, a young man working in Rahul's office pointed out. He was right in a sense, for after four years the Modi rule had begun to wane in the face of an unpopular demonetization and a badly implemented GST. The rather fickle middle class was scouting around for another hero and Rahul Gandhi's candidature gained just a little bit, in context. He came across as 'the public school educated average nice guy'. On the eve of the 2019 polls, he is still no one's first choice, but given the options, there are those who could vote for him rather than a Mamata Bannerjee or a Mayawati.

Rahul blames his Pappu image on the vicious campaign

carried out by trolls employed by the BJP whose main job was to 'abuse' him. At the Berkeley interaction he claimed, 'There is a BJP machine ... about a thousand guys sitting on computers. They basically tell you things about me. They tell you I am reluctant, I am stupid; they tell you all these things. You have seen me now. You guys can make up your mind.'

I don't know when he realized it but he'd hit the nail with the last sentence. He is as much to blame for his image trap, as are the trolls. In the earlier days, it was the Gandhi mystique with its impermeable aura that captivated the public. From Nehru to Rajiv and Sonia—'the Family' came with a pedigree of privilege that held its brand appeal in a feudal polity. But now in the age of transparency and ball-by-ball engagement, in the era of social media and 24x7 television, the pedigreed mystique has a reverse effect ; by shying away, it looks as if you have something to hide. So, the most crucial component of his make-over has been the demystification of Rahul Gandhi. By activating his social media profile, changing his Twitter handle from the aloof @OfficeOfRG to the more accessible @RahulGandhi he has broken down the wall between him and the public at large. Instead of an abstract entitled dynast, we are getting to meet the real Rahul, who has a wry sense of humor, who can take potshots at his opponent without getting abusive, and above all, whose view on the political events of the moment goes beyond women reservations, rural employment guarantee schemes and RTI. (Reference being to a particularly disastrous TV interview he gave on the eve of the 2014 polls.)

To counter the trolls, he's smart enough to play it droll. Take for instance, his reaction when a young journalist complained that whenever she tweeted something in favour of the Congress the trolls on social media attacked her, calling her Piddi. The reference was to Rahul's Jack Russell Terrier who has acquired a social media presence of his own after Rahul posted a video of his with a tongue-in-cheek comment that it was Piddi who wrote all his tweets since the trolls thought he was too dumb to write them himself. 'But Piddi is a very charming fellow, he is very intelligent and he also tweets,' replied Rahul with a delighted laugh.

One could argue that all this is merely the fluff, but, in politics the packaging is half the battle. What is interesting is that the BJP has since stopped referring to him as Pappu and has appointed a quick response team of senior cabinet ministers to counter Rahul. Despite this, Rahul's biggest challenge is from within. The onus is on him to prove that he is no paper tiger, that the guy on Twitter is the real deal. This is not going to be easy. Despite his 14 years as an MP, he has no backstory to define him. Unlike Modi, and the various other contenders for the PM's job, there is no Rahul Model. He has never been a union minister or a chief minister; his constituency doesn't boast of any major development project that reflects well on its third term MP, and whatever party post he has held so far, has been inherited not earned. He may have thrown his hat into the prime ministerial ring but to his allies and opponents alike, he still remains the untested and untried. And in politics, that's not a very bankable commodity.

It was Sonia Gandhi who decided that it would be her son Rahul and not his more politically inclined sister, Priyanka, who would take over the family business of running the Congress, and pulled him out of his corporate job in London once she had re-established the family hold over the party. After Rajiv Gandhi's assassination in 1991 the party slipped out of the hands of the Nehru-Gandhis for a brief period of seven years until Sonia took

over as party president in March 1998. In choosing a political
heir from the family, Sonia revived an old Congress tradition of
the father-daughter and mother-son combination in the party's
history: from Nehru and Indira, Indira and Sanjay, followed
by Indira and Rajiv to Sonia and Rahul. The family has always
had two members in active politics with the dynastic interns
breaking into the mainstream in their mid-30s and early 40s.
Indira became president of the party at age 42; Sanjay became
an MP from Amethi at 34 and Rajiv joined the party at 37. At
33, Rahul's entry was perfectly timed (born 19 June 1970).

And so, just as Indira had begun to groom her son Rajiv while
she was still in the saddle, Sonia began Rahul's apprenticeship
while she still held sway. But Rahul proved to be more stubborn
than his father. In an interview to *India Today*, Rajiv had said
then that he was joining politics 'to help Mummy' ('The way I
look at it is mummy has to be helped somehow': August 1980).

Like his father, Rahul too may have signed up for dynastic
duty but he was going about it in his own way. He sure confused
the hell out of everybody during his initial years when he spoke
about changing the very system that nurtured him. 'Just because
I am the outcome of a system doesn't mean I can't change
it,' he had said. What further exasperated the Congress was
his aversion to the party leaders. He shunned Sonia's coterie,
avoided the headquarter honchos and the party faithful, instead
set up his own team of young professionals at his residence at
12 Tughlaq Lane. A ticket seeker from Nawabgunj for the 2007
assembly polls, expecting to be quizzed on caste configurations,
was stumped when Rahul asked him the number of mobile
phone users in his constituency. What was even more incredible
was that Rahul knew the answer.

The party's Department of Publicity was reprimanded for its
lengthy pamphlets. Instead, Rahul asked for bullet points. At a

meeting of the Congress Thinktank on Future Challenges (set up for him by his mother), he wondered how they could attract 'new stakeholders' to the party and suggested that they talk about 'opportunities' instead of 'challenges'. After that, sundry Congressmen puffed up both their blow-dried hair and their corporate jargon. But the most effective symbol of how he was totally missing the context was the answering machine at his residence-cum-office where an officious voice answered with: 'Thank you for calling the office of Shri Rahul Gandhi. You can dial 1 for Hindi and 2 for English.' After which you were asked to Dial 1 for appointments and Dial 2 for others. If you wanted an appointment, you were asked to state your purpose 'briefly' after the beep. I was made aware of this contraption during a trip to Amethi where the locals cited this as an example to show how inaccessible their representative was. Fortunately the said machine did not last very long.

To his credit, the then freshly minted Gandhi scion didn't cut himself any breaks when he chose Uttar Pradesh as his first political task. With a little less than three years under his belt as an MP, Rahul took charge of the Congress campaign in the 2007 state elections. He did not give himself a walk-over by choosing an easy state where the Congress had a stronghold. Instead, he chose India's largest and Congress party's weakest state as his *karambhoomi*. This is a state where the Congress has been out of power since 1989. In 2002, the Congress held only 25 of the 403 seats and 8.9 per cent of the vote share. Under Rahul's charge, the Congress won 28 seats and 11.6 per cent vote share in the 2012 assembly. Later, in 2017, Rahul went in for an ill-fated alliance with the Samajwadi Party and the Congress was once again reduced to an all-time low of seven MLAs and 6.2 per cent of the vote share. If one was looking to Uttar Pradesh for the Rahul Model, then this was certainly not it.

Long back, writing for *India Today*, I had pointed out that while his grandfather may have written *The Discovery of India*, the grandson today has embarked on with his own version of Discovery tourism, as he pranced around the countryside dining with Dalits and sleepovers with tribals (March 2007). The tag caught on; especially when Rahul played the role of a political tourist to the hilt, down to stopping over at a local Wimpy's for a strawberry milkshake before a rally in Western UP.

On one of his roadshows in Kanpur, on a hot summer April evening in 2007, I managed to run alongside his car as it made its way through the city's crowded by-lanes. At the time, Rahul was the most sought after headline in the country and every reporter on the beat was looking for the elusive exclusive. He didn't respond to my political queries, but when I mentioned that covering his road shows was like working out at a gym, he immediately offered me a Diet Coke from the plastic blue ice box at the back of his Toyota Land Cruiser. I recall scribbling a mental note to myself: nice guy, prefers gyms to politics. Yes, it was a naive summing up of a situation, but I suspect I wasn't too off the mark. A collateral gain from all that gymming is that the double chin his grandmother wrote to her friend Dorothy Norman about has long vanished. (Letter dated August 1970, Indira Gandhi wrote: 'My Grandson Rahul is a darling. He has got rid of his wrinkles and still has a double chin.')

Rahul's political career had a dream debut. With his dimpled charm, public school mannerisms and the nostalgic connect of his surname the Gandhi scion soon became a darling of the media as well. He embodied a Kennedyesque legacy of power, glamour and tragedy. But it was also a legacy that he wasted during the UPA years by refusing to engage. And today, at a time when a disappointed India has moved on to another narrative, where pedigree doesn't hold the same allure as a chaiwallah,

Rahul has emerged from the sidelines, ready to connect. He now has to break from his own privileged past and compete in the more plebian narrative that Modi dominates. Or, as S. Prasannarajan, editor of *Open Magazine* put it so eloquently, Rahul's dilemma is that of 'Being a Gandhi in the Time of Modi'. That's a tough ask. He not only has to take down a powerful opponent but in the process Rahul also has to tell us what he, and the Congress under him, stands for. What is his idea of India? That is the only way he is going to be able to get the people of India to vote for him. As Siddharth Varadarajan Founding Editor, of *The Wire* pointed out, 'For Rahul Gandhi coming to power is essentially how good your speeches are or how good your alliances are, but not the nitty-gritty of mass mobilization.' His suggestion is that Rahul must look back at Gandhiji's Champaran Satyagraha of 1917, which helped the Congress establish itself as a mass movement.

What version of his surname does this latest 'Gandhi on the block' bring to the Congress table? Is he an institution builder like his great-grandfather, Jawaharlal Nehru? Is he as decisive and authoritarian as his grandmother, Indira Gandhi, with her socialist streak? Does he have Rajiv Gandhi's liberal and reformist outlook, or is his politics NGO-driven like his mother?

During his initial years, Rahul seemed more inclined towards his mother's socialist brand of politics, than following a pro-reforms model. Since his debut coincided with the Congress-led UPA Government taking office, both Rahul and Sonia became the alternate power centre for bleeding hearts, taking their cue from the National Advisory Council packed with academics rather than Dr Manmohan Singh's cabinet. The UPA's National Rural Employment Guarantee Act (NREGA) and even the farmers' loan waiver sailed through because the mother-and-son duo backed them. 'I see in his eyes his father's unfinished agenda. He wants a modern India, but also one that would be more responsive to the poor,' says Sam Pitroda, who has worked with both the father and the son. According to Pitroda, 'Rajiv was more extrovert, Rahul more introvert. Rahul is more analytical, he is more comfortable talking about systemic, logical stuff and not random conversations with no goal.' In other words, less small talk, more structured conversations.

While the UPA was in power—and during Rahul's first decade in politics—the unstated joke at the Congress headquarters was the more *jholawala* and disheveled your appearance, the more chances you had of striking a chord with the Congress heir. Often Youth Congress workers used to take off their Rolex watches and park their flashy cars at a nearby five-star and take an auto to a meeting with Rahul. There is this story of one Youth Congress leader who would inevitably come huffing and puffing for a meeting, and then ask for change to give to an auto (thereby successfully conveying the impression that she had not come in the comfort of a car).

Post the 2014 loss a cross section of Congress leaders met Rahul, both individually and in groups. They all agreed on one thing—the Congress could not limit its appeal just to the marginalized and the poor. It had to widen its arena to include the middle class, traders and corporates. Rahul is said to have told them that the one reason he took up the cause of the poor was simply because the needs of the corporates and the middle class were being handled by such ministers in the government as P. Chidambaram and Pranab Mukherjee, whom these sections could address directly. The poor had no such access. Congress leaders also told Rahul that while the Congress is a national coalition, especially of the SCs/STs/OBCs and minorities, a perception had gained ground that the party was catering only to these sections at the cost of the majority and the upper castes. They conceded that the Congress could not have ruled India for over five decades with the support of minorities alone, but also pointed out that there was a communication failure during the UPA years when the charge of minority appeasement gained ground. Especially after Dr Manmohan Singh's statement, 'Minorites must have first claim on resources' (December 2006). As a result, the Congress had vacated the entire space relating to Hindu concerns for the BJP. This is the space that Rahul's grandmother had dominated and one that he had to reclaim if he wanted to bring the Congress back to its original glory. As Rasheed Kidwai, author of *24 Akbar Road* pointed out, 'V.N. Gadgil, who was the Congress ideologue, used to say that even if all Muslims vote for Congress, the Congress is not going to get anywhere close to majority. The Congress has always been pro-Hindu but this flavour was missing in Sonia's Congress and therefore, in the Congress that Rahul has inherited.'

Consequently there have been some makeovers. After he took over as Congress chief, Rahul is busy attempting a course correction, visiting temples, scaling mountains (Mount Kailash), and displaying his janeu (sacred thread that Brahmins wear)— literally trying to showcase his inner Hindu. The idea is to pitch the Congress as a secular Hindu outfit versus the BJP as a 'fascist' Hindu party. (Fascist is a word Rahul uses often in connect with the RSS.) This led to a social media commentator remarking wryly, 'Earlier we were told that the BJP was Congress plus a cow. Now the Congress looks like BJP minus a cow.' Radhika Ramaseshan, consulting editor at *The Business Standard*, however point out, 'The optics of Rahul visiting temples and proclaiming himself as a Shiv Bhakt did work for the Congress in the Gujarat elections. We have seen the optics, now I am waiting for the articulation.' The articulation is where Rahul has to show both his commitment and his consistency.

In the run up to 2019, Rahul has also toned down his left wing rhetoric, actively shifting his focus from not just farmers and the marginalized, but also to the traders and the salaried middle class, criticizing the Modi government for demonetization, an unwieldy GST, and for slashing interest rates on small savings. Today if you ask him whether the Congress leans left or right, he quotes his grandmother who answered the same question stating: 'The Congress doesn't lean but stands straight.'

He may be standing straight but he also has to stand tall. For that he needs a vision. While speaking to NRIs in Bahrain at the Global Organisation of People of Indian Origin (8 January 2018), he was asked by a member of the audience to list three concrete—not generic—actions he would take if the Congress came to power. Rahul reeled off a list. The first was job creation by encouraging the small and medium scale industry. The second on his list was to reform education while affordable healthcare was the third. According to a member of Team Rahul, his prime focus is definitely going to be the MSME sector in small towns to revive job creation, even if it means restructuring the banking sector. Speaking earlier, on another occasion to the PhD Chamber of Commerce in Delhi (26 October 2017), Rahul had expounded on this theme pointing out that India has nearly six crore MSMEs in clusters across the country. In his speech he said, 'We need targeted cluster development programmes at a massive scale across the country. We need to link these small, micro and medium businesses to our banking systems ... Today they receive almost no bank credit even though they account for 40 per cent of India's economic output and half of India's exports ...'

As regards healthcare, Rahul is apparently critical of the

insurance-based American model for he feels that will only benefit brokers and those with connections, but not the poor. We are told that he wants to focus on the infrastructure, have an AIIMS or half an AIIMS in every district. However, the nuts and bolts are yet to be communicated to the public at large, as well as the fact as to why he didn't implement this when the UPA was in power. The one time I have heard Rahul speak about his healthcare plans was during the Singapore interaction where he was asked to comment on Modi's insurance-based healthcare model. In response, Rahul volunteered his vision saying, 'Healthcare in the 21st century is basically data. You're gonna move from a world of doctors to a world of data. It's like you had pilots earlier, now you don't have pilots. They call themselves pilots but they are basically system managers. Planes fly themselves but people need to be comfortable that there's a pilot sitting there. The entire thing is managed through GPS and through other communication systems. That's where the world of the doctors is going. Traditionally in India our idea has been healthcare for Indians. We've never seen the global healthcare opportunity. I can envision a world where Indian healthcare data is helping treat people in Singapore and Singapore is paying India for it.' However, I am not quite sure how much this impressed the moderator (Professor Danny Quah) who muttered something about this being 'a very exciting vision' and then gently nudged Rahul to another topic.

Rahul needs to make his communication style more pithy. He tends to over-simplify with too many examples that often get lost in the telling. Somewhat like Barack Obama's style, each speech of his will be interspersed with an anecdote that makes it personal. Only the anecdotes take too long to get to the point. Maybe, this is the right time to dig up that memo on bullet points that he tried to enforce within the Congress.

He also has a habit of picking on one theme and harping on it ad nauseam. Initially it was all about trying to bridge the gap between Bharat and India (this was when UPA was in power). This went on to his trying to change the system he was a part of. His experiments with democracy ended with holding elections to the Youth Congress where a well-entrenched system saw well-heeled dynasts bag most of the posts. His latest bug-bear is the RSS. All his interactions, both on and off record, end up being about how 'divisive and fascist' the RSS (and hence the BJP) is. But, there is a difference in being consistent and being boring. And Rahul needs to figure this out fast if he wants to retain his audience.

Having a plan is just half the battle. The other half is the messaging. As Dilip Cherian (Image Guru) once told me on my show *Roundtable* (NewsX), 'Rahul is up against the greatest communicator of them all, one who tells the masses that "I am going to put gas in your home, money in your bank and health insurance in your pocket". On the other side is the Congress President who may well have a better blue-print to deliver all these, but doesn't quite know how to communicate this to the voter. Consider this: it was only recently that we found out that he had helped Nirbhaya's family shift out of the slums to a flat in Dwarka and that he also counseled her brother to make something of his life. It was Rahul's intervention that helped the brother become a pilot. However, he told the family not to go public about his outreach as this was something he was doing on humanitarian grounds and not for political gain.

Rahul has been called many things; he is yet to prove all of them wrong but the one epithet few will dispute is that he has his heart in the right place. The rest of him is playing catch up! During the infamous interview he gave to television anchor, Arnab Goswami (2014) he had commented, 'I don't go into an election thinking, if we lose it's the end of the world. We lose some elections, we win some elections. The real thing is that it's a heart thing. It's a soul thing.' Yet, not everyone has the luxury of treating politics as an NGO. As BJP leader Ram Madhav said to me in another context, 'We are not here to do charity. We are here to win.'

Apart from what he reveals on social media, little is known about the Private Rahul. There is a close knit circle of friends and family around him, but few will talk to the media. Discretion is something the Gandhi scion values greatly. I guess trust doesn't come easily to someone who has seen both his grandmother and father die gruesome deaths. Rahul often talks about how his grandmother was shot by the very people who were guarding her, the same people he played badminton with every morning. Those whom I managed to speak to, describe him as 'sincerely earnest, not the dewy-eyed variety', but who is passionate about subjects that interest him. I'm told he is quite capable of dining at a five-star, taking a look at the bill and calculating how many poor people could be fed with the same amount. He's been spotted both at the capital's five-stars and also cafes like Sagar Ratna, seated usually with his back to the rest of the room, perhaps seeking brief moments of privacy that have evaded him since the moment of his birth. Points out an acquaintance who has interacted with him on social occasions but prefers to remain anonymous, 'On sartorial issues, I don't think dressing "up" is his thing. In fact, I find his suits a bit too "regulation" and nothing fancy. He probably looks best in a white KP (kurta pyjama), stubble in tow. I like the fact that he seems perfectly comfortable in a village hut or at a cricket match or at Wasabi. Even in restaurants, you'll find him in jeans, a sweater and sneakers. He certainly seems more regular than the "Abdullah, Omar Abdullah" Bond technique of, well, Omar. And I don't think you will see him on the cover of *GQ*!'

Governance, and putting systems in place, seems to be a favourite with this MPhil in development economics (Trinity College, University of Cambridge, UK). He does see his role as that of an 'enabler'. Rasheed Kidwai adds that Rahul sees himself more as a trustee than a wielder of power. In his conversations, Rahul is known to refer a lot to Michael Porter, a management guru with whom he did a brief stint in London before plunging into politics. But continuity is an essential enabler. Rahul's earlier hit and run brand of politics don't make the grade.

However, if you look at his own benchmarks he certainly has come a long way since 2014; he's no longer reluctant. He is not seen as a Pappu anymore. In fact, when he speaks, the BJP takes him seriously and issues a prompt reaction. He is also not just criticizing the BJP but he is also pitching an alternate narrative of what the Congress stands for, though the nuts and bolts of this still have to be worked out. The problem is that, in the world outside the Congress party, Rahul will not be competing against his own backstory but against those of Narendra Modi, Mayawati, Mamata Bannerjee and Akhilesh Yadav. Pitched against them, will his narrative hold? Therein lies his biggest challenge.

AKHILESH YADAV

The Bicycle Chief

Akhilesh Yadav was three years old when he was taken by the family accountant (Tewariji) to be enrolled at the local nursery school at Safai in rural Uttar Pradesh. There the boy who was brought up as Tipu by his grandmother and aunt (with an ailing mother and a largely absentee father hovering in the background) was asked his name. A bit flustered, Tipu admitted that he had no formal name. S.N. Tewari, the accountant, gave him a choice of three names. 'I liked Akhilesh the best,' he recalls with a smile. And Akhilesh it has been ever since. Of course, when he became Uttar Pradesh's youngest chief minister (CM) at age 38 in 2012, his supporters reverted to his nickname shouting with glee—'*Tipu Ban Gaya Sultan!*'

So while he is a dynast he has had to pretty much figure out his legacy right from the start. Even when he was the CM, he was not allowed a free hand with his father and a coterie of uncles calling the shots. It was Mulayam Singh Yadav (his father), Shivpal Yadav (father's brother), Ram Gopal Yadav (their cousin) and Azam Khan (a powerful Muslim leader) who ruled by proxy. Akhilesh was left with the ceremonies of office but not the power. The dominant joke in Uttar Pradesh then was that the state was being ruled by 'four-and-a-half' CMs.

Towards the middle of his tenure, somewhere in 2014 a national magazine referred to his rule as '*Andher Nagri Chaupat Raja*' (confused ruler, chaotic state). Always more sensitive to national headlines than local ones this was a 'Mirror Mirror on the Wall' moment for Akhilesh. He had ridden to power on his *Kranti Rath* (Wheels of Revolution), promising change, presumably for the better, but the wheels of change had got stuck in the politics of the same.

Akhilesh realized that in order to give himself a fighting chance in the state polls due in 2017 he had to change the narrative. And do it fast. So he did two things. One: he put development projects on a fast track. A 326 km long state-of-the-art expressway connecting Lucknow to Agra was flagged off and completed in a record time of 23 months; work began on a metro in the capital city of Lucknow and a river front with landscaped parks and cycle ways was sanctioned on the banks of the Gomti. Apart from these, a last minute push saw the chief minister go into overdrive and flag projects worth Rs 60,000 crore during his last month in office. An appropriate new slogan—'*Kaam Bolta Hai*' was coined to showcase Akhilesh as the new age, development-oriented neta. No matter that it was a slogan set more on foundation stones than completed works, it showed the right intention.

However, Akhilesh Yadav had a bigger problem at hand. He realized that whatever initiatives he had taken in terms of development were over-shadowed by the image of a CM held hostage by his father and uncles. Accordingly, six months before the polls Akhilesh began to distance himself from the 'old guard' culminating in a dramatic face off in December 2016. Even though he rebelled against his father, he did so in a respectful and reluctant tone, thereby giving the impression of one who had no choice. 'My revolt against my father was not planned or deliberate. It was forced by circumstances. If I win I will attribute my win to my father,' he told me in the middle of the 2017 state election campaign (*NewsX* Cover Story: Campaign Trail with Mr & Mrs Akhilesh Yadav). This won him kudos in the court of public opinion.

Another factor that prompted him to rebel against his father was the influence his 'Amar Singh Uncle' had over Mulayam. The portly figure of Amar Singh looms large over the Yadav family saga. A powerful Lutyens' Delhi networker, Amar Singh became friendly with Mulayam in 1996 when the latter was a defence minister in the Deve Gowda government.

Soon the dhoti-clad Netaji became a regular add-on at Amar Singh's flamboyant bashes in Delhi's five-star hotels, exchanging his socialist credentials for a socialite tag. This did not go down well with Akhilesh, Ram Gopal Yadav and Azam Khan. The family bided its time and when the Samajwadi Party (SP) was defeated in the 2007 assembly polls, the trio began voicing their apprehensions against Amar Singh with Azam Khan leading the charge. Eventually in 2009 Mulayam and Amar Singh parted ways. However, less than a decade later Amar Singh was back in Mulayam's life and Akhilesh was fearful of losing his grip over the party (and his father) once again. As he told his friends who chided him for taking on his own flesh and blood: 'What could I do? I had no choice.'

By making this a fight against the outsider Amar Singh, instead of his father, Akhilesh managed to convert the headlines from a legacy grab to legacy preservation. His little revolt may have come too late for his party's fortunes in the 2017 assembly as the SP was reduced to an all-time low of 47 seats. But at 43 years, it was not too late for Akhilesh himself. Even in defeat, Akhilesh showed a remarkable capacity for reinvention backed by a strong survival instinct. Less than a year after his assembly drubbing he reached out to his father's arch rival—the Bahujan Samaj Party (BSP) leader Mayawati and struck an alliance with her against the Bharatiya Janata Party (BJP) for the Lok Sabha by-polls in Gorakhpur and Phulpur held in March 2018. The duo defeated the BJP and once again Akhilesh was back in the reckoning as one who should not be underestimated. Especially when he repeated this formula and combined with the Rashtriya Lok Dal (RLD) to wrest the high profile Kairana seat from BJP two months later.

But before we go to the thrilling finale, let us dwell on the beginning which had a deceptively auspicious start. It was the elections of 2012 that saw Akhilesh emerge from the shadow of his father, a former chief minister and the country's ex-defence minister, Mulayam Singh Yadav. Old man Yadav had cut his teeth on socialist politics and was groomed by stalwarts like Ram Manohar Lohia and Raj Narain. He eventually formed his own party—the Samajwadi Party—in 1992. With Muslims and Other Backward Castes (essentially the Yadavs) as its voter base, the SP swept Mulayam to the Chief Minister's Office in 1992—his second term as CM but first as the head of his own outfit. Mulayam had been CM once before from 1989–1991 when he was part of Chandra Shekhar's Janata Dal.

When in power Mulayam Singh went out of his way to favor his party vote bank. Yadavs—which constitute just 8.5 per cent of the electorate (2011 census)—were given key postings at police stations and government offices. Since Mulayam was a former wrestler, muscle power became closely identified with the party. Local dons and history-sheeters had access to the top echelons of the party. It was in this scenario that Akhilesh made his leadership debut when he was made state president in 2009. Interestingly, it was Amar Singh—and not Akhilesh's father—who suggested that he should be elevated. Sometime after the SP lost the 2007 Assembly polls to Mayawati, the party's top leadership met for a dinner at Amar Singh's Lodhi Road residence in Delhi, which was attended by Mulayam Singh Yadav, Jaya Prada, Jaya Bachchan and Ram Gopal Yadav. It was there that Amar Singh suggested that the politics of the new age also needed a new age neta. He then pointed to his twin daughters and said that they are the voters of tomorrow. And asked one of them which serials they watched on TV. The reply was *Hannah Montana*. Then Amar Singh in his own impeccable logic replied: 'See even Akhilesh's daughters are the same age and through his kids he is in touch with what the young watch and want.' He proposed Akhilesh's name as the party president, and everyone agreed except Mulayam Singh. Perhaps he was not quite content to let *Hannah Montana* be the deciding factor in such a crucial discussion. He simply said that he would consult the party ideologue, Janeshwar Mishra.

Mishra agreed immediately and gave Akhilesh his whole-hearted support. In fact, it is Mishra and not Mulayam who has been the father figure in Akhilesh's life. 'When I became president he told me that you are not a leader right now. But work hard for two years, then I will come to your rally and raise a slogan of "Akhilesh *Zindabad*" in your support. That is when the others will accept you as a leader,' recalls Akhilesh with a nostalgic smile. And adds with a refreshing candour, '*Kitna bada dil tha unka*' (What a large heart he had). 'Who does this in rajniti?' implying 'Who raises slogans in support of a junior in politics?'

It was also Mishra who gave Akhilesh his first lesson in political authority when the 35-year-old continued to touch the feet of his party seniors even after being state chief. 'How will you discipline them if you keep showing them deference?' pointed out Mishra. 'But at least allow me to touch my father's and your feet,' protested Akhilesh. Later, when he became the CM, one of the first orders he issued was to set up the 376 acre Janeshwar Mishra Park in the heart of Lucknow. Modelled on London's Hyde Park, the Rs 168 crore project was ready by August 2014.

Akhilesh began his apprenticeship with several 'cycle yatras' across the state to propagate the party symbol (which is a cycle). This was also a time when the SP was in opposition. Since the old guard did not accompany him on these excursions (one yatra was a 250 km long stretch so it would've been impossible for any of his uncles to keep up), both Shivpal and Mulayam had no clue of his popularity. Quick to realize the subliminal value of brands, the youth icon peddled hope claiming he was riding the 'umeed ki cycle' (cycle of hope).

Finally on the eve of the 2012 assembly polls when SP was hoping to cash in on the anti-incumbency of the BSP government and make a comeback, Akhilesh undertook a rath yatra across the entire state. Mulayam Singh flagged off the Kranti Rath and Uncle Shivpal donated Rs 5 lakh to the cause, thinking that '*ladka hai, ghoomta rahega, pak jayega*' (He's still a young lad, let him gain experience, or be frustrated—the phrase can be read either way).

Akhilesh did more than just gain experience. He won over

the cow-belt which soon began seeing him as the symbol of a progressive SP. The party of Mulayam had a Luddite aversion to computers, resisted the English language and promoted history-sheeters. Here was a graduate in environmental engineering, who carried the latest Blackberry, responded to BBMs and the English language. The first sign that the SP got of politics unusual was when Akhilesh over-ruled his father to deny the history-sheeter D.P. Yadav a party ticket. Akhilesh was on his Kranti Rath en route to Haiderganj in eastern UP when he was asked to comment on D.P. Yadav's entry. 'The SP will not admit anyone with such a tainted image,' he said firmly. Initially his father's reaction was to rebuff the son but as the media picked up the story proclaiming the arrival of a new age leader, one who could easily trump Rahul Gandhi's youthful credentials in the cow-belt, Yadav senior kept quiet. This proved to be a key turning point in the way Lutyens' Delhi saw Akhilesh.

As the national media reached out to the newest socialist on the block, Akhilesh laughed and told me: 'It looks as if Delhi has finally discovered me.' Yet he was smart enough not to provoke the party faithful. Though he speaks fluent English, he has never given an interview in English, answering in Hindi even on English channels. As for his party's aversion to technology, he waves that aside saying, 'We only oppose technology that displaces professionals like artisans and weavers. I am pro-computers, but these can be in Hindi or Urdu. Why only in English?'

The campaign Akhilesh ran was low on glitz but high on tech. At a time when the SP office in Lucknow still hadn't installed computers, catchy slogans and campaign tunes came out from the computers of a war room set up by Team Akhilesh. These were immediately cleared by the CM himself via his iPad and BBM. Akhilesh's favourite campaign at the time showed a plodding elephant (the elephant being the party symbol of his state rival Mayawati). Suddenly a youth with a red cap (the red cap is a SP brand identity) cycles past, and overtakes the elephant with a cheeky ring on his cycle bell.

When the results came in, it turned out that the cycle rider with the jaunty cap won. Akhilesh's dual-appeal worked, both with opinion makers in Delhi and the crowd in the cow-belt. This was also an election where another scion, Rahul Gandhi was hoping to make his mark. Like Akhilesh, Rahul too was all over the countryside, descending from his chopper at rally grounds, rolling his sleeves, wearing a stubble and an aggression that the Congress mistakenly thought would charm the cow-belt more than Akhilesh's personal connect on the ground. During the campaign, Bhupendra Yadav a tea stall owner in Pratapgarh, summed it well when he told me, 'When Rahul speaks about the farmers' problems it looks as if he is reciting something he's been told. When Akhilesh speaks, it looks as he is one of us, he knows the problems.'

Unlike Rahul whose initial speeches sounded like patronizing sermons, Akhilesh knows how to work a crowd. This was evident from his 2012 rath yatra—he would wave to a truck-driver parked along his rath and try to guess his village from his accent. 'Look that's a Samsung camera, even SP workers have that now,' he would tell another youth trying to take his picture, trying to make the point that the party was now in with the latest technology. He would suddenly wave to a youth standing at the fringe of his rally and ask, 'Didn't I recruit you into the SP?' Even back then Akhilesh knew the reverberating power of a simple gesture.

His eldest daughter Aditi would sometimes accompany him on his trips along with her lilac knapsack and iPad. Her father would often rummage into her rucksack and share her stash of chocolates with the media on the bus, cajoling her with promises of more. He knew he had to keep all his constituents happy.

Akhilesh met his wife Dimple Rawat, an upper caste daughter of an army officer, in college. 'We met here in Lucknow in the cantonment area and then we got married. Don't ask me what happened in between,' he says with a sheepish smile. The truth is that while as a father Mulayam had no objection to Dimple, as a political leader he was not in favour of his son marrying a Rajput girl. At this point it was Amar Singh who supported Akhilesh. 'This is true. Amar Singh Uncle told my father if this wedding has to take place ensure that it is a grand affair. It will silence the critics,' admits Akhilesh. Sure enough, the wedding on 24 November 1999 was a lavish affair hosting the then Prime Minister A.B. Vajpayee, chief ministers of different states, cabinet ministers and Bollywood stars. 'The only time the crowds moved away from the dais was when Sridevi was spotted at the entrance,' laughs Akhilesh.

The couple have three children, Aditi and a pair of twins—Arjun and Tina. Dimple may be the low profile half of the power couple, but she is both his confidante and advisor. In 2009 Akhilesh persuaded her to contest her first election and a very shy Dimple emerged on stage doing little more than wave. She lost that to the Congress who fielded cine star-turned-politician Raj Babbar against her and got Salman Khan to campaign. But she won her second election (2012) unopposed, for by then her husband had learnt the art of political management, and ensured no one stood against her. However, her third election (2014) was a win against the Modi wave and by the time the 2017 Assembly rolled by, she was the party's star campaigner. 'She's helping me by reaching out to the women voter thereby doing half my work,' Akhilesh would tell the media with a proud smile. Some would say Dimple had the tougher job, for during

Akhilesh's chief ministership women voters had been angered by the deteriorating law and order in the state. Over time, and with the exit of the older generation, Dimple has come to play a more assertive role. She is seen at Akhilesh's side at party meetings and being a Lok Sabha MP she is fast becoming the 'national' face of the party. When negotiating an alliance with the Congress for the 2017 polls it is to Dimple that Priyanka Gandhi had reached out.

But, let's get back to the 2012 campaign. By the time Akhilesh's Kranti Rath had covered 9000 km and 215 of the state's 403 constituencies, an alternate narrative was taking shape, much to his father's surprise and Uncle Shivpal's obvious dismay. The crowd had begun looking at Bhaiyaji (as they called Akhilesh) as the next Netaji (that is what Mulayam is known as). Congress leader and analyst Surendra Rajput pointed out: 'Akhilesh was seen as a pocket-book edition of Mulayam Singh.' And then quipped, 'Pocket books always sell more.'

Even before the last ballot was cast in Uttar Pradesh, I wrote the cover story for *India Today* (magazine). The Hindi edition had Akhilesh's picture with the caption: '*Tajposhi ki Tayaari*' (Ready for Coronation). We had declared him CM even before the final vote had been cast. Unfortunately, his party took a little longer to do that even though the SP swept the election with 224 of the state's 403 MLAs.

There was a reason for the delay. The opposition came from within. Uncle Shivpal threw his own hat in the ring claiming that it was not Akhilesh's poster boy appeal but his own organizational team that was responsible for the win. Some of Akhilesh's supporters even put a copy of *India Today* on Mulayam's desk at his party office and peeped anxiously from the windows outside to see if he would get the message. The affable Ashish (Sonu) Yadav who handles the local media for the SP, remembers how at first Mulayam did not even glance at the magazine when it was placed before him but once they had all left the room picked up the copy and smiled when he saw the cover proclaiming his son as the next CM. Later it seemed that the 72-year-old Mulayam had changed his mind—or had been persuaded to—for he still did not announce Akhilesh as the party's choice for CM. Instead he told his colleagues that he was keen to become CM for the fourth term simply so he could equal his bête noire Mayawati's record; she too is a four-term CM.

Hearing this, an angry Ram Gopal Yadav who was batting for Akhilesh snorted and said, 'CM record *banne ke liye nahin bante hain*' (Don't have to become a CM just to create records). After Janeshwar Mishra's demise Ram Gopal had donned the mantle of a party ideologue simply because he carried the nomenclature of Professor and was considered the '*padha-likha*' (literate) face of the party.

At this point it would be imperative to understand the netaji-betaji (father-son) equation. When Akhilesh was very young, and his mother Malti Devi was still alive, Mulayam met his second wife, Sadhna. The SP patriarch also has another son Prateek with Sadhna. According to an SP insider, 'The equation between father and son was never intimate. Akhilesh would not meet his father for three to four days and when he did the conversation was minimal.'

Akhilesh was sent off to a boarding—Dholpur Military School in Rajasthan—and graduated in environmental engineering from Mysore University after which he went to Sydney where he furthered his studies on environment impact assessment. In fact, the first time he realized that his father was someone 'important' was when his father came to visit him at his school and the UP chief minister's helicopter touched down on his school grounds.

Finally, it was decided that Akhilesh would be the CM and that the name would be proposed by Azam Khan (a Mulayam loyalist) at a meeting of the party's National Executive. Knowing his cousin all too well, Ram Gopal did not leave any scope for a last minute coup by Mulayam. Before the proceedings began, he took the mike and announced firmly: 'Now Azam Khan will propose Akhilesh Yadav's name as the next chief minister.'

It turned out to be a pyrrhic victory. Akhilesh may have got the CM's chair but it was Mulayam and his two chachas (Ram Gopal and Shivpal) who ran the government. After the swearing in, the entire cabinet was taken to Subrata Roy, a powerful Lucknow based industrialist's residence for dinner. This sent a strong message that despite the new age CM, the old power-brokers were back in business.

It was soon clear that it was not Akhilesh but the old guard that was running the show; whether it was choosing his own chief secretary or the posting of a low level bureaucrat, the decisions were taken by Mulayam and his brothers. Between them, Ram Gopal and Shivpal divided UP into their respective power zones with the former getting western UP and the latter eastern. When the young CM began to distribute the 18 lakh free laptops that were part of his campaign promise, his father asked him to remove his (Mulayam's) face as the screen saver as he was anti-technology. Later when Akhilesh began work on his pet project—the Lucknow to Agra Expressway—his father scoffed at him asking how many poor people will travel on the expressway? When two young girls were alleged to have been raped and murdered in Badaun, all Netaji had to say was 'Boys will be boys'. This was not the progressive face of governance promised by Akhilesh. Was the father trying to scuttle the son? Certainly Mulayam displayed little paternal pride in Akhilesh's success. According to a SP leader, 'Whenever anyone would praise Akhilesh to Netaji, he would be asked "Are you a chamcha [sycophant]?"'

That Akhilesh had lost control of the narrative was most evident after the 2013 Hindu–Muslim riots in Muzaffarnagar that claimed over 50 lives. A month later, he was busy organizing the family's annual Saifai Mahotsav that is held every year on Mulayam's birthday in the family stronghold. Bollywood stars such as Salman Khan, Ranveer Singh, Madhuri Dixit and Alia Bhatt were flown in. When the media pointed out that the money wasted could have been spent to rehabilitate the riot victims they were banned from the event.

When the 2017 election drew near and the time came to roll out his rath once again (this time he called it Vikas Rath— Chariot of Development) the pragmatic CM knew that he had very little to offer the public. Perhaps this realization was another factor that made him take on the old guard.

Whatever the motive, Akhilesh slowly began distancing himself from his Uncle Shivpal and father. What made things worse was the return of Amar Singh. As if on cue, Mulayam began to distance himself from the son, stating obliquely at a party function at the SP Party Office on 15 August 2016 that he was the one who had founded the party and he was still the party's best face. This was the first sign that the father was not planning to make his son the CM face in the next elections. Later, Akhilesh got to know that Mulayam had been negotiating with the Congress (via Amar Singh who took him to meet Priyanka Gandhi) for an alliance to stop Akhilesh from becoming the CM again and instead projected himself as the CM candidate. Was Amar Singh working to break the party and get revenge on the trio that was responsible for his ouster? Especially Azam Khan whom he felt spearheaded the move to oust him, wondered Team Akhilesh. If so, why was Mulayam playing along?

'Akhilesh was not surprised,' says Udaiveer Singh, a party colleague and a junior from his school. 'By then he could sense that his father was being manipulated by Amar Singh to grab the chief minister's chair once again.' The party was divided between father and son with the majority favouring the rising star. 'Party leaders used to meet his father and then go to Akhilesh and say, *Hamne do jhoot bole hain netaji ko* [We told two lies to Mulayam]. One was that the 2012 polls were won on his name not yours. And the second is that he can win the votes for us in 2017, not you,' recalls Udaiveer.

Akhilesh fired the first salvo by expelling two state ministers close to his Uncle Shivpal on corruption charges. His father immediately demanded that they be reinstated. Akhilesh obliged but the bugle of revolt had been sounded. In October 2016, Akhilesh moved out of 5, Vikramditya Marg—the house that he shared with his father and stepmother Sadhna in Lucknow. He shifted to a house next door—4, Vikramaditya Marg. Interestingly while the two houses had separate gates there was also an inter-connecting entrance on the inside, leaving the door open for reconciliation.

The break-point came at a National Executive meet on 24 October that was open to the media. Speaking from the podium Akhilesh pleaded with his father to take his side against Shivpal and Amar Singh. '*Meri aap se koi narazgi nahin hai, lekin aap ke khilaf koi saazish hogi, apki party ke khilaf koi saazish ho toh meri mazboori hai bolna*' (I have nothing against you but if someone conspires against your party I have to speak). It was an emotional plea from a son to his father, from a political junior to his leader and would have swayed many a politicans, but not this one. Mulayam Singh responded by openly chiding his son from the public podium.

❖

Was this the moment then when he was at his lowest that Akhilesh decided to reach for the highest? On 5 November he took out another rath yatra from Lucknow to Unnao telling his supporters that the procession should be so long that when his Mercedes driven bus touches Lucknow the last car of the cavalcade should be leaving Lucknow. Although the Mercedes rath broke down midway, he completed the yatra on a SUV cheered on by crowds along the entire route. This gave him the confidence to take on his father, the old guard.

In December, when an adamant Mulayam (who was also the national president of the party) issued a list of candidates for the assembly elections next year, dropping key members of the CM's cabinet, an angry Akhilesh hit back with his own list where these names were included. Mulayam then suspended his son from the party for six months.

Akhilesh pushed for a show of strength. He hosted a lunch attended by over 200 MLAs who expressed faith in his leadership over his father's. A somewhat naïve Akhilesh thought the leadership issue had been settled and went next door via the interconnecting door between the two bungalows to call on his father. A more pragmatic Ram Gopal called a National Convention next day in order to cement Akhilesh's stamp over the party. This convention marked a turn-around from the one held two months ago where Mulayam had treated Akhilesh as an errant school boy, scolding him in front of the entire party and national media. Neither Mulayam nor Shivpal attended this meeting on 1 January 2017.

Presiding over the podium, Ram Gopal announced that Shivpal had been sacked as the SP state unit chief. More importantly he announced that they now had a new national president—the father had been replaced by his son. As a loud cheer went up, Akhilesh took the mike. He spoke briefly and in a voice poignant with emotion. '*Main jitna netaji ka samman pehle karta tha usse dugna main ab karoonga*' (I will double my respect for my father), said Akhilesh. His tone was respectful but finally he had shown the audacity and gumption his supporters had been clamouring for. It was not just a new year for the SP; it was also the beginning of a new era.

There followed many trips to the Election Commission as father and son fought for the party symbol—the cycle. Elections were due in February and March, and the symbol was needed for the nomination papers. Team Akhilesh claims it had Plan B ready; they would have opted for the motor-cycle, thereby indicating that the SP was moving into a newer, more youthful age. But it was the cycle that both were after—for this was the symbol that the party's traditional voter identified with. More importantly the party's funds were also frozen, for whoever gained control over the party would have access to these funds and it was rumoured that over Rs 500 crore lay in the bank. The EC finally decided in Akhilesh's favour on 17 January 2017.

The pre-occupation with the family feud instead of strategizing for the elections was one reason for the SP's defeat. Another mistake Akhilesh made was in aligning with the Congress. While the family feud was on he had agreed to a tie-up with the Congress. Though the denouement left Akhilesh on a strong wicket he still honored his commitment to the alliance, even giving in to the Congress's demand of 105 seats. His supporters saw this as an excessive amount pointing out that the Congress held only 28 MLAs at the time. Akhilesh told the media that his was a '*bade dil ki dosti*' asking 'What is the point in doing dosti with a kanjoos?' (Why be miserly in friendship?). BJP leader and Cabinet Minister Arun Jaitely commented wryly that this was a fatal mistake as Akhilesh had given away 105 seats to a 'non-party'. Did Akhilesh keep the alliance so that the minority vote would not be divided?

The alliance with the SP was negotiated by Priyanka Gandhi and her brother Rahul. The Congress played tough and called off the alliance twice when its demands for a large chunk of seats were not met. For Akhilesh there was the added pressure of Amar Singh negotiating an alternate alliance with the Congress with Mulayam as the CM face. Plus he had to get on with the business of campaigning as the SP was left with only three star campaigners—Dimple, Azam Khan, Jaya Bachchan—and himself. So he gave in to the absurd number of 105 seats. However, after that his patience ran out as the Congress delayed announcing candidates and campaign dates. 'I know Rahul is a national leader, but in UP I am the bigger party so I am the big brother in the alliance,' he told me at the time.

Mulayam did not campaign for the party. The party faithful remained with Akhilesh. An old slogan that went *'Jiska Kaam Kayam Hai, Uska Naam Mulayam Hai'* (The one whose work speaks, his name is Mulayam) was reworked to *'Jiska Kaam Kayam Hai, Uska Baap Mulayam hai'* (The one whose work speaks, his father is Mulayam). Rationalizing the defeat, Akhilesh says: 'Because of the family fight we could not build a definitive narrative for the voter. The public did not hear me talk about development. They instead heard the BJP talk about *"kabarsthan-shamshaan ghat"* [graveyards vs funeral pyres]. We did not have the emotional glue to keep our voters together.'

To appeal to the aspirational voter the focus should ideally have been on the development work undertaken by him such as the Lucknow Metro (this especially impressed the youth who boasted that they would soon be travelling in the same style as those in Mumbai or Delhi). 'I still remember, at the time Javed Usmani (then chief secretary) was very keen that instead of a metro we have a BRT system for buses. But I wanted to build something new age. If we build a BRT then at some point we would have to replace it with metros.' He blames the centre for delaying the security and safety NOC that had to be issued by the Union Rail Ministry which is why the Metro could not be listed as one of his completed projects.

The trophy certainly was the 326 km long Lucknow-Agra expressway. Navneet Sehgal, the CEO of the project, claims: '7500 acres of land were taken from farmers without agitation. This is a six-lane green-field expressway, but it has eight-lane structures so if you want to expand the road tomorrow to take in increased traffic, you can do so.' The launch had its share of drama with six Sukhoi jets landing on the expressway. 'The Air Force had requested a space for planes to land in case of emergency so a 3 km landing strip has been incorporated in the expressway,' says Sehgal. Points out Udaiveer Singh, 'Akhilesh firmly believes that where there is development, there is growth. Infrastructure has been his focus always. He says, "Double the Speed, Triple the Economy." As CM he made roads, new power houses, worked to cut the transmission losses in power supply. He also invited film stars to shoot in the state as seeing these locales on the big screen helps promote tourism to the area.'

The Gomti river front in Lucknow was developed on the lines of the Thames waterfront prompting local headlines to claim, 'Lucknow ban gaya London' (Lucknow becomes London). Incidentally Europe is a favourite holiday destination for the ex-CM and his family. 'The one major achievement of distributing laptops, building expressway, the metro, was that it changed the image and perception about our party,' says Akhilesh. 'If you want a benchmark of how a road should be then Expressway is it. We also built mandis along the expressway so the farmer feels part of the growth story. We also joined the 50

state district headquarters to the expressway via a four lane for
better connectivity.' A perfume park and an aloo (potato) mandi
was planned in Kannauj, mango wholesale market mandis in
Lucknow, while Ramdev was given 500 acres in Mainpuri for
a food park.

Akhilesh put his environment and engineering degrees
to good use during the planning of the expressway. (He has a
Bachelor's and a Master's degree in Civil and Environmental
Engineering from St Jayachamarajendra College of Engineering,
Mysore, as well as a Master's degree in Environmental
Engineering from the University of Sydney, Australia.) When
the National Highways Authority of India did not okay the
environmental clearance for a cemented access bridge over the
Ganga, Akhilesh suggested a steel one instead and the project
was not held up due to lack of clearances. Points out Aashish
Yadav, his media consultant, 'Akhilesh often says that first
America built roads and now roads are building America. He
tried to do the same for UP.'

The SP had also announced a pension scheme whereby two
saris were given away to women belonging to BPL families.
Akhilesh instead suggested they give Rs 500 a month so that
the women could use the money on health, children's education
or their own wardrobe. Pragmatically he also conceded that the
party was in danger of committing political suicide if it didn't
get its fashion sense right. 'Some women don't wear saris, some
wear only salwar-suits. Then there is the problem of getting the
colours right. I was trying to figure out a way to avoid this *jhagda*
(fight),' he said in all earnestness and pointed out that the SP
managed to help 55 lakh women by transferring money online
to their accounts.

When the election results came in, Akhilesh held a press
conference, gracefully accepting defeat. 'People may not have

liked my expressway and this is why they voted for the bullet train,' he said with a wry smile that did not reach his eyes. (PM Narendra Modi's pet project has been to bring the bullet train to India.) When new CM, Yogi Adityanath, held purifying rituals before moving into the CM's official residence at 5, Kalidas Marg, Akhilesh's sense of humor ran out and he remarked caustically: 'When we come back in 2022 I will get a fire engine to spray ganga-jal on the house.' There was a part of Akhilesh that was hurting. He had taken a great deal of pride in restoring the CM's bungalow in 2012. At the time when he moved in he had been horrified by the garish pink on the walls ('Some of the walls even had tiles on them, the kind you see on bathroom floors,' whispered an SP colleague with a shudder that would go down well at a Good Housekeeping seminar). Pink was the favourite colour of Akhilesh's predecessor Mayawati. When I met Akhilesh during the 2017 campaign, he took great pride in showing me around the CM's official residence which was now tastefully done up in grey with wooden panels, stating: 'We get dignitaries from the world over calling on us. This is a house that will do the host proud.' And then added wistfully, *'Poori ladai iss ghar ke liye hai'* (The entire fight is about this house).

He may have lost the lease on 5, Kalidas Marg for the next five years but there is little denying that he will make a comeback. An interesting aside to the political war was the real estate feud between Yogi and Akhilesh, for after losing the latter moved to his government accommodation in 4, Vikramaditya Marg. Since this was government owned, he was soon served an eviction notice; well, as soon as he defeated the BJP in successive by-polls. Akhilesh moved to a three-bedroom rented accommodation but the state government accused him of wrecking the government bungalow before he vacated it. A visibly upset Akhilesh held an hour long press conference pointing out the inconsistencies in the case against him—such as the charge that he filled the swimming pool with sand. Only, he said, there was no swimming pool at his house! The accusations hurt for he sees himself as a creator rather than a destroyer. If he wasn't a politician he would have made a very good architect for he has a keen eye for design, and had a say in every project undertaken by his government; some of which are now being 'inaugurated' by the current government.

Akhilesh has not wasted time since his defeat in self-pity but in consolidating his hold over the party. He was also one of the first regional leaders to suggest the idea of an alliance to take on the rising might of the BJP. In an audacious move, the first person he reached out to was his father's bête noire Mayawati— whom he refers to as bua (father's sister), even telling her at a chance meeting in Parliament's Central Hall during the 2017 Monsoon Session that the SP, BSP and the Congress needed to come together with other like-minded parties to defeat the BJP. He hinted that if she wanted to be PM, she had his support. Later, he explained to his aides, that unlike her, he had age on his side. For the record he is quick to rule himself out from the prime ministerial stakes saying: 'My focus is on 2022 (the next UP state election) and not 2019. For me UP is the bigger trophy.'

Reaching out to the BSP would be unthinkable in the SP of old, but Akhilesh has been quick to react to the changing times. He had realized that the party's main enemy is not the fading BSP but the rising BJP. He persuaded Mayawati to support the SP in the Gorakhpur and Phulpur assembly by-polls against the BJP in March 2018. This was a historic first and only he could pull it off because Mayawati nurses a deep hatred of the Yadav Seniors, blaming Mulayam and Shivpal for locking her up in a state guest house in 1995. But with Akhilesh there is no such baggage of the past. The gamble paid off, for with the BSP's support, the SP candidates romped home in both the seats. Sounding older than his years, Akhilesh told the media, 'Vahi vyakti safal hota hai jo puraani baat bhool jata hain' (Only that person is successful who can forget past bitterness).

I met him for a cup of coffee served along with barfi and dry fruits at his home in Vikramaditya Marg on the eve of the Gorakhpur and Phulpur results. He was in a mood to talk, from Kumbh Melas to Art Deco. I steered the conversation towards his newfound friendship with the BSP. 'The alliance is a good move and from this a new path for the future may be found. If the BJP can form alliances why can't we. Some people say you have opened your cards very early, but I am happy,' he told me. And this was a day before the results came in. Then, perhaps because he was free from the campaign trail he shared another line of thought with me, 'If the fight is on religious lines, we shall always lose to the BJP. If the elections are fought on caste lines, we shall win.'

It's easy to see where he is coming from. In a country where the Hindus are in 80 per cent majority the BJP will always win a polarized vote. This is one of the lessons Akhilesh had learnt from the UP assembly loss. The Congress and the SP had come together to keep the Muslim vote from splitting. In hindsight, Akhilesh realized that this sent out the wrong message to the Hindus. He also reminded me that it was ironic that the SP was being painted as an anti-Hindu party as the Yadavs were the original Krishna vansh, and pointed out that he prayed to Lord Krishna and had an idol of Hanuman at his house. Recently I have seen him repeat this at various fora. He has also commissioned a 50 feet bronze statue of Krishna (conceptualized by him) at his hometown Saifai, to be unveiled on the eve of the 2019 elections. The statue depicts Krishna as 'Rathangpani' (one who holds the chariot wheel as a weapon) referring to the episode in Mahabharata when Krishna picked up a chariot wheel to attack Bhishma. This is the only time during the war that Krishna had picked up a weapon. The choice of the statue, his harping on the Krishna-Yadav link is not just to woo the caste vote. It is also to ensure the BJP doesn't have a monopoly on the Hindu vote.

Well, he has a game-plan, and for luck, he has his broken nose. An old football injury has left him with a crooked nose. 'This is my good luck charm for only successful people have broken noses,' he says. Maybe he has a point. The only other politically broken nose belonged to Indira Gandhi; and she certainly was the original comeback queen.

RAM MADHAV

The Saffron Evangelist

What happens when you combine ideology with pragmatism and convention with innovation? Well, you get a leader skilled in real politick—you get a Ram Madhav.

It was in July 2014 that the Rashtriya Swayamsevak Sangh (RSS) sent one of its sharpest minds on deputation to its political wing—the BJP. Usually the RSS pracharaks (title given to those who propagate) work as backroom boys and provide mission markers for the BJP. Rarely do they lead from the front but Madhav would be an exception. He joined the BJP, high up in the hierarchy as a general secretary and was given two portfolios—the North East and Jammu & Kashmir (J&K). Both were difficult tasks as the BJP had a negligible presence in the North East and was considered an anathema in the Valley.

Yet, within a year, Madhav delivered a BJP government in J&K and Assam. Within four years, the North Eastern states of Arunachal and Manipur had saffron flags flying. The former was a crafted win whereby the ruling Congress government was toppled and replaced by a BJP coalition (December 2016), while the latter was a nimble-footed electoral grab whereby the BJP managed to form the government with the support of regional allies, even though it wasn't the single largest party (March 2017). These were followed by the first ever BJP government in Tripura, and BJP-supported coalition governments in Meghalaya and Nagaland by March 2018; all this, under Ram Madhav's watch. Since the North East and Kashmir are border areas, the BJP with its stridently nationalistic outlook and hard-line against immigrants had always been regarded with suspicion by the locals. Given that, this breakthrough was all the more remarkable, especially by an RSS man. 'The BJP will do anything democratically possible to win elections,' says Ram Madhav. 'We are not in politics for charity but to win elections,' he adds, thereby cementing his conversion from the RSS—which sells itself as a cultural and a social organization—to the not-so-altruistic BJP.

It's always difficult to pin down Ram Madhav for a long chat because his iPhone is always buzzing with calls from the North East, Nagpur and across continents. (By the way, he is an Apple geek. Interestingly I found a love for technology cutting across party lines with Madhav, Rahul Gandhi, Milind Deora and Omar Abdullah sporting the latest iPhones, more for the sheer rush of technology than a style statement.) However, over coffee and lots of mithai I managed to meet him for several short chats. Whether you meet him for a meal of curd rice and parathas or just a cup of green tea, there will always be something sweet on the table; his sweet tooth is also evident in the names of his two pugs—Vanilla and Chocolate!

After the North East the BJP handed him yet another difficult state to turn around—that of Andhra Pradesh where the party has never been in power on its own. Madhav was given charge soon after the ruling Telugu Desam Party broke its alliance with the BJP in March 2018. Andhra is also the land where he was born (East Godavri district on 22 August 1964). His *janambhoomi* had suddenly become his *karambhoomi*. But the latest assignment also begged one pertinent question—was Madhav being set up for a fall? There are those within the BJP who have not taken too kindly to his mercurial rise. However, Madhav has two things going for him—the RSS backing and a working equation with the prime minister. In today's BJP, that's a good enough safety net. I use the net metaphor deliberately, because every net has its holes. Here, I should add a third factor that Madhav has going for him—which is the thrill he gets from the 'Mission Impossible'. I ran into him soon after he was put in charge of Andhra; he was on a flight to Srinagar to resolve a coalition issue there while I was on my way to interview Omar Abdullah. But even while he was headed to the country's northernmost tip the iPad in front of him had Andhra Pradesh on its screen. When I commiserated on him being handed a hot potato, he replied that to the contrary he was quite confident that the state would shore up the BJP's numbers in the 2019 general elections. (Since the BJP lacks a strong leader in the state, and knowing the way the party operates, I am sure Madhav must have already identified a local regional leader to ally with.) There is a view that during the 2014 Modi wave the BJP had peaked in the North, especially in Rajasthan, Madhya Pradesh, Gujarat, Bihar and Uttar Pradesh. The party was looking for new territories to make up its numbers in the coming elections. Both the North East and the South are on Modi's aspirational agenda and this is where Madhav plays a crucial role.

Madhav's rapport with Narendra Modi stands the test of time. He'd been a frequent visitor to Gujarat on RSS work and interacted with the then CM. He's been 'impressed' (his words) with Modi's methodical work style, especially the way he ran his 2012 election campaign. Later, as a national executive member of the RSS, Madhav pitched in on then prime ministerial candidate Narendra Modi's 2014 campaign that saw the BJP win 282 of the 543 Lok Sabha seats. It was the tech-savvy Ram Madhav who pushed the RSS to overcome its Luddite aversion to technology and procure as many as 60 Lenovo Yoga tablets. These were then filled with crucial voter data developed by Team Modi. The data-enabled tablets were then distributed to the RSS's prantpracharaks; a prantpracharak is in charge of 15–16 districts. They perform the key task of spreading the RSS message. Madhav's team made the pracharaks familiar with the Bharat Vijay app—literally meaning, a Win for India. This contained polling booth data based on voting patterns of six previous national and assembly elections. 'By the time I was deputed to the BJP I was already half-way into politics,' says Ram Madhav, who views his career graph moving along a line of 'natural progression', rather than a cut and paste job.

Interestingly, in 2006, much before Modi's candidature as the PM face gained formal currency, Madhav had zeroed in on him. This was at a time when BJP patriarch L.K. Advani had projected himself as the party's PM candidate for the 2009 elections. But, even as far back as then, Madhav was amongst the very few who realized that this particular star was now flickering, and in its stead another was rising on the horizon. The Wikileaks (US cable>84043 dated 2 November 2006) quotes the then consul general in Mumbai, Michael S. Owen, stating that: 'The RSS's Ram Madhav told Embassy New Delhi ... going so far as to say that Modi's ascendancy is not a question of if but when, and the USG [United States Government] must start considering now how it will deal with Modi when he becomes head of the BJP and leads the party's electoral campaign in the national elections scheduled for 2009.' Today, many within the BJP are claiming that they were the first to spot Modi's potential but Wikileaks backs Madhav's first mover advantage.

Ram Madhav's prophesy came true in 2014 and not 2009, but it revealed two facets about the RSS strategist. One, of course, that he could differentiate the (dead) wood from the trees in a manner of speaking (i.e., choosing Modi over Advani), and second, he could nudge decision making within the RSS. This kind of heft only comes with trust and a track record of credibility, and Madhav had worked for nearly four decades to achieve this.

These were interesting decades of apprenticeship. Ram Madhav's association with the RSS began as a young volunteer when as a balpracharak he was carrying messages to and fro from RSS leaders during the Emergency. 'Messaging remains his special skill' notes *The Economic Times* in a recent profile. Madhav's father Surya Narayan was a state secretary of the Jan Sangh in Andhra Pradesh and was jailed during the Emergency. Theirs was a middle class household, living in the East Godavri district with Madhav's mother Janki Devi teaching Sanskrit at a local school. Madhav attended RSS shakhas as a child and is named after two RSS sarsanghchalaks (chiefs)—Keshav Baliram Hedgewar and

Madhav Sadashiv Golwalkar. First nurture then nature led him to the RSS way.

While in the eighth grade, Ram Madhav got some of his classmates together to form a 'Thinkers' Club' called Pradeepti (meaning 'light'). The group met once a week at his house to discuss either a book or an article in the newspaper. Huddled in a circle, sitting on wooden chairs, it would be an intense articulation of the national narrative as perceived by 13 year olds. 'Looking back, I can say this was when it all started,' recalls Madhav.

By 'all' he meant a way of life that taught him how to deliberate, debate and also, propagate. Books, gadgets and think tanks are essential tools for someone whose mind is constantly challenging every book he's reading or every conversation he's having. So it was not surprising that soon after he joined the RSS, Ram Madhav rounded around 100 'intellectuals' from the RSS in Secunderabad (Hyderabad) and started a discussion group called The Thinkers Meet. The English name was an anathema to the Sangh that abhorred western titles. The idea of debate also did not go down too well with some of the traditional Sangh leadership that prefers dogma to dialogue.

But you cannot stop an idea whose time has come. Soon after, in 1989, the RSS formally established PragyaBharti, an intellectual's club which was comprised of Sangh heavyweights such as M.G. Vaidya, Murli Manohar Joshi, S Gurumurthy, Dattopant Thengdi and K.R. Malkani. The surprise name here was that of Ram Madhav who, at age 24, was the youngest member of the group. 'Either by design, or by accident, I was included. And my "intellectual innings" continued,' recalls Madhav.

He used the PragyaBharti platform to host debates and intellectual face-offs that pre-dated our prime time television shows today. One such regular was Arun Shourie (journalist and writer) who took on a representative of the Catholic Bishops Conference of India on a debate on religious conversions. Essentially an argumentative Indian, Ram Madhav is much happier meeting those with opposing ideologies than those who agree with him. Nothing makes him happier than the banter of a good debate though I am not sure if the same can be said for the person on the other side of his sharp, sometimes aggressive and always unapologetic, defense of both the parivar and the party.

Later, in 2000, Madhav was sent to Delhi as a joint spokesperson to assist then spokesperson M.G. Vaidya. At the time the RSS needed an articulate voice to allay apprehensions about the organization which was essentially seen as a fundamentalist, rigid outfit run by men in khakhi shorts. That was also the time of the Ram Janambhoomi movement—a BJP led agitation for building the Ram Mandir in Ayodhya that had toppled a masjid to make its point. Saffron was a colour that needed a lot of explanations, some spin and a broader brush. The bespectacled, English speaking Ram Madhav was the right ideologue for the job.

Dressed in telegenic Fab India kurtas, his iPad and the latest smart phone in hand, he met journalists over cups of coffee at local cafes and tried to erase the stereotyped image of a narrow-minded Sanghi. I recall when I once pointed out that it was almost an anachronism to see a RSS leader using the latest technology, he retorted saying, 'There is a difference between being modern and being western. I may be wearing a kurta-pyjama but I am sufficiently liberal, democratic and open to criticism. In that sense, I am modern. But at the same time, being modern should not be confused with being westernized. The two are not synonymous. Look at China, it is modern. But do you see a KFC or a McDonald's there?'

The suave Sangh apparatchik remained an RSS spokesperson during the tenure of the first BJP-led government at the centre, when Atal Bihari Vajpayee was the PM and did most of the fire-fighting during the 2002 Gujarat Riots. He was also manning the mikes during L.K. Advani's Jinnah moment. This is when the Hindutva hardliner Advani tried to do an image make-over during a visit to Pakistan in 2005. Standing before the tomb of Mohammed Ali Jinnah, he described the founder of Pakistan as 'secular' and an 'ambassador of Hindu-Muslim unity'. This understandably created an uproar back home. As the RSS spokesperson, it was Ram Madhav who had to articulate the Sangh's stand on Advani who was also then the BJP president. He was deputed along with other senior BJP leaders such as Venkaiah Naidu for crisis management. As soon as Advani landed in India, the media was outside the airport waiting to question him. A chit was handed to Advani which said, 'protocol should not be mistaken for policy'. The crisis managers were handing Advani a face-saving argument. For reasons of his own, Advani chose to ignore this advice.

While in Delhi, Ram Madhav saw an opportunity to further build on the Thinkers Club model and came up with the India Project in 2005 with many right wing leaders on board, such as BJP leader Vinay Sahasrabuddhe and right leaning journalists, Swapan Dasgupta and Ashok Malik. The India Project was mainly an academic exercise to promote a certain viewpoint but the idea soon caught on as its meeting began to be attended by both the Sangh and the BJP heavyweights, with the then CM of Gujarat, Narendra Modi, hosting one such event in Ahmedabad.

The success of India Project in turn inspired him to set up the India Foundation. Co-founded by Ram Madhav, the organization unabashedly describes itself as a 'premier think tank that can help understand the Indian civilizational influence on contemporary society'. To understand the power it wields, one has to take a look at the career graph of its board of directors. Of the 13 members, four went on to become ministers in the Modi government with two cabinet ministers—Suresh Prabhu and Nirmala Sitharaman, and two ministers of state—Jayant Sinha and M.J. Akbar. A fifth became a BJP general secretary (Ram Madhav) while another is a Rajya Sabha MP (Swapan Dasgupta). One of the founder trustees, Shaurya Doval, is the son of the all-powerful National Security Advisor Ajit Doval.

With the BJP government in power at the centre, conclaves hosted by India Foundation became a power destination for top editors, defense officers, religious heads, and other thought leaders. It goes without saying that an invite from India Foundation gets top of the line attendance from the Modi cabinet. 'The idea is to create an environment conducive for people to mingle and ideate,' says Madhav. But encouraging debate was not the only reason for organizing these conclaves.

Madhav and his colleagues clearly felt that in an India that had for long been in the grip of the left of centre, the right wing too needed institutional support. The secular line of thought already had established think-tanks, clubs and water holes all over the country. Those espousing a reactionary train of thought did it in a very defensive, in-your-face manner, creating more apprehension than support. If one had to sell an idea or an ideology it had to be packaged right down to the most casual detail. Such as whether the India Foundation should offer cocktails or not at its conclaves! Incidentally it does, since former army chiefs, foreign strategy experts and academics who are invited prefer their single-malts over a glass of roohafza any day. The spirit of *Atithi Devo Bhava*—the Guest is Supreme— prevailed!

The topics discussed at India Foundation meets vary from

defense to dissent, from national narrative to social media, to the idea of Indian womanhood. The delegates at these events are from various professions, geographies, faiths and ideological affiliations. But no surprises here, the topics, more often than not are in sync with the thinking of the Modi government. Take for instance, India Foundation's decision to espouse the 'One Nation, One Vote' concept. Modi has also been lobbying to combine assembly polls with general elections.

S Prasannarajan, editor of *Open* magazine wrote in October 2017, 'There's a lot more to the man who has also become the official patron of the intellectual Right. As the head of India Foundation, a think tank for the Right, he plays a key role in the making of a counter-establishment of the mind to take on the Left. Writer, speaker, networker, conscience keeper and evangelist at large, Ram Madhav continues to be the Sangh Parivar's chosen man to bring ideas and ideology together for the cause.'

Much like the equally 'modern but not westernized' Modi, the street-smart Madhav is quick to grasp the importance of social media. He was quick to understand the power of Twitter—both to convey a message and a snub. Such as his put-down to Rahul Gandhi that went viral. This was in response to Rahul Gandhi's statement that the 'RSS promotes mediocrity'. Madhav immediately shot back with a tweet: 'RSS leaders are upset with Rahul's comment. They say we never promoted him.' It was a tongue-in-cheek retort that went down well with the Modi 'bhakts' on social media.

Being audacious may not be something that he learnt in the RSS, but in Modi's BJP it is paying him rich dividends. Only he could have pulled off the politically antithetical alliance between the

People's Democratic Party (PDP) and the BJP in J&K; or tied up with the Bodoland People's Front (BPF, a pro-Bodoland party influential in lower Assam) to win the Assam polls. The backstory of the PDP-BJP alliance is particularly interesting because it involves both strategy and a bit of gumption.

Ram Madhav was given charge of J&K exactly four months before the state polls in October 2014. The state was handed to him when its in-charge J.P. Nadda moved to the cabinet. When asked how a hardliner like him would handle the Valley, Ram Madhav stated enigmatically: 'I am not a hardliner or a softliner, I am a pragmatist.' Luckily he had been visiting the state as a pracharak and had built a network that included both intellectuals and IB officials. His goal was simple. 'We knew we would sweep Jammu but it was crucial to open an account in the Valley and to show a BJP presence there.' A break-through came early when he managed to rope in former separatist leader Sajjad Lone onto the BJP platform, after engineering a meeting between Lone and the PM.

The BJP won 25 of the 87 seats in the state while regional parties, the PDP and the National Conference (NC) won 28 and 15 seats respectively, with the Congress getting just 12. Although Madhav had managed to more than double the BJP's tally from 11 in the last assembly, he still failed to win a single seat in the Valley. The BJP still remained an outsider in Kashmir.

In order to push BJP's chances as a stakeholder in government formation, he used the media to build the right perception. The art of spin is a skill the RSS excels in and Madhav learnt his lessons well. Carefully planted edits in newspapers and equally carefully planted speakers on television debates argued that any non-BJP government in the state would in effect ignore the mandate from Jammu. (The state's seats are divided with 46 in the Kashmir Valley, 37 in Jammu and 4 in Ladakh.) The BJP got all its 25 seats from Jammu, while PDP got 3 from here and a bulk from the Valley.

The two regional parties in the state—the Omar Abdullah-led Jammu & Kashmir National Conference (JKNC) and the then Mufti Mohammed Sayeed-led PDP—could not put aside their regional egos to come together on one platform. First the BJP approached the JKNC but it proved to be a frustrating exercise as its leaders said yes in Delhi but backed out in Srinagar. It was then that Madhav & Co. began the 'laborious' process of reaching out to the PDP. This was to be an audacious experiment, for of the two regional parties, the PDP was more sympathetic towards the militants and the separatists. The RSS was against the alliance but eager to notch a win for the BJP. Reading between the lines, Madhav went ahead with the alliance. It still took 40 days for PDP to say 'No' to the Congress and 'I-Do' to the BJP. Initially it seemed as if Madhav had pulled off the impossible and indeed he might have put together a very unlikely but workable coalition but for the sudden death of the sitting CM Mufti Sahab in January 2016. After that the BJP had to deal with his mercurial daughter Mehbooba as heir apparent.

If the alliance lasted nearly three years it was only due to deft political manoeuvres. Madhav was always aware of the fact that the day the coalition breaks, knives will be out for him regardless of the kudos he got when the BJP formed its first government in the troubled border state. Sure enough when the BJP broke with the PDP, it was Madhav who was fielded to do the firefighting, telling the media that 'the government had withdrawn from the alliance but not the state'.

The break-up added to his latest charge—the unwinnable state of Andhra—does signal pitfalls ahead for this resourceful pracharak. However, few can find fault with his other portfolio—that of delivering a saffronized North East to the BJP. He is fast acquiring the reputation of having a Midas touch during elections, reminding his colleagues of the Arun Jaitley and Pramod Mahajan magic during the Vajpayee era.

As mentioned earlier, while it is the norm for RSS pracharaks to be deputed to the BJP, most are low-profile individuals who prefer to work through back channels rather than take the lead and step on sensitive egos. Ram Madhav has neither the inclination nor the temperament to make these politically correct concessions. Perhaps part of his confidence comes from the fact that he is simply following the lead set by another RSS pracharak who has taken the BJP by storm—Prime Minister Modi himself. Nonetheless, he has managed to ruffle some very sensitive feathers within the party who are wary of his mercurial rise. His equation with BJP President Amit Shah is hard to define; though on the surface the two seem to have a cordial rapport with Shah deputing Madhav as a firefighter in the South after his success in the North East and J&K. Apart from Andhra he was also deployed to Karnataka during the recent state polls, in the Hyderabad-Karntaka region, because of its Telugu speaking population. The party increased its seats in this belt from 6 to 20+ in the May 2018 polls.

Yet it is interesting that despite delivering various states for the party he has not been rewarded with a Rajya Sabha seat and hence been kept out of the Modi Cabinet as well. If this worries him he doesn't show it. He has a habit of redefining himself as the situation demands and apart from the portfolios allotted to him, keeps himself busy on the seminar and foreign policy network. He prides himself on being a foreign policy buff and when he first came to the capital as the RSS spokesperson, had reached out to Diplomatic Delhi, interacting with heads of missions. One reason for this was to negate 'the misconceptions' they had about the RSS. He organized an interaction between the mission heads of the EU countries and the RSS Chief Mohan Bhagwat. As many as 27 ambassadors came for the dinner to meet Bhagwat. This was perhaps the first meeting between a RSS Chief and the Western world. He's also been a regular visitor at the US State Department, ever since his first interaction in 2006 when he was grilled about the BJP's role in the 2002 Gujarat riots and the 1992 Babri Masjid demolition.

Later, as BJP general secretary, he continued meeting foreign heads of missions, often inviting them to breakfast meetings where they get to meet key policy-makers and cabinet ministers. 'The idea is not to depend on the media to communicate but to talk to them directly and explain our policies,' he says. So he's organized interactions explaining such diverse issues as the GST, the impact of the UP election win, Triple Talaq and all the twists and turns in the Ram Janambhoomi movement.

His networking on the international arena stood him in good stead when Modi became PM and held his NRI events. He was part of the team that was deployed for Modi's Madison Square Garden event, where he was able to tap into the network he'd nurtured as a pracharak. Apart from showcasing Modi's Visa Power there is a rationale behind these Modi-Wows-the-Diaspora events. The Indian diaspora is roughly 25 million across the world and the idea was to motivate it to lobby legislation in favour of India as well as solicit FDI. Madhav points out: 'Outside the purview of hard-core government engagement on foreign policy, such interactions are useful tools for diplomatic engagement. The PM's popularity helps in creating community unity and helps the diaspora connect with their homeland. It should not be seen as a partisan event.' The last point is not necessarily true because the shrewd prime minister does use these events to shore up his own image by targeting the opposition back home, but that's clearly something the BJP is not going to lose any sleep over. Madhav has also been involved with Track Two diplomacy, such as when he went to China before the Chinese President Xi Jinping's visit to India in September 2014 and later to Israel to prepare the ground for the first ever Indian prime minister's visit to the country in June 2017.

Having authored *India-China: Uneasy Neighbours*, Madhav fancies himself as a sort of Sino-India buff. He argues that India needs to 're-orient its strategy from west-ward thinking to east-ward approach' and that a new non-Western counter-narrative is needed to establish a new global order in the 21st century. Like the rest of the BJP he is quick to dismiss Nehru's foreign policy as being weak kneed. 'After Independence we believed in certain romantic ideas like Panchsheel, Non-Aligned Movement, *Hindi Chini Bhai Bhai*. In international relations you cannot be romantic. You cannot be merely idealistic. You have to be cold bloodedly pragmatic,' he said, speaking at a seminar organized by the India Foundation in 2015.

During an interview to S Prasannarajan in *Open* magazine, Ram Madhav put the shift in the political narrative after Modi came to power in a global context. 'For the first time, you find people owing allegiance to a non-Congress nationalist school of thought that have come to occupy all the constitutional positions in the country. It is no mean achievement. There is a coherent and well-developed thought process behind this massive achievement. What the so-called ideological Right needs to do is to find proper articulation of it. Essentially it needs boosters and amplifiers. It needs to believe in co-option, as there are many intellectuals in the country who identify with the core thinking of the Right, yet they are outside the organisational structure of it. Globally also, non-Left and non-neo liberal ideas find more traction today. In a way, borrowing from John Micklethwait, I would say that we are living in a Right world today.' (20 October 2017)

Maybe there is a point to the argument that this enterprising pracharak-turned-politician has found his 'right' place in the BJP working outside the confines of government, channelling opinion and mobilizing support through his various initiatives instead of being part of the Modi cabinet. For in the world according to Chanakya, the Thought Leader will always be a notch above The Policy Executor.

HARSIMRAT KAUR BADAL

Firebrand from Punjab

In Punjab, they call her Bibaji, which means good girl. Harsimrat Singh Badal knows how to be good but she can also be very bad, especially when it comes to taking on her political foes—the Congress—for she will never forgive Indira Gandhi's party the horrors of the 1984 riots. She was a young college girl in Delhi at the time, and lived through the terror of hiding in her servant's quarters with her two brothers and an 85-year-old ailing grandmother. 'We were locked inside, with my mother begging us to try not to even breathe so that the mobs plundering and ransacking our house in search of us could not find us. Many sisters of our community were not so lucky ... a community that has helped build and protect India by shedding its blood was targeted by its own people on the basis of their turban and long hair,' she said in the Parliament as a first time MP during her maiden speech on 2 December 2009. The Congress was in power at the time but that didn't stop this Punabi kudi from pointing her index finger across the aisle straight at the Treasury Benches.

Anger at the Congress has been the cornerstone of her growing up years and segued quite naturally with the politics of her in-laws. Politics was never her end-goal, though she should have seen it coming when she married Sukhbir Singh Badal, heir to the Shiromani Akali Dal (SAD), son of Parkash Singh Badal. 'The understanding when I got married [November 1991] was that Sukhbir would never join politics. He had completed his MBA and it was expected that he would handle the family business. But destiny had other plans. Two years later he was into politics and eighteen years later, so was I,' she says.

Together they are Punjab's most influential power couple. He is the president of the SAD and a former deputy chief minister of the state while she is the feisty face of Punjabi politics in New Delhi. Currently, she is also a cabinet minister for food processing in the Narendra Modi government at the centre. What adds to the power buzz is that this is a combination that has the future chief minister of Punjab. In fact, in order to take a holistic look at Harsimrat's politics one would also have to understand where Sukhbir is coming from and where he plans to take the SAD.

I have interacted with both on many occasions, and while Harsimrat is a television anchor's delight, with her telegenic outfits and snappy sound-bites, Sukhbir takes time to warm up; though when he is provoked he delivers the deadlier punch. I was told to begin with development issues for, with him, that's the ice breaker. He is passionate about the work he undertook as deputy CM and his main grouse is that the media deliberately chose not to highlight this, instead focusing on some of the juicier allegations levelled against him by his opponents. More on this later, but if you are going to travel in swanky SUVs, build seven star resorts and fill the state cabinet with your relatives then even the most bizarre accusations tend to stick. Perception is three-fourths the battle in politics. This is the lesson that this generation of the Badal clan can learn from Sukhbir's dad, who has been described as the Nelson Mandela of India.

Regardless of what he promised Harsimrat while taking their wedding vows, Sukhbir sees his joining politics as a natural career progression. 'Our family has a history with the people of Punjab going back over seven decades. The people see a continuity, and a safety and security with our family. So it is a commitment to the people, and to the workers. Whether you like it or not, you are a part of it,' he says.

It is Harsimrat who is the accidental politician. And being Harsimrat, her reason for joining politics will catch you off guard. 'It was Captain Amarinder Singh who convinced me,' she says with a sparkle in her eye at the memory of a good fight. The Captain is the current chief minister of Punjab, the Badals' arch rival in the state and clearly the most unlikely sponsor of Harsimrat's political launch. She explains with a smile, 'He came to our hometown and challenged us by making his son contest from there. He threw down the gauntlet and said we will finish off the Badals, if they have guts let them fight me.' She adds, 'That was it. I didn't want to contest, but the challenge of a fight like that was enough to get me going. I am a Sardarni and love a good fight.'

This was in the 2009 Lok Sabha when the Captain's son Raninder Singh contested from Bhatinda constituency which lies in the Badal stronghold. Contesting the election did mean a break from the Badal family tradition for as Harsimrat says, 'Womenfolk in our family don't contest polls but they do canvass for their men and nurture their constituencies.' But when Raninder's candidature was announced, both Sukhbir and Parkash Singh Badal were otherwise engaged as deputy chief minister and chief minister of Punjab respectively. This left only Harsimrat free for the Lok Sabha contest. Her on ground connect as the Badal Bahu worked, for she won that battle with a margin of 120960 votes—the highest in the 2009 Lok Sabha.

Currently the SAD is smarting after a drubbing in the 2017 Assembly elections where it was reduced from 56 to 15 MLAs. Sukhbir's father, the five term chief minister, Parkash Singh Badal, has now retired from active politics, effectively handing over the reins of the party to his son. This is now Sukhbir's time to consolidate a comeback in the next assembly polls, due in 2022. He would love to give his father that one last win if he can, for the 90-year-old still remains the party patriarch. Most recall Parkash Badal's never-say-die spirit caught so well in a memorable put down he gave to the media in the 2017 polls. When a reporter asked him if he was fit to run for office, he asked caustically, '*Bhaj ke dikhawan?*' (Should I run and show you?)

The solemn Sukhbir is certainly not a novice who has just come into his legacy. During the last ten years of the Akali Dal led government in Punjab it was Sukhbir who was calling the shots—especially when he replaced his father as party president in 2008 and became deputy CM a year later. He is also credited for the 2012 win when the party defied all norms to make a comeback, for this was the first time in the history of the state that Punjab voted a party back to power. At the time, Sukhbir had told the media that 'the art of contesting elections has changed and one must adapt to the trends to be successful'.

Party leaders acknowledge Sukhbir's role in the win, for he took his fathers' party, steeped in traditional vote banks, and nudged it towards the new age aspirational vote bank. Says Naresh Gujral, who is the first Hindu MP from the party, 'By focusing on not just Panthic issues but also development issues such as skill development, industrialization and infrastructure, we reached out to the youth who felt hopeful.'

SAD is a party that was founded on religion, controlling most of the Sikh gurudwara committees. It is one of the oldest regional political parties in India and was part of the independence movement since the 1920s. Its priority was protection of the Sikh minority. Since then the SAD splintered into many groups with Parkash Singh Badal finally forming his own party—and this remains the most dominant Akali Dal today. Over time the party's appeal has broadened from its Panthic Sikh identity to a broader party of Punjabis. 'The SAD still represents the Sikh community at large—around the world, I would say. We made it a Punjabi party. Do you know that in the last assembly [2012] there were more Hindu MLAs in the SAD than any other party in Punjab? In politics, you have to represent everyone,' says Sukhbir.

Both Sukhbir and Harsimrat are seen as belonging to the forward looking progressive generation that talks development along with its religious agenda. Of the two, Harsimrat is perhaps of a more religious bent for she assiduously does the *paath* (prayers) every morning. His friends say Sukhbir has become more religious after marriage. In a recent TV interview when he was asked what he did the first thing each morning, Sukhbir replied: 'I do the *paath.*' Then he asked the TV anchor who was also a Sikh, 'Don't you?' When the anchor mumbled that he had been brought up in Dehradun, Sukhbir persisted with a playful smile, 'Don't they say their prayers in Dehradun?' So, don't be fooled by the serious look on his face for within lurks a school-boyish sense of humour.

What did the SAD do right in 2012 and wrong in 2017 when it's margin dropped drastically by 41 seats? Sukhbir doesn't have to think hard for an answer. 'In 2012, the difference between us and the Opposition [the Congress led by Captain Amarinder Singh] was that we believed in a positive agenda and they followed a negative agenda. We went to the people with our work, telling them what we had done.'

He is bitter about what he clearly calls a media-managed hype against the Akali Dal that painted Punjab as a drug haven. 'Now that we are out of power why is the media not talking about drug abuse in Punjab? If 70 per cent of our youth are on drugs they should be lying on the roadsides or in de-addiction centres. As you drive into Punjab did you see any such person on the road? Name one drug lord who has been caught since the new government has come in?' he asks with an eloquent shrug. However, he is quick to add, 'Winning and losing is up to God, development of Punjab is my passion. But people always want more, even if you give them too much, they want more.' The last line caught the frustration of this MBA from the California State University in Los Angeles—for no SWOT analysis taught at the fanciest of colleges, can explain voter behaviour.

Yet Sukhbir maintains his education is his most effective governance tool. Born 9 July 1962, he studied at The Lawrence School Sanawar, and completed an MA in economics from Panjab University followed by his MBA. 'Whether you are running a company or a party, you need both exposure and management. The MBA degree that also teaches governance tools like SWOT analysis, flair for technology and being adept at social media, all help me run the party better. In the end, it is all about management and people skills,' he says, merging his new age education with his traditional lineage with ease. 'If I hadn't gone abroad I would not have been exposed to expressways and international airports that I have tried to replicate here. If you live confined in a village and don't go out, then you won't know how to develop a state,' he adds with an earnest smile. This is also the longest speech I have heard him give!

One pet project of the Sukhbir Badal government was to link all the towns with four to six lane expressways. 'You can cross any corner of Punjab to reach the other end in two to three hours,' says Sukhbir. Urban infrastructure was a key focus area for Sukhbir, perhaps because he realized that while the Badals had an edge over the emotive vote bank in rural areas, they lagged in the urban constituencies. 'When we took office in 2007, only 30 per cent of towns had sewage water supply, when we left office we had covered 95 per cent of towns,' says Sukhbir. According to him the need of the hour is the CEO-cum-CM model. 'It is the only way, just as the CEO works to make his company number one, we work to make our state number one. Think big and you will achieve big. If you want to make Punjab the best state, what do you need?' It's clearly a rhetorical question for he provides the answer. 'You need ideas not money. Ideas will get you the money.' Especially if it is an idea backed by the brand name—Badal! 'The projects of ITC, TCS, Pepsi and Infosys that you see today were initiated during our government,' points out Naresh Gujaral. He also adds, 'Sukhbir is very decisive. Once he commits to something he is good for his word.'

Sukhbir is very proud of his Invest Punjab policy which came in for praise by the World Bank. The principle behind this is the concept of One Office/One email/One month to get clearance for any project. 'For 28 departments we had one office and one page application forms which would be cleared in one month. Anyone investing more than 5 million rupees could go to our Invest Punjab office in Chandigarh and get not just approval but also land allotment. It's all computerized, no dealing with officials and paying bribes,' says Sukhbir.

An equally proud Harsimrat points out, 'He is a planner. His father used to always say, set your own goals, don't try and compete with opponents. Ten years ago, Punjab had 10–12 hours of power cuts when Sukhbir said I will make it a power surplus state; and he achieved it, though everyone laughed at him initially. He said I will create roads in concrete four to six lane expressways, he has delivered that. Once he decides to do something he achieves it. Most of his plans are so huge that people find it hard to believe that he will deliver but he does it.' She pauses and then adds with a smile. 'Knowing the guy, he has a track record of delivering.' And who could know 'the guy' better than his wife who is at his side, both at home and on the political battle field as well.

It's easy to see the chemistry between the two Badals. She is the firebrand, at times politically incorrect, but one who never hesitates to pull any punches. He is more measured with his words and actions. Those who know Sukhbir say that, unlike his wife, he is not the one to wear a grudge on his sleeve and can be diplomatic if the need arises. The feud between him and Captain Amarinder is not just political, it is also personal. In 2003 when Amarinder Singh was the CM, both Sukhbir and his father were imprisoned in a disproportionate assets case based on a PIL. They were kept in a cell reserved for inmates on the death row. Sukhbir has called this nothing less than a political vendetta. He states, 'The PIL has since been dismissed by the courts. Till date has anyone found anything against me in the last ten years? False cases have been registered and we have been acquitted.'

Yet, right before the 2017 assembly elections in Punjab, he shared a dais with his bête noire—Captain Amarinder Singh—at a media conclave. The two made small talk and traded quips, with the Captain even pointing out how he sent Sukhbir Diet Coke while in prison. This did not go down well with Harsimrat who watched the interaction on TV at home. For her, an enemy is an enemy, both on the campaign field and off it. Sukhbir, however, has his own rules of engagement. Once when asked by the media why he had greeted the Captain at a wedding in the traditional manner by touching his feet even though the latter had sent him to jail, Sukhbir had replied with a simple statement: 'It's in our culture.' For his part the Captain too is much more wary of the outspoken Harsimrat than he is of the Akali Dal president.

The convent-educated Harsimrat (born 25 July 1966) clearly skipped the Bible lessons on forgiveness at her school. Textile Design was more her forte and perhaps her career of choice. She is always dressed in pastel pinks and restful reds, but that could be a diversion to underplay her feisty temper. She used her maiden speech in Parliament to bring up the 1984 riots. Later she discovered that she was always being targeted by the Congress benches. 'Whenever I spoke, Congress leaders and even ministers were on their feet trying to interrupt me. I realized it was Sonia Gandhi [then Congress President] who was egging them to take me on. Why should the president of a party be insecure of a nonentity like me?' she asked, delighted at the reaction she'd evoked.

The couple have three children, but so far none of them want to go into politics. Then again, with the Badals, those are famous last words, for as stated earlier Harsimrat would be the last to have predicted a political future for her own self. But despite her non-political upbringing she was quick to adapt to the role of a 'Political Bahu'. In public she will never be seen without her head covered, always dressed in churidar-kurtas. 'I used to love wearing saris and jeans. But now I always cover my head as most women in the village have their heads covered. Moreover, being a Badal, I was also the bahu of the area. It's a sign of respect. Only thing I don't do is uncover my head when I go to Delhi because you can't be traditional here and modern in Delhi. I don't like having dual personalities. People in Delhi say it's regressive, but I am not a hypocrite. I am what I am,' she says. It's an attitude that she wears with elan. The *Hindustan Times* rightly noted on 8 January 2017, 'She adds oomph to the demure dupatta-on-the-head look.' The one time when she wore a sari instead of the Punjabi outfit to a dinner hosted by the PM for the visiting President Barack Obama she got angry letters from Punjab saying, 'When you should be showcasing our culture and dress, you wore a sari.' That is when it struck her—back home she was seen as Punjab's brand ambassador in the Delhi court.

It's a badge she wears with pride. 'The Sikh community is small in number but it has always made huge sacrifices for our nation. During our freedom struggle, out of 2125 Indians killed by the British, 73 per cent were Sikhs; out of the 2646 people sent to Kaala Paani, 80 per cent were Sikhs; and, out of the 121 Indians hanged or executed by the British, 78 per cent were Sikhs,' she told the Lok Sabha on 2 December 2009.

Harsimrat was born a Majithia, a clan that traces it lineage to Maharaja Ranjit Singh's Majithia warrior generals. Her grandfather, Surjit Singh Majithia, was India's deputy defence minister in Jawaharlal Nehru's cabinet in 1952. However, 1984 was the turning point in the family's politics. Harsimrat's brother

Bikram Singh was a minister in the Akali Dal cabinet. During the 2017 elections the Aam Aadmi Party accused him of being part of a drug racket, a charge that both Harsimrat and Sukhbir are quick to rubbish, pointing out that none of these accusations have been proved in court, or outside. Sukhbir's sister Parneet Kaur is married to former Congress Chief Minister Partap Singh Kairon's grandson Adesh Pratap (Adesh was a minister in SAD cabinet). The coming together of the Badal–Majithia–Kairon families has seen a powerful consolidation of power and wealth. Interestingly, both Bikram and Adesh retained their constituencies in the 2017 drubbing.

'She may have begun as a reluctant politician, but now I call her an aggressive politician,' says Sukhbir. 'Yes, I've been told to cool down and calm down in Parliament,' admits Harsimrat. And then simply shrugs indicating clearly that it's not going to happen anytime soon. She even refers to her backbencher style of politics on the campaign trail, exhorting crowds to chant with her, she points out, 'I can shout louder than all of you when I am taking on the Congress in Parliament.' But Harsimrat had the last laugh—with the Akalis in a minority in the Punjab assembly, now it is Sukhbir who has to fight for his share of time on the floor of the House, and sometimes even shout to make himself heard. 'So once in a while now when I see him shouting I remind him of his own advice to me,' smiles Harsimrat.

It is a media delight to get the couple together on the same dais. Both their politics and their chemistry seems in perfect sync, with one often seamlessly finishing off the other's answers—usually that one is Harsimrat. But Sukhbir—or Kakaji as he's known in rural Punjab—has a wry sense of humour, delivered with the perfect deadpan look that gives him the edge. Earlier the media was wary of his gruff and serious demeanour but over time he has become famous for his one-liners. For instance, at a media event when questioned about dynastic politics, Sukhbir retorted, '*Ghora lain lage vi pedigree dekhde ho*' (You even see the pedigree of the horse you buy).

While she is definitely the more talkative Badal, he is the one with a plan—whether it is how to strategize for the party or decide where the family would go for a vacation. When asked what she would do if she wasn't into politics, pat comes the reply, 'I would be a homemaker, squabbling with him as to why he's come home late.' Perhaps that's the real reason why Sukhbir pushed her to join politics because if you ask him who wins the fights at home he will promptly tell you, 'She does.' A response which promptly draws a smile from her. 'Well that's the only place I can win with him,' she points out with a laugh.

I recall meeting her as a first time MP when I was doing a story on women dynasts. At the time she told me, 'The benchmark of my politics is that my father-in-law should not be ashamed of me. People should not say Badal sahib ki bahu (daughter-in-law) and shake their heads', she'd said. However, as you may have already guessed this is no demure daughter-in-law but a Punjabi firebrand who knew even then how to wrangle the odd concession from her powerful father-in-law. It was at her initiative that Parkash Singh Badal had announced the recruitment of women in the police force. She also 'persuaded' Sukhbir to revive the popular game of kabaddi by holding an international competition in Punjab in 2011. 'Of the 17 teams, four were women's teams but the prize money was Rs 2 crore for the men and Rs 50,000 for women. I fought with Sukhbir against this bias,' she says. In private it's Sukhbir, but in public she calls him Sukhbirji as that's how Punjabi men are traditionally addressed by their wives. 'He loves it,' says Harsimrat, with a delighted smile.

There are certainly no gender biases in this combination, and regardless of what she says, it's easy to see which one of the two usually gets to have the last word.

July 2017, Nitish Kumar, the chief minister of Bihar and Janata
Dal (United) leader who had come to power with support from
Tejashwi's party—the Rashtriya Janata Dal (RJD) had broken
the alliance. He replaced them with the BJP and continued in
government. But worse was to follow for Tejashwi. For a few
months, later in January 2018, his father and RJD chief Lalu
Yadav was sent to the Birsa Munda Central Jail in Ranchi to
serve a 14 years sentence after being convicted in a multi-
crore fodder scam case. Incidentally, even Tejashwi has been
accused of accepting bribes in exchange for granting illegal
favours to a private hotel company when Lalu was the railway
minister in 2006. The fact that he was around 15 years old at
the time hasn't stopped the Enforcement Directorate (ED)
from routinely interrogating him. 'It is fortunate that I am not
married, otherwise the CBI and the ED would be questioning
my in-laws as well,' remarked Tejashwi with a smile.

Some would say that his father's misfortune saw the making
of Tejashwi Yadav because it is only after Lalu was jailed that the
leadership mantle fell on him. He had to step up and not just
placate the party faithful but also convince his opponents that the
RJD was alive and kicking. When I pointed this out to Tejashwi,
he commented that it was not his father's misfortune but the
opportunistic attitude of Nitish Kumar that was responsible for
his coming into his own, saying, *'Log kehte the, pehli baar chunav
lada, pehli baar deputy CM bana* [People used to comment that
I became deputy CM soon after fighting my first election], my
opponents and those who did not know me used to question
how will he handle such a big responsibility.' It was not so much
his performance as deputy CM but the way he handled his
role as leader of the opposition that won him national aplomb.
Overnight he was stripped of his ministerial office, and after
leading an all-night dharna outside the governor's residence,

Tejashwi walked into the state assembly to speak at the trust vote moved by Nitish Kumar and his new-found ally—the BJP. 'There was no time to prepare a speech as we were busy all night doing a dharna, but what I felt I presented before the house at the time. *Jo bhi tha*, I spoke naturally, and no, I didn't feel nervous, why should I? We had done nothing wrong, they were the ones looking nervous and guilty,' he said, when I asked him about that famous speech that certainly saw the making of a leader.

In a 45-minute performance that was televised nationwide, Tejashwi lashed out against Nitish, whom he now refers to as Paltu Uncle (one who is always changing sides). The speech was high on theatrics and acerbic in its attack against Nitish's *vyakti vishesh* (individualistic) brand of politics. Speaking almost extempore with an occasional glance at the sheaf of papers in his hands, he addressed the Treasury benches as 'Boss'. He reminded them about their 17 years of association, which Nitish summarily broke one fine morning in June 2013 by sacking all the 11 BJP ministers from his cabinet. '*Jis tarah se doodh mein makkhi hoti hai, uss tarah se makkhi ko nikal deeya gaya, vaise aap logo ko nikaal diya gaya* [He removed you from his government, as one would a fly from a glass of milk],' said Tejashwi flicking his fingers at an imaginary fly. He also taunted Nitish saying that while he would always respect him as an elder he would never respect his politics. The speech and its delivery had a Lalu-esque touch but the voice was modulated and had a gentler cadence than his father's trademark aggression. Those wondering why the veteran leader had chosen his youngest and yet untried son as his heir apparent, got their answer that day. 'With every crisis a star is born,' noted RJD spokesperson Manoj Jha. Agrees Siddharth Varadarajan founding editor of *The Wire*, 'He certainly has had greatness thrust upon him. If the RJD sweeps the next assembly he will be the youngest chief minister of any state ever.'

an introvert, deeply religious and ritualistic. He is also known as Kanhaiya, after a snapshot of him dressed as Lord Krishna went viral. It is also clear that he is not content to playing second fiddle to his younger brother as is apparent by the 'I Am Lalu' poster he has splashed on his social media sites. A fiery orator—both of Lalu's sons have inherited his eloquence—Tej Pratap has taken to blowing a conch before speaking at a public rally and tries to imitate Lalu's rustic appeal. The catch is that while Lalu is rustic, he is not inelegant; and though a fiery speaker, Tej Pratap sometimes comes across as aggressive and unpolished. The difference between him and Tejashwi is that while the latter can modulate his voice to suit the occasion, the former comes across as either sullen or aggressive. Both have their own appeal when addressing rallies in the cow-belt, but in one-on-one interactions, the younger son comes across as more savvy. Signs of sibling rivalry came to the fore as soon as the limelight shifted to Tejashwi with Tej Pratap commenting wryly that he had no issues if his younger brother got married first since he was any way more popular with the girls, being the deputy chief minister.

Ironically, it was after Tej Pratap's own marriage that the sibling rivalry became public with Tej Pratap tweeting that he was feeling side-lined within the party as 'certain party people don't listen to me'. While ostensibly this was in reference to some of his candidates being ignored for party posts, it was also clear that he was demanding a greater play within the party. His mother Rabri Devi hastily managed the optics by getting both brothers to feed each other *mithai* at a public event but there are those who have noted that Tej Pratap's little revolt happened soon after his marriage to Aishwarya Rai, the daughter of a RJD MLA, who harbours political ambitions herself and plans to contest the 2019 Lok Sabha elections. 'There is no issue between us, I think the media is getting affected by saas-bahu serials to okay too. I am not into day to day rituals like him, if you pray in your mind that's ok. It depends on person to person. There is a God but I believe that *ghanti bajane se sab kuch theek nahin hota* [solutions don't lie in ringing temple bells]. You have to work also.'

Unlike other dynasts, most of whom have an elite foreign university education to spiff up their credentials, Tejashwi is a Class 9 drop out. Always a back-bencher he preferred the playing fields to the classroom and dropped out of school to play national cricket. That this is still his first love was evident when I asked him: 'Tell me how it all began.' And he began with his cricket career not political one. And though he didn't notch up any remarkable milestones, his cricketing stint is something he is proud of. His Wikipedia page (the modern day backgrounder) has a section dedicated to his cricketing achievements. 'My parents never forced me to do anything whether it was studies or cricket, all they said was *jo karo mann se karo, dil laga ke karo* [whatever you do give it your best]. I wanted to represent the Indian cricket team which is what every player wants to do. I was the Delhi Captain for the Under-15 and Under-17 national teams and played in the Under-19 team when Virat Kohli was the captain.' He was also part of the Delhi Daredevils Team during the first four seasons of IPL. Once, when debating the controversies surrounding the IPL, Lalu commented wryly: 'My son Tejashwi is part of the Delhi team. But all he has done is to carry water to the field. They don't give him a chance to play.' He also played a couple of Ranji Trophy matches when he had to give up the game due to 'ligament problems in both my ankles'.

It's because of cricket that he spent most of his teens travelling out of Bihar, but in 2010 he was in Patna during the state assembly polls.

The way Tejashwi tells it is that one morning as his father was on his way to the party office to address a press conference, he decided to accompany him. 'I thought *dekhte hain kya hota hai Papa ke press conference mein—bahut kum mauka milta tha* [let's go and see the press conference]. In any case, I got little time to spend with dad as I used to be in Delhi and travelled a lot, so I went with him. The media was there obviously and Dad introduced me. But the media presented it as if Laluji has launched his son.' However, according to a journalist present at the time the launch looked more planned than accidental 'for there was Tejashwi smartly dressed in a pant and shirt, quite unfazed with our questions'. Then again, that is also how Tejashwi usually is, at any given point in time. Soon after Tejashwi began campaigning for the party. He says, 'Where Papa could not go, the candidates called me because it was presented to them that I had been launched into politics. So I thought *chale jaate hain* [let me go], the Ranji Trophy season had just finished so I thought if I can be of help then why not.'

Does he now have any regrets that he did not complete his education? 'At the time I felt that now is my chance to play cricket, for I can continue my studies any time later. But see, I could have easily got a *farzi* certificate like Smirti Iraniji or Modiji but I am accepting that I didn't complete my school, I was a true cricketer,' he says with a mischievous smile, taking a dig at the controversies surrounding the educational qualifications of both Smirti Irani and the PM. He adds, 'Later on I realized you need a basic qualification. However, a degree doesn't mean *aapke paas puri qualification hai* [that you have all the qualifications], *theek hai* [it's all right], that was my mistake and I admit it and if I get any opportunity or chance then I will try and study further also.' I think the last bit was added to assuage my middle class sensibility which has a problem with the idea of a school drop-out becoming a deputy chief minister in 21st century India.

Interestingly, soon after our meeting I noticed a social media post on Tejashwi's timeline where he had put up a picture of his meeting with Congress President Rahul Gandhi and underneath the picture was a caption: 'Bliss was it in that dawn to be alive, but to be young was very heaven.' It's a quote from a William Wordsworth poem on the French Revolution; and though the revolutionary potential of either of the two young men (although separated by almost two decades) is yet to impress me, the enthusiasm and the acquaintance with Wordsworth, however, was heartening.

With the opposition getting together on one platform to take on the BJP in the 2019 general elections, it is interesting to see the bonhomie between the GenNext leaders that are now at the helm of their parties. Tejashwi, for instance, has a connect with Rahul; the two of them were seen lunching at a restaurant in Delhi's Defence Colony Market some time back. He also has an equation with the two scions from Uttar Pradesh—Akhilesh Yadav and Jayant Chaudhary. 'Rahul told me he'd take me out to lunch sometime, so one day I called him and said I am free so he said let's go. People should meet like this, it is good as common problems can be discussed ... Akhilesh, Omar, Jayant, Hemant, Soren, we are all in touch. We do talk about the economy and state of the nation, the loss due to GST and demonetization, and the arrogance of the BJP,' he said.

Of all, Tejashwi is the youngest but he is also the most sought after because unlike for the others, his father's vote bank is still intact (in the 2015 state elections, even though it was clear that Lalu Yadav would not be the CM candidate, the RJD got

the largest number of seats, even more than the JDU, though
Nitish Kumar was the chief ministerial face of the alliance).
Of course, Lalu's party is limited to Bihar but the state offers a
large chunk of 40 MPs to the Lok Sabha kitty. The only danger
would be from within, if Tej Pratap plays into the BJP's hands
and splits the party.

When I asked Tejashwi if he endorsed his luncheon
companion, Rahul Gandhi's candidature as prime minister, he
said, 'See who will be PM is a secondary question. First question
is to defeat this government and *chutkara paana hai* [be free of
them]. People want to be free of this tanashahi and Emergency
rule, where all the agencies from CBI to ED are being misused.
The people of this country are seeing the PM's silence on mob
lynching, atrocities against Dalits and BJP ministers supporting
rapists. Instead of a one way *Mann ki Baat* [a radio programme
hosted by Prime Minister Narendra Modi], there should be
kaam ki baat.'

That didn't quite answer my question so I tried another
tack, asking him how it felt to be doing business with the same
Rahul Gandhi who had embarrassed his father by tearing up an
ordinance (passed by the then UPA Government) that allowed
those who had cases pending against them to contest elections
until they were actually convicted of the charges. (Lalu fell in
this category.) Tejashwi's reply came with a slight smile. 'How
do you only relate the ordinance to my Dad? Does it matter in
today's India if he tore it or not. People should worry about
the current situation not whether he tore an ordinance or not.
That was in the past. Worry about the now. We have to face it all
together. Rahul is an alliance partner. Soniaji and my Dad had a
very good relationship. *Theek hai* [It's ok]. We are the NextGen
and there are some things which I would hesitate to say in front
of Soniaji but not with Rahul. *Sab theek hai* [Everything is ok].'

On that note he offered me some digestive biscuits that had come along with the tea!

As I munched, he added, 'I don't understand why there is a problem if the opposition is getting united and with good reason. Why should we fight *alag-alag* [separately]? If the BJP can fight with 40 allies then so can the opposition fight together and unite against the BJP. Modiji and Amitji have only three to four agendas: Hindu vs Muslim, Ram–Sita, Pakistan, Kashmir and stone pelting. Have they kept any of their promises?'

Talking about fulfilled promises, he is all too eager to narrate his achievements during the 18 months he was in office. I suspect part of the eagerness also comes from a sense of hurt at the criticism about his ability to hold onto some pretty heavy-weight portfolios, for apart from being deputy chief minister, he was also in charge of the road and building construction departments. 'But if you compare my work it was much better than any department handled by Nitish. Other departments used only 15–20 per cent of their allocations to sanction work; I used 100 per cent of the funds allocated to sanction projects,' he said. He is also proud of the fact that he got the central government (which was led by the rival BJP) to clear projects that were stuck at their end. 'The Central Road Fund for Bihar was Rs 200 crore, I got that increased to Rs 1000 crore. In addition, 53 Railway Over Bridges [ROBs] that had been stalled since 2010 got cleared.' Seeing that I did not quite get the enormity of what he had achieved he explained, 'The NHAI guidelines for land acquisition differ from the state ones. Because state governments used to give four times the compensation as compared to NH road projects; the central projects got stalled as no one wanted to give up their land for a lower price. I met the minister in Delhi and said, let the price be the same as that's recommended by the state. All your projects are stalled because you cannot acquire land so you need to change your guidelines. So they agreed that whatever price was suggested by the Bihar collector would be paid for the land and that the centre would give the extra money.'

He added with a flourish, 'In 18 months I built 5000 km of road without a single charge of corruption against me during these months,' and sat back in his chair, looking at me expectantly. When I didn't react, he leaned forward again and pressed his point: 'People say that I have assimilated disproportionate assets—that too when I was 13 or 14 years old. By that logic when I was handling three ministries, I should have done so many more scams, worth thousands of crores. Yet during these 18 months I made strict policies to prevent corruption. I made a proposal that no files related to the award of contracts would come to the minister. Everyone knows what happens with these files, and had I disposed of them or I would have been framed. *Anyway kitna cement, bricks lage ga* [how much cement, bricks will be used], to give extension to contractors. This is not the work of a minister but the engineer. I made a committee under the principal secretary to take these decisions. Since mine was a nodal ministry, others like Rural Development and Irrigation were also affected. This was a way of closing *sabhi dukaane jo chalti thi* [corruption]. Those affected have spread stories about me being corrupt but it is the people's court that is the ultimate decider.'

If Tejashwi thought that I wasn't paying close attention to what he was saying—my recorder was doing the needful—he was right. For in the middle of his impassioned speech, one thing struck me, that despite his lack of educational degrees, he was genuinely concerned about new age issues like performance, deliverability and image. I don't think his father would have spent so much time explaining his performance parameters because for Lalu his vote bank mattered more than problems of perception and image.

Tejashwi has often told the media that the one thing that worried him when he was touring the country playing cricket was the negative image of Bihar in the rest of the country. But aren't his parents to be blamed for that as well, for both Lalu and Rabri have ruled the state for almost 15 years between them? He dismisses criticism against his parents saying, 'It was propaganda. There is an image about Bihar that is contrary to the facts. When my Dad became the CM, at that time Patna's Gandhi Maidan and the railway station were mortgaged. My father got Bihar out of that mess that Jagannath Mishra (Congress CM) had put it into. Also, earlier, Bihar and Jharkhand were one and all the industry, sports and cultural associations were in South Bihar which have gone to Jharkhand. When the state was split, Mom asked Atal Bihari Vajpayee who was the PM then to give special status to Bihar. Nitishji was a central minister then and he tried to stop it saying they will get the credit.'

That's his story and he is standing by it. He went on to add, 'There was a lot of difference between the 90s and today. That time the paramount demand was for social justice, that development should not be just for a few but for everyone. It should reach the villages where people were not able to even ask for their rights. They only became more demanding once they were given the basics.'

Is he going to play the same politics of caste as his father? For in the end that is the vote bank that is propelling him to power, is it not? 'We are not playing any politics. The MY word [Muslim-Yadav] was not coined by my dad but by the BJP to limit us. They want that the Extreme Backward Classes should be unhappy and not vote for us. When we talk of reservations it's not just for Yadavs and Muslims, it is also for Dalits and Extreme Backward Classes. Everyone should get their share according to their population.' According to him the next election will be fought on the principles of 'Ambedkar, Gandhi and Mandal versus Golwalkar and Godse'.

From caste politics he moves on to the politics of religion, asking, 'Why are only Muslims secular and not Hindus? A Muslim can be both secular and communal, as can a Hindu so don't mark them into silos. This is their agenda to divide us. It is not right to say that the word "secular" is anti-Hindu, and only about Muslims and Pakistan.' I asked him if he was also trying—like Rahul and Akhilesh—to change the perception that his party was pro-minority at the cost of the majority vote? 'We want to take everyone along. When Amit Shah and Nitish Kumar play caste politics you say they are doing marvellous social engineering but when we talk, we are casteist. We want to include the back-benchers of society along in the development story.' He cites the example of former Bihar CM Jitan Ram Manjhi, a Mahadalit who belongs to the Musahar community. In September 2014, Manjhi had claimed that a temple in the Madhubani district of Bihar was cleansed after his visit. Relating this incident, Tejashwi asked, 'When he visits a mandir why do you wash the mandir after his visit? We are not against any caste but we are against this kind of a *soch* [thought process] that allows only Brahmins to head both temples and the RSS. Why not other castes? Of course, Boss, if there is a poor amongst the upper caste then he too should be given reservations. That is also a part of our demands, but you have to also fight a mind-set.'

One point his mind is set upon is that he will never do business with Nitish again. He blames him for pursuing the cases against his father, and says, 'If I do another alliance with him then people will accuse me of being a *paltu* [making a U-turn].'

Finally, as he was seeing me off, I asked him what he did with his day offs. He laughed, saying that between ED summons and party work, he barely gets any time off. Adding in a lighter vein, 'God forbid some disaster occurs and you are watching a movie, the media will go overboard saying—look there was a catastrophe but he was busy watching a movie!' He was referring to the fact that a television channel wasted an entire hour of prime time discussing the fact that Rahul Gandhi had gone to see *The Last Jedi* the evening the Gujarat and Himachal assembly results came in [2017].

Maybe, in today's hyper-critical world, he has a point there, Boss!

OMAR ABDULLAH

Cub-e-Kashmir

It's a carpe diem moment for Omar Abdullah. Years ago, his grandfather Sheikh Mohammad Abdullah, the Sher-e-Kashmir, had written in his autobiography, *Flames of the Chinar*: 'The historical relationship between individuals and events is subject to two interpretations. Some believe that individuals make history while others contend that historical forces create individuals. I believe that reality lies somewhere between these two extremes. Unless given an opportunity individuals cannot prove themselves.' Today, Omar stands at such a cusp where both character and circumstance will come into play.

The Chinar leaves are still smoldering in a Kashmir that was misgoverned by a most unnatural alliance formed by the

regional People's Democratic Party (PDP) and the national
Bharatiya Janata Party (BJP). The alliance came together on the
audacity of hope, but three-and-half years later (June 2018), the
audacity was reduced to bluster and experience trumped hope.
At a time when the Valley is desperately looking for a credible
leader, Omar Abdullah can be sighted on the horizon. Therein
lies opportunity. Does he have it in him to step into the Valley's
leadership gap?

Omar has been tried before and found wanting. But today, his
chief minister-ship (2009–2015) which seemed unremarkable
at the time, has acquired a nostalgic sheen. What is equally
important is that Omar seems to have used the intervening years
as a grooming period to shore his credentials. There were those
who found Chief Minister Omar Abdullah to be inexperienced,
overtly sensitive and lacking an on-ground connect. In a state
where even a day's trip to New Delhi marks the traveller as a
RAW agent, Omar spent far too many weekends in the capital to
build trust in the Valley. However, in Opposition, Omar seems
to have made himself a check list of What-Not-To-Do. Instead
of the airport's exit lounge, he is now seen touring the Valley
often dressed in the ethnic shalwar-kameez.

When I landed in Srinagar to interview Omar for this book, I
did the 'journalist-thing' and asked my cab driver in Hindi what
he thought of his former CM. He replied in English, spending
the first few minutes cursing the government at the Centre, past/
present governments of the state for capitulating to a regime in
New Delhi that cared little whether graduates from the Valley
got jobs or not. Finally, about Omar specifically, he said he liked
him the best because he was so reactive and empathic—albiet
on social media!

Some more conversations in the Valley revealed a similar
line of nostalgia. There was a perception that Omar had matured

in Opposition. Translated in Kashmiri-speak this meant that he appeared more mindful of local aspirations and had stopped toeing the Centre's line. During the 2014 election campaign—which Omar lost as the sitting chief minister—I had visited Srinagar for my show, *Cover Story*, telecast on NewsX (29 November 2014). At the time, Naaem Akhtar, PDP Leader who went on to become the minister of education, had told me, 'Omar doesn't know anybody in Kashmir. He hasn't studied here, he hasn't been brought up here, he hasn't even played here.' Political analyst Sheikh Mohammad Quayoom too had made a similar observation in the show, 'When you compare Farooq with Omar, the former is more closely linked with the people, call it his rhetoric, theatric whatever. Farooq will enter a village home and go straight to the lady who is cooking rice and say pour some for me. I have seen him do it, and that is more important for a Kashmiri than the road you are building outside his house. Omar is Western educated and has a certain social reticence. That doesn't gel well. You have to come and sit with me on my paddy land and have my cup of tea. I will come and embrace you, an old lady will come and kiss you on your forehead. If you think this is going to your next bout of influenza, well that doesn't gel with us!' But during the disastrous PDP-BJP experiment, Quayoom pointed out, 'Omar was certainly much better as a leader of Opposition than he was a chief minister. For one, he did not jump the gun as he did as CM.'

I went to meet this improved, non-jumpy Omar at his residence at 40, Gupkar Road. A small steel gate let me inside the fortress like walls guarded by armed guards, to a manicured lawn with cane chairs where I was greeted by the affable Tanvir Sadiq, Omar's political secretary. By the time Omar arrived, dressed in dark blue track-pants, I was about to sip my coffee brewed for me by Tanvir. 'You do know that he does this for very few people,' remarked Omar. In an instant the brew that I was nonchalantly sipping was upgraded to Special Status. In Kashmir, everything comes with a perspective as I was about to learn.

Now, there is an unofficial rule book for doing interviews. You always begin with the soft questions. Maybe it was the belligerent ghost of my Kashmiri Pandit grandmother, but I went for the jugular. Switching on the voice recorder on my mobile phone, I remarked, 'People say you lost the 2015 elections because you did not have the same connect with the locals as your dad.' The smile remained but a shrug gave the game away. 'Look, I am what I am. I never claimed to be as easy communicating with people as my dad. Criticism is something you take as it comes. You are only as good as your last election. When the chips are down, all the stories come out. Suddenly Yogi is not a good administrator or as great a crowd-puller as he was in Gujarat and Tripura, just because he lost two by-polls recently.' Omar was alluding to the fact that despite being the BJP's star campaigner pan-India, the UP chief minister managed to lose two Lok Sabha by-polls in his own state, including one from his former constituency in March 2018.

Before he started treating me as his next bout of influenza, I went back to the rule book, and told him how 'Omar the Opposition Leader' was perceived as more mature than 'Omar the Chief Minister'. 'Omar any day is more mature than Omar the day before,' he said. 'Every day you learn something new about yourself, about the situation and people around you. That is, if you are willing to learn. If you approach life with the misplaced belief that you know everything you need to know, then you will stagnate. I am confident enough in my own abilities to recognize that there's nobody I will meet who I can't learn something from.'

The tone is certainly more measured than it was five years ago. The CM who walked around with his resignation in his pocket has now decided that it's best not to take every comment personally. The hair on his head has greyed with good reason. 'You come to realize very soon that the exuberant I'll-change-everything-in-a day mind-set is not practical. The reality is very different. You have to work the system to achieve what you want to. You also have to know that you will not achieve a 100 per cent of what you set out to achieve and therefore you have to be realistic, not just in your goals but also realistic in what you communicate to the people in terms of promises,' he says. Adding, 'I have learnt it's better not to mislead the people. I know that it makes for bad politics but I honestly rather have people angry with me in the short term for saying no, than be angry with me in the long term for saying yes, and not being able to deliver.' There is something refreshing about his candour. What I liked about him was also the fact that after the BJP-PDP government collapsed he did not rush to cobble a coalition stating simply: 'We did not have the mandate in 2014 and we don't have the mandate in 2018.'

Omar became chief minister on 6 January 2009. Since the National Conference (NC) had 28 MLAs in the 87-member house, it took the support of the Congress with its 27 MLAs to form the government. Dressed in a black sherwani, the then 38-year-old took oath as the youngest CM of the state. Farooq Abdullah regaled the media with lyrics from the popular Hindi film song, '*Papa Kehte Hain Beta Bada Naam Karega*'. A more sombre Omar restricted his sound-bites to stating that his top priorities would be 'good governance and reaching out to the people'. Given the Abdullahs' three generational friendship with the Nehru-Gandhis, there was much hype that this management graduate could have some of the answers to the Valley's problems. Perhaps that was too glib a reading of the situation. Some of Omar's biggest challenges lay in the past as much as in the future. In Kashmiri politics, an Abdullah is both the text and the context.

The Abdullahs have held sway over the Valley ever since 1932 when Omar's grandfather formed Kashmir's first political party—the Muslim Conference. Later, after a conversation with Jawaharlal Nehru, he transformed it to the more inclusive National Conference and spearheaded a popular Quit Kashmir agitation against the Dogra rulers on the lines of the Quit India movement against the British. Since independence, the family has monopolized state politics, and were a part of any government formation (with large chunks of governor's rule in the middle), until the launch of the PDP in 1998. It is an open secret that the PDP was propped up by the Centre with the sole aim of weakening the one party hold that the National Conference had over the Kashmiri voter.

When I asked Omar if the NC paid the same price of doing business with the Centre that the PDP is now paying, he replied, 'It's not just the NC but J&K has paid the price for it. Look at the machinations and intrigues of establishing the PDP with overt and covert GOI support around when the NC passed an autonomy resolution in the assembly [26 June 2000]. It is also a fact that [intelligence] agencies continue to prop up individuals with a view to dividing the votes. There is a lot more intelligence agency driven intrigue in J&K than in any other state. So I would say the whole state is a victim of that, not just my father, not just the NC. My grandfather had always warned people that New Delhi will never be comfortable with a strong single voice emerging out of J&K, particularly out of Kashmir. They would always want to prop up and support multiple voices because it suits their scheme of things to have a number of mid strength voices rather than a really strong voice. This is again something that's borne out by evidence over the last 20–30 years.'

Omar used his stint in Opposition to undo his image of being the Centre's favourite go-to Kashmiri. In September 2016, when unrest broke in the Valley after the killing of militant Burhan Wani, Union Home Minister Rajnath Singh took an All Party Delegation to the Valley for talks. (Wani was a Hizbul Mujahideen commander, also known as the poster boy of militancy due to his appeal with the Valley's restless youth.) The BJP and the PDP squabbled over inviting Hurriyat leaders to the talks. It was Omar who touched a chord with the locals when he criticized the CM for failing to engage the separatists. Speaking to the media he said, 'You need to open channels of communication to address the political nature of the problem. You cannot tire this agitation out, you cannot crush it and you cannot buy out a solution to it. You have to address it politically.' Omar has maintained that the problem with Kashmir is political not administrative, it cannot be solved with economic packages or subsidized rice. He echoes his grandfather's line that a solution without talking to either the separatists or Pakistan is not possible.

As he told former editor and columnist, Vir Sanghvi, when he appeared on his weekly political show, *Virtuosity*, 'It is simplistic to say stone throwers are doing it for money, a few maybe but majority are for ideological reasons. They don't see their future with the Union of India. They do not believe that the accession of J&K to India was the right step and they would like to correct that. I do not agree with either their premise or their methods but it would be foolish to deny it.' (15 April 2017)

Quayoom agrees saying, 'The difference between Omar and Mehbooba is that he doesn't identify himself with the militants. He may condole their deaths but if anyone is seen as a nationalist, secular leader here it is Omar. And that's both a good and a bad thing.' He adds, 'Of late Farooq has been playing the soft-separatist card. Omar would never do that.'

The idealistic Omar has also talked about setting up a Truth & Reconciliation Commission between India and Pakistan. I recall his speech at the New York University (NYU) where he stated: 'I understand a Truth & Reconciliation Commission is a post conflict measure. But how long do you wait? Do you wait till the absolute last gun has gone silent? Because that may be a very long wait and possibly this is an interim measure that will actually allow you to come even closer to a final solution' (India and Pakistan: A Subcontinental Affair, NYU, October 2013). The only name he could come up to head this, was someone like Nelson Mandela.

Meanwhile, when I asked him if he had a blue-print for resolving the Kashmir crisis, he pointed to the National Conference's Autonomy resolution. The crux of which is a return to Kashmir's pre-53 status. Presidential orders since then have eroded several special privileges given to the state when it acceded to India, giving leeway to central laws such as the Armed Forces (Special Powers) Act over those of the state. 'We have acceded not merged with India. We don't want internal autonomy from Pakistan or Russia or America but from India, where we have already been guaranteed greater autonomy by its Constitution,' says Omar. Adding, 'This was the sovereign promise made to the people of J&K. You cannot deny that Maharaja Hari Singh wanted J&K to be an independent country. He did not accede to either India or Pakistan in 1947. He wanted an independent J&K. His hand was forced by the invasion but even then he negotiated a special status for J&K. That special status is part of the reason why J&K became part of the Union and you can't sort of take the line that J&K will continue to be a part of the union but the terms on which the accession took place we will erode those. That's blatantly unfair.'

I asked him about his equation with the Congress which didn't pay heed to many of his demands as CM, even though both were alliance partners, such as the removal of AFSPA, despite Omar making a public statement that it would soon be removed (*The Hindu*, 21 September 2011). He remembered the incident all too well, telling me, 'I was on the right side of the argument, the situation warranted it and I had the support of the minister that really mattered—Mr Chidambaram. Both of us ran into a brick wall at the time—AK Antony [then defence minister] and Mr Pranab Mukherjee who was then finance but had earlier held defence so he had the exposure to the same thought process that Mr Antony was privy to. The PM was unwilling to overrule two of his senior most ministers. I dare say if he had taken that decision, who knows politically things might have been very different, and I don't mean for the NC but for the state as a whole, in terms of the current state of alienation that you see, the anger on the streets.'

Is there any rule book in dealing with the Centre, I ask. He replies candidly, 'The Centre is not a unitary force or a single unit. Are you dealing with the Congress or with the BJP...? There is no single way to answer a question like that. I had no problems in dealing with Dr Manmohan Singh, Mrs Gandhi or Rahul for that matter.'

In boarding school language, he and Rahul Gandhi are 'family friends'. Nehru was a staunch supporter of Sheikh Abdullah until they disagreed and Nehru threw him in jail. Farooq too has had his share of accord (pun intended) and discord with both Indira Gandhi and her son Rajiv. As for the GenNext, both Omar and

Rahul share the same pedigreed background, a boyish love for gadgets, bikes and an interest in geo-politics. The buzz in the Valley is that Omar became the chief minister only because Rahul made that a condition of Congress support to the NC government. Until then it was expected that Farooq would be the next chief minister. He had even hinted as much on a few TV interviews immediately after the results. But almost overnight Omar's name was finalized. The general perception was that Rahul had pushed for Omar's candidature.

When I tried to cross-check something that I thought was a given, Omar denied it outright claiming he was not Rahul's but his father's choice for CM. 'They [Congress] don't get to choose. I don't get to decide who the Congress' face for PM or CM will be and similarly the Congress doesn't get to decide who their allies will put in any position. Who the NC's CM candidate is or was is a decision only the NC will take. At no point in time did the Congress have a veto as to who would or would not be CM candidate of the NC.'

Noting the skeptical look on my face he shrugged and added, 'I'll tell you this much, if the Congress had at any point of time told us to choose A instead of B there would have been no alliance. I would never have tied up with a party that told us they would rather have me than my father. That is out of the question. And in all fairness to the Congress that conversation never took place.' Then why hasn't he denied this earlier? His response is typically Omar. 'I was never asked. Why deny something that's not been asked. If I deny everything that people talk about that's all I'll do every day.'

The legacy question for Omar is a many layered one. He has to deal not just with the past but also the present for his father's larger than life persona looms over both the party and the state. Appearing on the show *Rendezvous with Simi Grewal* (1999) along with Farooq, Omar had spoken about living under the shadow of a flamboyant father. Farooq has always been something of a show-man, whether it was his much publicized golf games or the time when he gave actress Shabana Azmi a ride on his Ducati. When Simi asked about his father's playboy image, Omar retorted that he'd heard all the rumours while in school, including the one that his father was getting married to the actress Rekha and added with a smile, 'I never had so many friends self-inviting themselves to my home for the summer holidays wanting to meet my stepmother.'

Since he is just the opposite of his gregarious father who was known as the Disco Dancer CM, every media interview of Omar has him fielding a question on the comparison. Appearing on NDTV's *Follow the Leader* show with Nidhi Razdan (November 2003) he admitted, 'I am not a gregarious outgoing person. I hate the thought of going to a disco with everyone analysing my every move ... [I am] fond of shaking a leg but on my own, I am fond of music.' After a pause, he added, 'and of staying alive on campaign trail.' He can joke about it, while listening to Dire Straits inside his bulletproof SUV, but the fact is that the Abdullahs do live under the shadow of a gun. The father and son never travel in the same vehicle even if they are headed for the same rally. As babies, Omar's two sons, Zahir and Zamir, were wheeled out in their prams with armed security walking behind them; whether they were in New Delhi or Srinagar. (Omar is now separated from his wife Payal.) It is only when he goes abroad that he revels in the normal everyday activities like hopping onto a tube or hailing a cab for himself.

So one could see where he was coming from when he dished out a snub at the NYU in October 2016. While participating at a conference titled 'India and Pakistan: A Subcontinental Affair Conference', he was confronted by a somewhat hostile Pakistani girl who pointed out she came from Azad Kashmir where she'd had a very 'happy and peaceful' childhood since there was no need for any heightened security in the area governed by Pakistan. To which Omar replied, 'The fact that you don't have any security means that there are no terror camps operating on my side of Kashmir and sending them to your side. They're operating on your side of Kashmir and coming across to my side. Your politicians are not facing terror attacks on their lives because of what we are doing. I am. Please don't tell me how happy you are. You are happy because we are not interfering in your day to day life.' Not only did Omar get applauded at the event but a video link of the same has got over 222,238 hits on YouTube.

Omar spent the first eight years of his life in Essex, England, for his mother Mollie was an English nurse when she met Farooq, then a practising doctor in England. The family moved back to Srinagar in the '70s when Farooq decided to join politics. When Mollie realized that teachers at the local school were fawning all over their pedigreed student, she insisted that Omar be sent to a boarding school in another state. He was sent to The Lawrence School, Sanawar in Shimla after which he completed his BCom (Hons) from Sydenham College, Mumbai University, and an MBA at the University of Strathclyde, Scotland. This is also a time when he met up with other political dynasts. While in Mumbai he stayed with NCP chief Sharad Pawar and his daughter Supriya, while Sukhbir Badal, son of the former Punjab CM, often drove Omar to Sanawar from Chandigarh (Sukhbir is an alumni). The imprint of his public school upbringing is very much there in his politics. Such as when he told me about how some of the state Congress leaders worked against him even though they were were part of his cabinet. When I asked why he didn't complain about them to Sonia Gandhi (since he had a good equation with her) he said in all earnestness, 'In school we were taught not to tattle!'

Politics was not his first career move, as he opted for the corporate sector and worked with ITC Global Holdings. He contested his first Lok Sabha election at age 28 in 1998. He explains, 'One of the reasons why politics did not seem like an option when I graduated college was the basic situation in J&K. The assembly had been dissolved. It was only in 1996 the political process resumed and I contested my first election two years later.'

Omar's debut in politics was at the national level; he won the Srinagar Lok Sabha seat thrice—in 1998, 1999 and 2004. At the time of his joining politics his father was the state chief minister and soon after the National Conference joined the NDA in 1999. Omar became the youngest minister in Vajpayee's council of ministers joining as minister of state for commerce in 1999 and later on as minister of state for external affairs in 2001. Omar has fond memories of his ministerial stint, especially since the BJP of Atal Bihari Vajpayee was not as strident a Hindutva outfit as the one lead by his successor Narendra Modi.

Omar's political legacy, his quick grasp of both policy and protocol soon earned him a space in the prime minister's official aircraft as he became an essential part of the PM's diplomatic outreach whenever Vajpayee travelled abroad. I met him at that time to do a story profiling him as 'India's Best Calling Card', arguing that he was being showcased globally as a success story from Kashmir. Omar had replied, 'I would like to think it is more than just my being a Muslim. I'd like to think my work contributes to it. But if that's the case, then so be it. Plus, my being from Kashmir shows that not all Kashmiris are militants or pro-Pakistan' (*Outlook*, 18 June 2001). What also got a mention in the international media were his aviator glasses, cutaway collars, dimple-knotted ties and matching handkerchiefs.

His stint as a union minister however was short-lived. During the 2002 anti-Muslim Gujarat riots, an upset Omar met the then PM Vajpayee and offered to resign. His resignation was not accepted. Omar waited and resigned 10 months later in December 2002 to concentrate on party work.

The fact that he did not follow his instinct and resign during the riots will always be one of his greatest regrets. In another context he told me, 'I've normally found that if I go with my initial gut instinct nine times out of 10 I am right. If I sit down to think about my initial instinct, analyze it and subject it to cross examination I tend to get things a little wrong. My initial instinct is not correct a 100 per cent of the time but it's definitely correct a lot more times than it is wrong.'

Six years later, Omar got a chance to set the record straight. This was during a parliamentary debate on the Indo-US Nuclear deal (23 July 2008). Speaking from the heart he simply stated, 'I am a Muslim and I am an Indian and I see no distinction between the two ... I did not resign when my conscience told me to and my conscience has still not forgiven me.' The speech went viral on YouTube and instantly propelled Omar to national recognition. Farooq himself saw it online since he was in London at the time. It also paved Omar's way to debut both in state politics as the media took note that the Cub-e-Kashmir was growing up.

Omar's first stint as CM was clearly his grooming ground when he made all the mistakes of a fresher. Take the incident when the bodies of two young girls—Asiya and Neelofar—were

fished out of the Rambi Ara stream in Shopian, near the twin
camps of paramilitary Central Reserve Police Force (CRPF)
and Jammu and Kashmir Police (JKP) in May 2009. The locals
immediately suspected foul play by the CRPF. The state police
however claimed that this was a case of death by drowning.
Contradictory reports coming from doctors and administration
added to the anger which spilled onto the entire Valley as
separatist leaders played up the unrest.

In the midst of this, Omar held a press conference where
he took the Centre's line and attributed the deaths to drowning.
Even though a CBI enquiry eventually supported this theory,
Omar was branded as one who was covering up for the security
forces. With this specific case in mind, I asked Omar if there were
any lessons he'd learnt from the past. He admitted he should have
been more circumspect. 'That is what I was told [drowning]. You
can put that down to inexperience, there were a dozen different
ways I could have answered that question. The one that I chose
was perhaps the least appropriate one.' Then adds after a pause,
'As it turns out the CBI enquiry bore out what I'd said at the
press conference but by then the damage had been done.' This
is where the lesson on perspective comes in—for in the Valley
every moment comes with its own truth.

There were other incidents too. For instance, the June 2010
violence where the Indian army claimed to have killed three
Pakistani infiltrators but which later turned out to be a case
of fake encounters of three local youths from the Baramulla
district. About 110 people died in the protests that followed,
including an 11-year-old boy, Tufail Ahmed Mattoo, who was
hit by a stray tear gas shell. Overtaken by events, Omar could
not control the mass anger that erupted in the Valley against
the killings. Later, he told Harinder Baweja of *The Hindustan
Times*: 'I went into a shell in 2010.' He added that he lost the

elections in 2014 because he was 'punished for not responding to innocent deaths' (13 July 2016). That interview took place in the aftermath of the riots after Burhan Wani's death and Omar pointed out that Mehbooba was making the same mistakes in 2016 that he did in 2010. However, he added, 'Mehbooba openly called for my resignation in 2010 but I'm not going to do the same. It's a difficult situation for her to deal with.'

But he is right in that his inaction both during the 2010 riots and the handing of Afzal Guru (2013) lost him credibility in the state. His dilemma was evident when he addressed the state assembly in May 2013, saying: 'I can't understand why so many are keen to occupy the CM's chair which I find myself in. I keep asking myself this. Crowds are fired upon even though as far as my information goes no militants were present ... Is this why we are flying this country's flag? So that I have to keep apologizing to my people? So that I have to keep accounting each time my people are fired upon? Decisions are taken elsewhere to hang someone but the responsibility is thrust upon me.' (English translation of his speech)

The earnestness of his speech may have won him empathy but it did little to reassure the people of the state that they were in safe hands. PDP Leader Naeem Akhtar commented, 'Omar came as a new idea but unfortunately he botched it too soon.' Writing in *The Indian Express* (27 July 2014), Deputy Editor Muzamil Jaleel pointed out: 'Over his six years in power, Omar's failure to get any change on AFSPA would become a metaphor for his inability to stand up to New Delhi where the Congress, his party's coalition partner, lead the UPA government and where Rahul Gandhi was considered a friend of his.' When asked by Jaleel why he'd not been able to live up to his political promises, Omar told him, 'No other state in the country is as affected by outside factors as ours ... If there is a breakdown of electricity, people come out on the streets to protest and start shouting slogans of *azaadi* [freedom]. I tried my level best, but there are lots of things that were outside my control.'

Somewhere down the line, Omar must have realized that while he was keeping the government, he was losing his base. The alliance had fared miserably in the May 2014 Lok Sabha where for the first time the NC failed to get a single seat in the state (the Congress too got zero). He finally called off the alliance in July, on the eve of the November 2014 state polls.

Looking back Omar says, 'Towards the end some of the state leaders in the Congress had made it untenable for the alliance to continue. The Congress had made up its mind that it was the party in power in perpetuity in J&K and that all they had to do was choose between the NC and the PDP but they would perpetually sit and occupy the corridors of power.' He adds, 'Once the parliament election results came out and we had the horrible results that we did, a lot of state Congress leaders secretly started visiting Mufti Sayeed's residence and cosying up to the PDP. In that situation it made sense to just go it alone and let the chips fall where they did. Am glad the results came as they did because it proved once and for all to the Congress that they were not indispensable, and that they needed—particularly at the state level—to behave like a reasonable and mature ally.'

He may have to do business with the Congress again, if the next round of assembly elections throws up another hung house. After the 2014 results Omar had offered a tie-up with the PDP to keep the BJP out. 'It was the PDP that said no to us,' he reminds me. However, in the aftermath of BJP–PDP collapse, he has ruled out possibilities of any tie-ups.

Omar has made his anathema to Narendra Modi's BJP abjectly clear. Those who follow his hugely popular posts on social media (at last count his Twitter following had reached

2.96 million) will note how he is constantly fact checking the Modi government and pushing the secular parties to get their act together.

When the BJP swept Uttar Pradesh in the 2017 state polls, he had tweeted in despair: 'At this rate we might as well forget 2019 and start planning/hoping for 2024.' Given his close equation with Rahul, many were surprised by what came across as a criticism of the Congress leadership. Shaking his head Omar says, 'I am not critical of him but as a member of the Opposition, there are times when my frustration with the single largest Opposition in the country sort of spills over.'

Omar has a rather realistic approach towards a non-Congress, non-BJP Third Front that is mooted by regional satraps. 'Look, if anyone is going to take the fight to the BJP it has to be the Congress. It's the only one with a pan-India presence. The rest of us will fight the BJP in our own small corners. I will fight them on six seats in J&K, I will not go beyond that. Some of the Opposition leaders will fight on a bigger platform. Mamata Banerjee will fight them on 42 seats in West Bengal but she will not fight on a seat in Bihar or Maharashtra. So, occasionally I vent my spleen so to speak, but it's always with the best of intentions. Thankfully, things have changed. We are more vocal in our arguments. I have always maintained that for the first couple of years we can keep telling people all the wrongs that PM Modi is doing; but we need to now start projecting an alternative. It's not good enough to say agriculture is in distress, we now need to also say this is what we should do to correct it. It's not good enough to say Modi is not generating jobs. We know that, but what are we going to do to about it?'

This prompts me to ask him my next question. How does he plan to generate employment in the strife-torn state? 'The single biggest resource J&K has is its water and its ability to generate electricity using that water. It's only when we have investment in place and we generate electricity that we can sell to the rest of the country that we will be able to in some limited way improve our fiscal position,' he says. But again reiterates his point that unless the political situation normalizes, any sort of economic measures—be it reforms or doles—can only take you so far. Even when Rahul Gandhi brought a delegation of industrialists comprising Ratan Tata, Kumar Mangalam Birla and Deepak Parekh to Kashmir in October 2012, Omar was skeptical of the move. 'Quite honestly, I realized the futility of it even then. Nobody was going to invest in J&K, particularly not in Kashmir. We are perceived to be an extremely unsafe and uncertain place. Gone are the days of the license permit raj when you could tell industrialists where they have to invest,' he points out.

Maybe it's a sign of the changing times, but to know all about Sheikh Abdullah I read his autobiography. To get an insight into his grandson's line of thinking, I checked out his Twitter timeline. His tweets are a sharp, sometimes tongue-in-cheek commentary on the political and social happenings in the country. In fact, Omar's digital persona reveals a certain audacity that is hidden underneath his formal, political identity. He gives one of his rare smiles, when I quiz him about his digital life, saying candidly, 'I enjoy it. I am a little more reserved and careful now than I was initially but that comes with the fact that Twitter has become a lot more hostile. I think the advantage of anonymity and physical distance emboldens people who would be far too cowardly to react the way they do if they were standing in front of you. But I still think it's a great medium to get one's message across.'

For now he's sticking to 280-character messages to get his point across. Take a look at this acerbic put-down to a particularly tiresome troll: 'If I type this tweet out more slowly than I did, will it help you better to understand what I wrote [14 December, 2017].' While his dad Farooq will hold court with his Urdu couplets, his sheer charm and booming laugh, Omar has a wry, sometimes self-deprecating, most times caustic wit, that is very British—and also one you don't want to get on the wrong side of.

Like most of liberal India, he is also troubled by the on-demand-nationalism that has currently gripped the nation. He points out, 'India is too large and too diverse to have one single thought process cutting across everybody. At the end of the day we're all Indians. That fundamental point will remain the same. But unfortunately that space to differ is shrinking. The fact that I want autonomy for J&K is seen as anti-national. The fact that I want a sustained dialogue between India and Pakistan is seen as anti-national.' He comes across as a decent public school boy wanting to play in the political *akhaada* (dirt pit), but also wanting to play away from the mud. Recently, on 24 March 2018, when BJP Leader Himanta Biswa Sarma commented that 'Rahul Gandhi may be a good human being but he isn't a good politician,' Omar immediately tweeted in response: 'Speaking purely for myself if being a good human being and a good politician are mutually exclusive, I'll choose to be a good human being any day of the week.'

In the murky world of Indian politics, this can be both a good and a bad thing.

JYOTIRADITYA SCINDIA

The Technoroyal

Jyotiraditya Scindia was on the stage, minus his ubiquitous dark glasses, his eyes sparkling with the sheer challenge of the moment. Lashing out at the incumbent BJP state chief minister, Shivraj Singh Chouhan, he said: 'When I think of him [the CM], I am reminded of a popular film song from the '80s. The film was *Hum Kisise Kum Naheen*, and the song goes like this,' he paused for effect, and then broke into a singularly off tune rendition of a popular Bollywood song—'*Kya Hua Tera Vada, Vo Kasam, Voh Iraada*' (What happened to your promises and all your intent). The song, about broken promises, touched a chord with the villagers gathered there, who began to clap. Flashing a mischievous grin, Scindia reversed the mike so it faced the crowd, and asked them to join in.

This was at a Congress rally in rural Madhya Pradesh, during the 2013 assembly polls. But, compare this impish campaigner who did not hesitate a second before belting out a Bollywood song in front of total strangers (he may have been off tune but he was perfectly tuned in to the mood of the people he was addressing), and contrast this to his earlier persona as an investment banker. After his graduation, he spent a year in New York and the next four years in Mumbai as part of the four-member team that set up Morgan Stanley's Investment Banking branch in India.

But destiny had other plans. In September 2001, Jyotiraditya's world came 'crashing down' when his father, Madhavrao Scindia, died in a helicopter crash. Scindia Senior was a Congress leader, a former cabinet minister and a close confidante of Rajiv and Sonia Gandhi. Some would add, also a man who could have been prime minister. His death was a loss not just to his family and to the people of Gwalior, but to the Congress party as well. It was then that his son was asked to join the party in 2001.

That is how the then 31-year-old Jyotiraditya (born 1 January 1971) became the third generation Scindia to join politics. His grandmother Rajmata Vijayaraje Scindia was one of the founding members of the Jan Sangh—a right wing political outfit that later became the Bharatiya Janata Party in 1980. It's a party that was formed in opposition to the Congress, and initially Madhavrao contested his first few elections from the Jan Sangh but joined the Congress thereafter. Ever since then the Scindia family has been divided amongst the two national parties, with Madhavrao's sisters Vasundhara Raje and Yashodhara Raje in the BJP.

Jyotiraditya is the 11th titular Maharaja of Gwalior. Even in 21st century India there are those who refer to him as Maharaja, especially in the Gwalior–Morena–Bhind belt (that sends 34 MLAs to the state assembly). 'I am not comfortable being called

Maharaja,' he said. And added, 'My father always believed in his work speaking for him. Yes, he came from a certain background that both he and I are extremely proud of. But my legacy is very clearly my past. I live in the present and work for the future of my people.' Yet, in his constituency Maharaja is what the locals refer to him as.

I was meeting him at his official residence in New Delhi for this conversation. I had also covered some of his campaigns and his speeches in Parliament and the first thing that struck me each time was his ability to connect. Not just as an articulate speaker but also the way he shifts his focus entirely on the target audience—even if it's an audience of one. The interview began with him asking me the questions: What was the book about? What would I be focussing on? And would I prefer coffee or tea? The impression he conveyed was that, at that moment in time, nothing mattered more to him than to get this conversation right. Ironically, the pressure then was on me to get the questions right!

The Maharaja question certainly didn't make the grade. Jyotiraditya—his friends call him Bal or Jyotir, others call him Aditya—pointed out that his family originates from a small village in the Satara district of Maharashtra called Kanherkhed. 'We started out as the sarpanches of the village so it's a very grassroots, son-of-the-soil driven origin from which we have risen. It's a village with which we still maintain close ties,' he explains. But, fortified with a sip of coffee I persisted. Can you seriously get away with the grassroots card when your family home is a 19th century palace sprawled over 12,40,771 sq. feet in the heart of Gwalior? He looked around his study, at his desk with a computer connected to a printer, to the shelves lined with books and mementos and commented wryly that he spent more time here, shunting between Parliament, his constituency Guna, and, of late, the rest of Madhya Pradesh. He also claimed that since he spent most of his childhood at school and colleges away from Gwalior, the 'royalty' tag was something he never got quite used to. The label that he says he is more in sync with is an investment banker turned politician; or even a technocrat of sorts.

Considering that both the BJP and the Congress were a part of his legacy, was there any confusion as to which political party he would choose? He replied, 'I think that when you decide your course, you must understand what your core beliefs and values are. Then there must be a synergy between your value system and that of the institution you choose to be a part of; if there isn't, then there will be dissonance, maybe not today but somewhere down the road. Therefore, for me, my core values are clearly liberal, a secular outlook, an agenda of social empowerment and a model of economic growth. All of these find a great degree of resonance with the values of the Congress party.'

The short answer is that he is very comfortably placed within the Congress, fitting in well with not just 'all of the above', but he also embodies a paradigm of leadership that both Sonia Gandhi and her son Rahul want to showcase. Here is a professional-turned-politician, who understands the nuances of governance and has won every election he's contested. The fact that his father is a former Congressman of course has its own home court advantage in a party that prefers the familiar to outsiders.

Initially when Congress President Rahul Gandhi was reluctant to assume the mantle of a party chief, there was a buzz that the party should instead promote either Scindia or Sachin Pilot (the Rajasthan state chief) to the top job. Both are seen as progressive, articulate faces of Congress Tomorrow. Both were also quick to scotch such speculation. And wisely so, for the Gandhis (first

Sonia and then Rahul) are reluctant to promote a strong, young face that may one day become a potential challenger.

But there were other more pragmatic aspirations. In the run up to the 2018 assembly elections in the state of Madhya Pradesh, the Congress needed to project a credible chief ministerial face. The BJP has been holding sway in the state since 2003, for three consecutive elections. Scindia made a pitch for the top job, camping in the state for months, taking on the BJP-led government for a spate of farmer suicides, holding rallies across Madhya Pradesh and winning by-polls in the Guna-Gwalior belt. But he was also contending against two veterans—former Chief Minister Digvijaya Singh and nine term Congress MP Kamal Nath.

Knowing well that at least one of the two was fiercely opposed to his becoming the CM face (and perhaps hoping that his party chief Rahul Gandhi would support his own candidature), Scindia pushed for the party to project a credible face to take on the BJP's sitting CM Shivraj Singh Chouhan. He explained his stand saying, 'People in India want to know whom they are vesting their trust in. Back in the '80s what mattered was 80 per cent your party symbol and 20 per cent your face. Today its 80 per cent the face of your candidate—you see this when you see many an independent candidate winning.' All were sound points, but aware of the infighting between the three state leaders, Rahul Gandhi refused to name a CM candidate outright. He instead opted for a neat balancing act between experience and youth by appointing the 71-year-old Kamal Nath as the Pradesh Congress Chief (PCC) and Scindia as the Campaign Committee Chief. The edge went to the veteran for it is usually the state chief who gets to be CM. One reason being cited is that unlike Nath, the (much) younger Scindia had age on his side, and could wait his turn. Another more obvious reason, of course, was that with a young party president at the helm can the Congress afford to promote potential challengers?

'Today it's not the issue of rescuing the Congress in MP as it is the issue of rescuing MP from the BJP,' said Scindia firmly when I tried to pin him down on his leadership goals. In a smart move, he opted for rhetoric over the definitive. 'At the end of the day, what is your goal?' he asked and proceeded with the answer. 'Number One, without the party there is no "you". If you are convinced of principle Number One then principle Number Two follows, that it is not X, Y or Z but it is the union of the energy and the strengths of the leaders of the party that matters.' That sounded more like a political theorem than an answer coming from his gut, but I let him carry on. 'And so therefore this concept of "yourself" and "your team" has to be—and am using this word purposefully—this has to be obliterated. It has to be collective. That's the changed thinking that we have to take to the battleground. For me whether it's Kamal Nathji, Digvijay Singhji or whoever is not important.'

Considering that this was a conversation we'd had before Nath had been made PCC chief, I'd have to hand it to him for being politically correct. There was nothing he'd said to me *then* that he'd have to unsay *now*. That itself shows the makings of a seasoned politician.

During the 2014 Lok Sabha polls when the Congress was reduced to its lowest ever score of 44 seats, Scindia was the only 'young' leader from Team Rahul (apart from Rahul himself) to retain his seat. He was also one of the more articulate, bilingual speakers, and often led the Opposition attack against the Treasury Benches. His speech during a debate on nationalism won him praise across party lines for he took on the fiery Smirti Irani, then cabinet minister for HRD. Considering that as many as 24 of the Congress' 44 MPs came from the South and the

North East, and could barely converse in Hindi, while the BJP made speaking Hindi a national and emotive issue, the message was as important as the medium. Speaking in impeccable Hindi, gesturing flamboyantly with his hands, Scindia gave Irani a run for her TRPs.

When I commented that he is more fluent in Hindi than most public school kids I know, he pointed out that it was thanks to his school, and also the fact that he accompanied his father on the campaign trail ever since he was 13 years old, that he was able to pick up the nuances of the language. With a perfectly serious look on his face, he added: '*Vartaman ke UP mein aur iss samay ke Uttarakhand mein bahut klisht Hindi boli jaati thi, hamaare hindi ke adhyapak badi klisht Hindi mein charcha karte the*' (In my school which was in the former state of UP and is currently in Uttarakhand, the teacher spoke chaste Hindi.)

His early education was at The Doon School in Dehradun. This was followed by studying economics at Harvard and an MBA at the Stanford Graduate School of Business. As a politician, however, he refuses to categorize himself as either reformist or populist. 'Why is one at the cost of the other?' he asks, before launching into one of his longwinded explanations. 'Sure we need to take hard decisions but that doesn't mean you don't create a safety net. At the end of the day you can only give from what you get. It's for you to decide—do you want a larger share of a smaller pie or do you want a smaller share of a larger pie? If you create the economic conditions so your country powers ahead at a 8 to 8.5 per cent GDP growth rate which the Congress was able to do for a decade—or rather two decades—the first being the first generation reforms that took place when Manmohan Singhji was the finance minister and the second as prime minister. As a result, you have raised this country to a two trillion dollar economy, and that enabled you to enlarge your kitty to spend on infrastructure, social justice and when the need arose, bring about a Rs 72,000 crore loan waiver scheme. So it's not one at the cost of the other, you can do both.' (No, there are no short answers with Scindia!)

One can, however, see the Stanford degree being put to good use, especially when he told a TV anchor in response to a similar reforms-versus-sops question: 'It depends on the dependent and the independent variable. Certainly a more effective social agenda will be driven by a higher growth. The independent variable is a higher rate of growth.'

Currently a 4th term MP, he was one of the New Age faces of the Dr Manmohan Singh cabinet when the UPA was in power. Scindia headed the Ministry of State of Communication and Information Technology (2008), Commerce and Industry (2009) and later on was upgraded to the Ministry of Power (Independent Charge) in 2012.

As the minister of IT one of his pet projects was Project Arrow—where he set about trying to reinvent the post office. In the age of internet and social media, post offices have lost relevance. Scindia converted these into community service centres that could be used for financial remittances, direct cash transfers for government sops, such as NREGA. He got the state-owned BSNL to ensure broadband connectivity for the post offices, roped in McKinsey to help restructure and began work on a pilot project of 50 post offices which increased to 5000 by the time he remitted office in 2009, taking him 'nine months to move from ideation to execution'. An endearing side story is that when he met with the workforce, the postmen complained that though they went door to door delivering mail, they had no allowance for shoes. Scindia okayed both an annual shoe and an umbrella allowance, as well as a 21st century bag that could be slung across their shoulders instead of the unwieldy sack to carry the mail.

His hands-on approach was also visible in the Ministry of Power where he hit the ground running since he took over in the aftermath of a colossal National Grid collapse. The brief given to the new minister was to ensure that this never happens again. Since he had Independent Charge there was no senior minister to buffer him. He put together a council consisting of ex-bureaucrats from the power and environment ministries, power producers and financiers to work out a solution. 'It was a target-oriented committee of 18-20 people who had clear responsibility of what needs to be delivered,' he said and added an interesting aside, 'I as the minister, and my secretary, would present to that committee every month what we had been able to deliver in terms of our targets in the last meeting. So I was accountable to them as much as they were accountable to us.'

It's a corporate style approach to governance. Putting systems in place is something he's been trained to do and something he clearly enjoys. The projects in his constituency are all monitored via spreadsheets and flowcharts. Apparently, he even has an internal monitoring mechanism for himself, telling me, 'every six months I judge myself, on what I have achieved and what new thing I can do.'

This was getting all too MBA-ish. While governance is about systems, politics is about beliefs. What then is the one cause he feels strongly about? He didn't have to look at a spreadsheet to answer as he reeled off a list of politically correct concerns, the most important being 'those that affect our secular ethos specially intolerance'. Taking a sip of his black coffee, he explained, 'The Congress has always stood for secularism, stood for every faith whether you are a Hindu, Muslim, Sikh, Issai (Christian). It has to be an amalgam. The word "secularism" has unfortunately been corrupted to sometime mean everything but Hinduism.' He added, 'Hinduism is a part of secularism because Hinduism— my religion—is a philosophy. It is not even a religion—it's a Darshan Shashtra [philosophy]. It is only in this great country that we have given birth to four religions—Hinduism, Sikhism, Budhism and Jainism. I am very proud of being a Hindu and my Hinduism certainly comes under the umbrella of secularism.'

I then asked him about his take on the politics of caste; that every politician, no matter which Ivy League institution they graduated from, has to resort to in order to win polls. Again he has a politically correct answer for me. 'Why do you and I use the phrase *Bharat ek guldaste ki tarah hain* [India is like a bouquet of flowers]? Because we've got to have every colour and every type of flower in that *guldasta*. Therefore, there must be representation of not only each caste but of every religion and every profession—why not a doctor, lawyer, an accountant, a farmer as well? They were all part of our freedom struggle,' he replied.

Certainly he is never short of an answer whether on the public stage or on the floor of the House, though he is at his uninhibited best on the campaign field. The formality that he reserves for the drawing rooms of Lutyens' Delhi is missing when he is in the hinterland. If his security cannot control the jostling crowds at his rallies, he cajoles them from the dais, calling out to a '*Hare ghoongat-vaali amma*' (Elderly lady wearing a green sari) to sit down with the promise that he will meet her after his speech. Sometimes, to control the leaders on the dais with him as they jostle for a seat in the front row, he tells them with an indulgent smile: 'In Parliament I prefer to sit in the back benches.'

Not quite correct, for he was House Captain and School Prefect at The Doon School. His father refused to send him to the family governed Scindia school in Gwalior, for fear he would get 'undue favours'. Instead he went to the elite boarding school that has schooled a prime minister, at least two chief ministers, and is clearly the playing field of political dynasts.

Apart from his work, he also takes his workouts very seriously, graduating from a chubby school kid to a toned member of Parliament. He claims that he likes to do a daily workout of 45 minutes to an hour. 'My passion is my workout. I believe it is extremely important to be fit. It helps you think sharp.' What about his time off? He is married to Priyadarshini Raje from the Gaekwad family of Baroda and the couple have a son and a daughter. Family is something he is not very keen to talk about in an interview about his politics. All he will say is, 'I believe it's important to spend quality time with my family, not quantity because as a public servant you don't have the luxury.' However, his son, Mahanaryaman, spent his last summer holidays campaigning for his father in the Gwalior-Chambal belt, much as Jyotiraditya did for his own father as a young school boy.

One reason behind the reticence to open his family for public scrutiny could be that there have already been too many headlines about the feud between his father and aunts over the Scindia legacy. His grandmother, Rajmata Scindia, too had her differences with her son; there was even talk of a Palace Rasputin in the form of her trusted advisor, Sardar Angre, who deepened the divide between the mother and son. Given the back story, I would say, trust is not something he gives away easily though he was accessible enough when I reached out to him for this meeting.

He is one of the few GenNext leaders I have not interacted with often and I soon had him disagreeing vehemently when I called him 'aloof' and accused him of hiding behind his dark glasses. He finally agreed to take my observations as 'constructive criticism' after making it clear that 'this is not the way I see myself'.

A keen cricketer, he prefers to bat than field, which doesn't surprise me for he is more pro-active than reactive in everything he does. As chairman of the Board of Cricket Control of India, Finance Committee, he didn't hesitate to ask for the resignation of the then BCCI President N. Srinivasan when the latter's son-in-law was implicated in a match fixing scandal in 2013. Calling a spade a spade is very well. But sometimes that can dig a few pitfalls?

'I know politics is the art of diplomacy,' he says. 'I have one life to live. I not only have to be true to you, I also have to be true to myself. And I do believe that in our country people want truth to be told. We are not infallible; we are here in this life to make mistakes. But the greatest mistake is, if you do not acknowledge that you have made a mistake. It doesn't make you smaller, it makes you even greater. And most important, you sleep well at night.'

His study has a map of India on one wall, a map of Madhya Pradesh on another. But what I found most revealing is that amidst various photographs of him at official ministerial events, there are as many as four caricatures of him hanging on a third wall. Well, that's one way of keeping it realistic, I thought as I walked away, wishing that New Delhi would see more of that impish campaigner instead of the Serious Scindia who talks algorithms, spread-sheets, dependent and independent variables.

HIMANTA BISWA SARMA

The Artful Negotiator

He is the insider turned outsider, turned insider again. That is the art of being Himanta Biswa Sarma. He may switch sides but whichever camp he joins, he soon becomes one of the prime movers—never the outsider for long. HBS, as he is popularly known in a world where initials are a power accessory, was the Congress party's rising star in Assam. For nearly a decade he was tipped to be the heir apparent to Tarun Gogoi, the septuagenarian chief minister. Then suddenly in August 2015, on the eve of a state election, the then 3rd term MLA quit the Congress and teamed up with the BJP. Sarma's popularity with the masses remained intact despite the changeover, and he is now the BJP's most potent weapon in the North East.

The rise and rise of HBS makes for a very interesting political tale.

Born on 1 February 1969, Sarma joined the Congress in 1993 when Hiteswar Saikia was the Assam CM. But it was during Tarun Gogoi's tenure that he emerged as the party's GenNext face in Assam. Everyone assumed that after Gogoi, it would be Sarma who would be projected by the Congress as its next CM candidate—and indeed Sarma thought it as well. He was Gogoi's Number 2, the de-facto chief minister, who dealt directly on his behalf with the other ministers in the cabinet, and also with the party cadres. This worked well till 2011 until Tarun Gogoi's 29-year-old son Gaurav—an engineer cum development worker—joined politics. Senior Gogoi asked his deputy Sarma to take Gaurav under his wings and train him. Himanta obliged but he soon got the feeling that young Gogoi's aim went beyond being an apprentice to Sarma. They were both after the same job.

Then came the 2014 Lok Sabha elections that saw the BJP sweep the country. The Modi effect was felt in Assam too where the Congress was reduced to a mere three MPs and the BJP won seven of the total 15 seats. This was a sign that the three term chief minister, Tarun Gogoi, was losing his grip on the state, more so when the Congress was defeated in the municipal elections that followed soon after the general elections. Himanta genuinely believed that given this situation, especially with the BJP making inroads in the North East, the party leadership would agree to a regime change in his favour. He claimed that he had the support of as many as 55 Congress MLAs (out of the party's total of 78). For the record, he underplays his own ambition. 'I did not want to be the CM myself as I don't believe in entry through the back door,' he says. Adding, 'But we did want the CM changed and suggested two other names to replace Tarun Gogoi.' (This may have been the short term plan but the long term goal was to ensure the CM's chair for himself).

An emergency meeting was called at the then Congress Vice President Rahul Gandhi's house in New Delhi sometime in August 2015. In attendance were Himanta, Tarun Gogoi and the party general secretary in-charge of Assam, C.P. Joshi. The way Himanta tells it, this meeting was the last push he needed to quit the Congress. He told me in an interview for NewsX that he was totally disillusioned with the way Rahul handled the meeting. 'He was distracted and more interested in playing with his pet dog, instead of neutralizing the issue.' According to Sarma, Rahul did not refer to the main issue at hand, which was his plea for a change of CM. Instead, when Sarma pointed out that it was he who had done the grunt work for the 2011 Congress win in Assam, down to choosing the candidates and the bulk of the campaign rallies, Rahul shrugged and said, so what? This irked Sarma but the break point came two seconds later.

'Then the dog came to my table and picked up a biscuit from my plate. I wanted my plate to be changed, I looked at him [Rahul] but he turned his face away,' recalls Sarma. Shaking his head in disbelief, he said, 'I got the impression he wanted me to carry on eating from the same plate.' Recollecting the moment still makes him smile in wonder. He added, 'Later, a senior journalist told me he had the same experience. He had gone to meet Rahul and had a fairly long interaction with him and just as he left the room he realized he'd left something behind and went back to fetch it. When he walked in he saw Rahul was so busy petting his dog that he didn't even acknowledge his [the journalist's] presence.' Since then, this story of Rahul and his dog has gone viral. It has also given Himanta an added USP in his new party—when it needs to counter Rahul Gandhi, the BJP often fields Himanta; and the ever obliging Himanta always has a juicy counter comment ready.

Those who know Himanta say that it was not so much

was not made the BJP's CM face in Assam. Therein lies the irony. From being Number 2 in the Congress, he went on to become Number 2 in the BJP. To Himanta's credit, he grit his teeth and set out to prove himself on the new turf, addressing over 269 rallies during the April 2016 state elections. He campaigned aggressively against his former boss, claiming that the then CM was too old and needed vitamins to survive. The attack was brutal but it was clear that Sarma wore his heart on his sleeve. Kaushik Deka, senior associate editor, *India Today*, who has closely covered Assam politics for over 15 years explains what drove Himanta: 'When he sets a target he accomplishes it. Here the target was to make Rahul Gandhi understand his worth. All he wanted to do was to pack off Tarun Gogoi and his son from Assam. He was like a man possessed. Taking revenge on Rahul was more important than becoming CM himself.' Later, Sarma acknowledged that his primary aim to defeat Congress in Assam, was driven by revenge and to give a befitting rebuttal to Rahul Gandhi's So-What poser. 'When I joined the BJP after a series of humiliations there was perhaps a sense of revenge on my mind, but that's over now. Today we are working for development of the North East and the BJP is the answer for this,' he told me.

Moreover, a pragmatic Sarma doesn't read the situation as exchanging one Number 2 tag for another. 'I was the Number 2 in Tarun Gogoi's cabinet but I was never acknowledged as such. Whenever there was a crisis they turned to me to deliver. But when there was an official function I was never called to the dais. I was never considered the Official Number 2. With the BJP, this is not the case. In the BJP I feel respected,' he explains pointing to the fact that when the central government introduced the controversial Goods and Services Tax (GST), he was asked to head the Group of Ministers of State (GoM) to streamline the tax. 'Never before has a minister from Assam been asked to head a national level GoM. Even in such small things there is a political message,' he points out.

The BJP rewarded him for delivering Assam by making him the convener of the North East Democratic Alliance (NEDA)—a platform formed by the BJP for the development of the North East states where all the chief ministers of the NDA-ruled states report to him. While development is the user word, the password is clearly saffronization, for the end aim of NEDA is to ensure the BJP comes to power in all eight states of the North East. It is a bold ambition because before Assam the BJP did not have a government in a single north eastern state. But soon after, Himanta along with Ram Madhav, the BJP general secretary in charge of North East, have ensured a BJP government in both Arunachal Pradesh (2016) and Manipur (2017). This was followed by a BJP Government in Tripura (2018) and BJP supported coalition governments in Meghalaya and Nagaland (2018). Mizoram is next on Sarma's target list.

He tailored his modus operandi to suit the needs of each state. In Arunachal the BJP engineered defections to topple a Congress CM and replace him with a BJP one. A somewhat similar plan of action was followed in Manipur after the 2017 state polls where the BJP got 21 MLAs as opposed to the Congress party's 28 MLAs in the 60-member assembly. But before the Congress could stake claim to government formation, Sarma had already approached the governor with the support of 32 MLAs, having 'persuaded' 11 MLAs from regional parties to throw in their lot with the BJP. In keeping with his exhibitionist style, when he went to stake claim, Sarma even had a Congress MLA whom he'd persuaded to switch sides, riding in the car with him. Since both Sarma and Ram Madhav follow the same ethos of ends justifying the means, it is an effective partnership. Ram Madhav has often stated, 'The BJP will do anything that is democratically accepted to win [elections].'

Sarma weighs his words carefully when I ask him if the ends justify the means. 'Maybe earlier yes, when I was in the Congress and I was asked to deliver I did so regardless of the means. But at this stage of my life I have realized that not only ends but even the means should be justifiable. Otherwise it's inviting unnecessary controversy.' When questioned further about the *means* he used to prop a BJP Government in Manipur, he called that the result of a 'fair negotiation'. Somewhat self-defensively he explained in a hurt tone, 'We negotiated only with our partners in the NEDA—most of the negotiation was conducted before the results came out. It was when Amit Shah [the party president] was campaigning in Imphal, he realized that there will be a shortfall of seats, so he instructed me to open doors of negotiation. I then talked to my friends from our regional allies.'

The tactics changed for the next set of elections that took place at the beginning of 2018 in Nagaland, Tripura and Meghalaya. The BJP was in power in none of these states. By now party President Amit Shah had realized HBS's potential and deputed a charter plane at Guwahati solely for his use during the campaign—and after. The BJP swept one state and supported a coalition government in the other two. The most spectacular win was in Tripura where the BJP crashed a Left dominated citadel to win 35 of the state's 60 seats. It was after 15 years that the Left rule in Tripura was obliterated and that too by a party that did not even have a functioning headquarter building in the state until the run-up to the elections. BJP's ally, the Indigenous People's Front of Tripura (IPFT), won eight seats. Sarma swung the alliance with IPFT over objections by most of his colleagues for the tribal-dominated party had been pushing for a separate state for tribals—Twipraland—something that the BJP is opposed to. This was a minor roadblock for Sarma. As he points out to the media (*India Today*, 19 March

2018), 'The BJP is also in alliance with the Bodoland People's Front in Assam who have been demanding a separate state. Such issues can be sorted out through talks.' The alliance with IPFT was crucial as it prevented the anti-Left vote from splitting. In Nagaland the BJP won 12 of the 60 seats but again, Sarma had already identified the National Democratic Progressive Party as an alliance partner. Since this is a Christian dominated state (93 per cent) the alliance was officially announced only after the polling with the BJP getting deputy CM.

While Tripura was a straightforward electoral win, Meghalaya showcased Himanta's finesse on the political trapeze. With just two seats in the 60 strong house, the BJP managed to be a part of the ruling coalition with a deputy CM in place. When the results came in, the Congress emerged as the single largest party with 21 MLAs. Mindful of its experience in Manipur where it had lost the state despite being the single largest party, the Congress rushed its big guns to the state— Ahmed Patel, Kamal Nath and Mukul Wasnik. It must have given Sarma some degree of satisfaction to outsmart those who had been his former colleagues and seniors. Even as the Congress leaders made frantic calls for allies, Sarma boarded his aircraft to Shillong (from Agartala where he watched the election results), whistling a song from an Assamese film in which he was a child actor—'Ek Dui Tini Chari, Juti Dilu Garu Gari' (One two three four, I've started the bullock cart). He knew he was on course as the battle had been won months ago when he had worked out a secret understanding with the regional National People's Party (NPP) that bagged 19 seats in the polls. Again, because it was a Christian dominated state (85 per cent) the alliance was not made public before the voting. A smug Sarma, however, states that it is the BJP's policy of not encouraging defections from any regional party in the North East that made the locals prefer an alliance with the BJP instead of the Congress. 'Amit Shah decided that after Assam we will not encroach on any regional parties. They should grow along with the BJP,' he says. The point to be noted here is the alacrity with which he credits his boss, the ruthless Amit Shah, for any smart move or policy decision.

It is this kind of backroom management that the Congress is missing, having lost out on Sarma. Party leaders recall the Rajya Sabha election of March 2010 wistfully. At the time the Congress had enough MLAs to ensure a single Rajya Sabha seat from Assam, but was keen to grab a second one as well. It was then that a call was made from the then Congress President Sonia Gandhi's office to Himanta Sarma. On the line was Ahmed Patel, political advisor to Sonia. Sarma immediately understood what was required of him. On the day of the voting, he arrived at the Assam Assembly with four BJP MLAs riding in his car, indicating that he had managed to 'turn them around'. The Congress won both the seats. The BJP cried foul play but Sarma's politics of hijack had won the day. The BJP-backed candidate and media baron Jayanta Baruah, lost the election. What must have sweetened the win for Himanta is that there is no love lost between him and Baruah who owns the Assamese media group Pratidin.

Sarma remembers the tale all too well as is apparent from the smile on his face but, raising his index finger, says in the firm tone of one who has made an important decision, 'Now if anyone asks me to get someone elected from the Rajya Sabha *by any means* I will refuse.' Along with stature he has developed a conscience. Having arrived, he now craves respectability. Acquiring a conscience is the first step in the makeover; fine-tuning his English and toning down his shiny suits, are corollaries.

Sarma's political graph shows the rise of a self-made man who learnt his craft on the streets, not on the pedigreed lap of a dynast. He joined the All India Assam Students Union (AASU) in the sixth standard. That was the time of the Assam agitation against illegal immigrants spearheaded by the then CM and Asom Gana Parishad leader, Prafulla Kumar Mahanta. Sometime during 1979–1980, HBS came in touch with Mahanta and his deputy, Bhrigu Phukan. A few years later, around 1987, he even flirted with the United Liberation Front of Assam (ULFA), running the odd errand for the separatist outfit. An interesting side story is that he won his first election in 2001 on a Congress ticket by defeating the then AGP leader Bhrigu Kumar Phukan from Jalukbari. After graduating from Guwahati's prestigious Cotton College where he was a two term general secretary from the AASU, Sarma went on to study law at the Government Law College and even holds a PhD in political science.

Having tasted agitational politics at such a young age, he was quick to realize that for him the lure was not the court room but the court of the people. In the early '90s when the government had begun its crackdown on the ULFA leaders, Sarma came in contact with the then Congress CM Hiteswar Saikia who was impressed with the young firebrand. On behalf of AASU, Sarma used to negotiate with Saikia regarding demands to upgrade Cotton College. Sarma's detractors claim that he then struck a deal with Saikia to join the Congress and dump the AASU. But Sarma denies this, pointing out, 'There is a section of Assam who wants to project I resigned from AASU to join Congress, but AASU is a student organization. After that you are free to join any political party, Congress, BJP or AGP. I chose the Congress, but waited for two years after leaving AASU to think through my options. I completed my law degree, kept in touch with Mr Saikia in my individual capacity but joined Congress only at the end of 1993.' He claims it was Saikia who made him 'want to be a good Indian and not just a good Assamese'.

Himanta's politically correct version does take the juice out of a story doing the rounds. Apparently when the AASU leaders were bargaining with the Saikia government, they had jotted down their list of demands on a piece of paper, marking which ones were negotiable and on which there could be no compromise. This paper reached Saikia (his detractors blamed Sarma for the leak), who in turn handed the sheet to his chief secretary who was bargaining with the union. This gave the government a good idea as to how far it could push the AASU. The next morning, when AASU leaders found themselves cornered, they spotted the same sheet of paper in the chief secretary's hands and knew that the leak had come from within. By then Sarma was ready to cut ties with the AASU and join the Congress.

So there is a ruthless streak in Sarma. It is this which keeps him ahead of the game. While his methods may raise eyebrows, his popularity remains intact with the public at large. 'What Saikia saw in him was not just a do-er but also someone with leadership potential, who inspired personal loyalty regardless of which platform he is on,' says Kaushik Deka of *India Today*. Even today, Sarma acknowledges Saikia as his political guru and refused to campaign against Saikia's son Debabrata in the 2016 elections. 'He is my *guru putra* (son of my guru) so I cannot attack him,' says Sarma. In the world of HBS there is a code of conduct in place. He makes it a point to categorise his loyalties, stating simply: 'Mr Saikia was my mentor but Tarun Gogoi was a senior colleague.' Hence the former's entire lineage gets his loyalty while the latter's son is collateral damage.

The BJP may have made Sonowal the Assam CM but it knows that the cut and thrust of the government is in Sarma's hands. He holds key portfolios of finance, education, planning and development, health and family welfare in the Assam government. It's not just politics but he's also well versed in the nitty-gritty of governance. He brought in transparency in teachers' recruitment process by initiating the TET (Teachers' Eligibility Test) which allowed anyone holding a degree to test for a teaching post. Those who clear the test can apply for the job via a transparent online process that has replaced the old system of bribes and patronage. This has endeared Sarma amongst the public as has his policy of making it mandatory for doctors to practice one year in rural areas before they can enroll for post graduate courses in Assam's government medical colleges. All bearers of hard luck stories are turned down with a resolute No, as Sarma fears that exceptions will soon become precedents to avoid the one year rural stint.

HBS makes the rules but also breaks them when needed. In 2009, as health minister in the Gogoi government, he was hauled up for riding a bike in a youth rally without a helmet. When questioned by the police Himanta countered, 'How will people see me if I wear a full mask helmet?' His gift of repartee (and electoral success) has made him a hit on the conclave and the cocktail circuit. But he still retains his grass-root touch, especially when it comes to crunching data and choosing his team. The BJP had given him a free hand in the 2016 Assam polls to choose candidates. But they were surprised with his choice for Bilasipara East in the Muslim-dominated Lower Assam. Sarma's pick was a Marwari, Ashok Singhi. When quizzed as to why he had fielded a Marwari in a constituency that bordered Bangaldesh and is populated by Bangaleshi Muslims, Sarma smiled enigmatically. After Singhi's win, he explained that Singhi was a contractor in the area and as most of the locals depended on him for a job, he had their vote. This kind of minutiae comes with a familiarity of the battle ground, and not by crunching data.

Those who know him cannot help but marvel at the ease with which he, a former leader of the Assam movement, is now peddling the cause of Hindutva. The Assam movement on which he cut his teeth, was one that fought for a composite Assamese identity and not a uniquely Hindu one. Yet, take Sarma's controversial comments on the Citizenship (Amendment) Bill moved by the Modi Government at the Centre. This bill seeks to amend the Citizenship Act so that Hindus, Sikhs and other minorities from neighbouring nations could be granted citizenship even if they do not provide the required documents. Local political outfits in Assam, such as the AGP and AASU have objected to this, fearing that migrants from Bangladesh would affect the state's demography, reducing the Assamese and other indigenous communities to a minority. Sarma waded into the controversy peddling hard core Hindutva. He commented that while Hindu migrants were welcome, Muslim ones were not. 'Who is our enemy, the 1–1.5 lakh people or the 55 lakh people?' he asked the media rhetorically at the release of his book, *Anya Ek Dristikon* (A Different Perspective) in April 2016.

Implicit in the statement was that while Hindu migrants from Bangladesh (the 1.5 lakh figure) were acceptable, those of Muslim faith (55 lakh) were not. When asked if it was the BJP's policy to differentiate between Hindu and Muslim migrants from Bangladesh (*Indian Express*, 2 November 2016), Sarma's reply was an unabashed: 'We clearly do. After all, the country was divided in the name of religion. Thus it is not a new thing.' In the book mentioned before, he creates a fear scenario, arguing that soon the ethnic Assamese community will be outnumbered by 'illegal' Muslim migrants.

That's his *Anya Ek Dristikon* and he expresses it without

any qualms. When I asked him if he was peddling Hindutva under duress or by conviction, Sarma was only too happy to explain. 'How can you differentiate Assamese identity from Hindu identity? First we are Hindu which has both an element of Sanatan Dharma and Sufism. Second we are Assamese, for we also have our inherent tribal culture. But the kind of Islamic thought that has been brought to Assam by Bangladeshi migrants is not Sufism and cannot be part of our identity.' Still, most of his former colleagues in the Congress can't help but chuckle to see Sarma metamorphosing into such a blatant Hindutva poster boy. Kaushik Deka points out, 'In his eagerness to defend his masters, he often ridicules public sentiment with his own brand of logic. That logic makes him a clever politician but not an endearing one. He wins the argument but loses public affection.'

Sarma disagrees, saying that it is not he who is talking a different tune but the Congress that changed post 2011. (Important to note here that this is the year when Gaurav Gogoi arrived on the scene.) Sarma states, 'From 2006–2012 Congress had positioned itself as a bigger nationalist party than any other, even the BJP. But after that Congress started deteriorating and practicing politics of appeasement.' That's his version of truth and he's sticking to it.

HBS learnt the art of messaging early in life. This was fine-tuned in 2008 when he acquired a television network—News Live. He used the platform to build his image. There have been charges of corruption against him but he dismisses these as 'political vendetta'. None have been proved in any court and neither have these charges worked against him in the court of public opinion where he is simply seen as one who delivers, even if it means rolling up his sleeves and getting his hands dirty to do the job.

Finally, many are asking what next for Sarma, for this is

KANIMOZHI KARUNANIDHI

Still Waters Run Deep

Between the headlines, and the backstory, falls the reality. For seven long years, in the world of newspaper headlines Muthuvel Karunanidhi Kanimozhi was accused in a telecom licensing scam. After 193 days behind bars in Delhi's infamous Tihar Jail and a long legal battle, she was finally acquitted by a special trial court. Hers was also one of the voices caught on the now infamous Radia Tapes where she's heard negotiating ministerial portfolios in Manmohan Singh's UPA-2 government for her party with the lobbyist Nira Radia. It is clear that Kanimozhi was the go-between for the centre and her father, then chief minister, the late M. Karunanidhi. The voice one hears on the tapes is both tentative and firm. Firm in that she knows the message she wants to convey, and tentative is the tone she uses to express her views.

Kanimozhi is the youngest child of the deceased DMK patriarch and some say, was also his favourite. Her mother Rajathi Ammal met Karunanidhi while she was part of his theatre group; they fell in love and Rajathi became Karunanidhi's third wife. His first wife Padmavathi had died, and he divided his time between his second wife Dayalu Ammal and Rajathi. While Kanimozhi is an only child, Dayalu has three sons, and one daughter. One of the sons, M.K. Stalin, was always considered Karunanidhi's heir apparent and became party president after his father's death. Those who look for compartments tend to label Stalin as Karunanidhi's political heir and Kanimozhi as his literary heir, for she's a former journalist, a poet and the prime mover behind the city's annual cultural festival—Chennai Sangamam.

But reality outstrips labels, challenges headlines and moulds its own backstory. Walking into the well-lit meeting room of Kanimozhi's bungalow in Chennai's CIT Colony, I met a leader whom I would later describe (notes to myself) as a very spirited and pragmatic politician. Dressed in her trademark cotton salwar kameez, wearing a bindi, gold ear-rings (more in the baalis range than jhumkas) and a wedding band, she wore no other accessories other than rubber chappals. The image that came across was of no-fuss-elegance rather than crumpled-cottons.

As we talked, I soon realized that neither the role of a wrongfully accused nor that of a poetess-turned-politician who dabbled in women's issues would define her. An economics graduate, the convent-educated Kanimozhi had definite views on a range of subjects—from capital punishment, renewable energy to the agrarian crisis. Although currently a Rajya Sabha member, she has also expressed a desire to enter electoral politics at the Lok Sabha level and not the state legislature. 'Let's see how things pan out, but I hope to fight the Lok Sabha,' she says, measuring her words with care.

She is pragmatic enough to realize that it is her brother who has the grip over the party's organization at the state level, but at the same time, there is a gap that can be filled at the centre. The DMK, like most regional outfits, needs an emissary who can negotiate funds, ministerial berths and other demands of the state with the central government. Of course this is a position that needs the trust of the party leader. The cordial but correct equation between Stalin and Kanimozhi can accommodate this role which complements rather than challenges his grip over the party.

'Stalin has worked his way to get where he is and deserves to be where he is. I don't think that it's because he is my father's son he is where he is. He has worked hard for it and is wholly deserving of his leadership position,' she says.

Counting from the time he was made a member of the General Committee of the DMK in 1973 to when he was nominated the party's working president in 2017, Stalin has had a nearly 45 years' learning curve. Some within the state refer to him as Prince Charles due to the rather long gestation period he had to undertake. After Karunanidhi's death in August 2018, a succession war broke out between Stalin and his estranged older brother M.K. Azhagiri (also Dayalu's son) who had been expelled from the party by their father in 2014. Kanimozhi wisely backed Stalin who is in control of the party organisation. She also has a sizeable following of her own in south-east and central Tamil Nadu.

Kanimozhi's entry into politics was accidental. After her MA in economics from the Ethiraj College for Women, Madras

University, she worked briefly at *The Hindu* as a sub-editor but left the job after her father became state chief minister for the third time in 1989. Those who have worked with her remember her as someone who was more interested in arts, music and literature rather than politics. She met her Singapore-based husband G. Aravindan at a literary event in Paris and moved there to edit a Singapore-based Tamil newspaper—*Tamil Murasu*. I asked her what made her shift from the literary to the political, but expecting the usual 'dynastic-compulsions' answer, I was not focusing on her reply, and so nearly missed the half-smile that she gave me in response. 'What?' I asked, curious now. She raised her eyebrows, and looked across the room at Manu Sundaram, the DMK national spokesperson who was also present. Usually affable, Manu played it enigmatic, and instead offered me some green tea.

Kanimozhi wouldn't elaborate further and we discussed the merits of tea over coffee for a while (apparently Manu is against coffee while Kanimozhi is still weighing her options). But later, over a masala dosa with a local source, I managed to extract the political 'masala'. The reference was to the fallout between the Maran family and the Karunanidhi clan. Murasoli Maran—Karunanidhi's nephew—enjoyed a close equation of trust with his uncle. From 1977 to 2003 he was the party's face in Delhi, and after his death this role was passed on to his son Dayanidhi who was also the cabinet minister for telecommunications in the UPA government from 2004–2007. But in May 2007, a Maran-owned newspaper, *Dinakaran*, had published a survey done by an AC Nielsen polling on who could be Karunanidhi's heir. The choice was between three of Karunanidhi's children—M.K. Stalin, Kanimozhi and their elder brother Azhagiri. In addition, another survey of the union ministers from the state was also published that showed Dayanidhi as the best performer, with

T.R. Baalu (a DMK leader close to the clan and a minster at the centre) in the third place. An angry Karunanidhi accused the Marans of creating a wedge between his family by pitting his children against one other. He also suspected that the Marans were pushing Dayanidhi's case in the leadership stakes by playing up a survey that showcased both his achievements and the divide in the family over the leadership stakes. The relationship soured. Dayanidhi was asked to resign as cabinet minister. Two months later, in July 2007, Kanimozhi was sent to New Delhi as a Rajya Sabha member.

'Right from its inception the DMK has sent a senior leader to Delhi as its face and to negotiate with the centre for more federal space,' points out A.S. Panneerselvan, who teaches politics at the Asian School of Journalism. 'In 1957 this role was played by E.V.K. Sampath who was Periyar's nephew, in 1962 it was DMK founder C.N. Annadurai, after his death in 1967 this role was played by K. Anbazhagan. Later, the Marans took over this role beginning with Murasoli Maran from 1977 to 2003. Being the face of Delhi is not an insignificant role, it is extremely central to the DMK's politics and the way it functions. It has to be someone you can trust, someone who can carry forward your ideological thrust.'

At the time of her political launch, Kanimozhi was 39 years old and blended well with the GenNext of various political parties—from Rahul Gandhi to Harsimrat Kaur Badal to Supriya Sule and Akhilesh and Dimple Yadav. Other DMK leaders such as T.R. Baalu belonged to an older generation. Kanimozhi fitted in well, and even went on to build her own equation with Congress President Sonia Gandhi, whom she says she has a lot of respect for. Kanimozhi certainly seems more comfortable with the Congress than the current day BJP, giving the impression that if the DMK has to choose between the two national parties she would nudge the party towards the Congress.'There is a lot of difference between the BJP led by Modi and Vajpayee's BJP,' she says significantly.

'The collective political wisdom of the state is that 2014 was an aberration. If the BJP had not won 70+ seats in UP it would not have got a majority,' points out Panneerselvan. 'India is moving towards a multi-party coalition arrangement and in it being a union minister is as important as being the chief minister,' he adds. Clearly he sees Kanimozhi emerging as the Number 2 within the DMK.

It was Kanimozhi who was the prime mover behind the DMK-hosted opposition unity bash under the guise of M. Karunanidhi's 92nd birthday celebrations in June 2016. Like all regional leaders, she is a firm believer in the rights of states in India's federal set up, and believes that the nature of India's polity calls for coalition governments rather than one party rule.

In terms of handling the allies, the way the Kanimozhi-Stalin equation works is, if there is an All Party Meeting in New Delhi or even in Patna, it is Kanimozhi who is sent as the DMK's emissary. However, if a Mamata Banerjee wants to talk about setting up a federal front, she picks her phone and calls Stalin. He takes the final decision but Kanimozhi is definitely an influencer; because she is family, because of her role as the 'Delhi Face' and because she could emerge as a legitimate Number 2.

While in the capital she stays away from the Page Three dinners preferring to keep her socializing to hosting idli-dosa breakfasts and attending the odd lunch. During her first stint in the Rajya Sabha she would rush back to Chennai every weekend to be with her then school-going son, Adithyan. However, her one favorite haunt in Delhi remains the Bahri & Sons bookstore in the capital's Khan Market. Or browsing around the DVD stores nearby so she could pick up a favourite Shabana Azmi movie (watched with subtitles for while she is probably the only one of the Karunanidhi clan to speak fluent English, she knows only a smattering of Hindi at best).

She knows that being the party's interlocutor to New Delhi is a two-edged sword. This has already led to her being embroiled in both the Radia Tapes scandal and the 2G case. The first records her negotiating with a lobbyist for cabinet berths for the DMK in UPA-2. Two things stand out here. One is that during the Manmohan Singh-led UPA Government, Kanimozhi was clearly the link between New Delhi and her father. She is heard explaining on the tapes, 'The prime minister is also very soft-spoken and dad can't hear that clearly also' (22 May 2009 conversation). The second fact that comes across is that she was not at all keen to see Dayanidhi Maran return to the cabinet. That she was pushing for A. Raja instead of Maran worked against her later when the 2G spectrum case was filed as the Central Bureau of Investigation (CBI) claimed collusion between the two. However, party sources claim that keeping Dayanidhi out of the cabinet was a party decision that she was implementing.

At that time, there was a chance of her getting a berth as a minister of state in UPA-2. She was keen on either the health or the environment ministry but once she realized that her elder brother Azhagiri was also interested, she decided to shelve her claims, pointing out that all the portfolios cannot go to the family. Political commentator R.K. Radhakrishnan, also associate editor at *Frontline*, who has covered the Karunanidhi family for two decades says: 'Senior Congress leaders including Pranab Mukherjee had reached out to her inviting her to be a MoS in their ministry, and use that experience as an internship to learn the ropes. But she did not push her case over her brother's even though she was the senior in terms of parliamentary experience.'

Later, in 2011, when the charge-sheet on the 2G Spectrum allocation case was filed, Kanimozhi was accused of taking a Rs 200 crore bribe in the form of an unsecured loan to Kalaignar TV by a realty company, in return for which the owners of the said company were to be given out-of-turn spectrum licenses by then telecom minister, A. Raja. Kanimozhi owns 20 per cent shares in Kalaignar TV while Karunanidhi's first wife Dayalu Ammal owns 60 per cent. Kanimozhi says the entire case was a 'political conspiracy to tarnish the image of the DMK'. She points out that she was only a director of Kalaignar TV for two weeks in June 2007 while the transactions took place between December 2008 and Febuary 2011. Moreover, she adds, she was not involved in the channel's financial dealings and there was no paper relating to a financial transaction with her signature on it. Regardless, she was sent to Delhi's Tihar Jail for six months on 21 May 2011.

That Karunanidhi's daughter would now be lodged in Jail No. 6, Ward No. 8 sent shivers down the political class' collective spine. A visibly upset Karunanidhi had called on her, leaving the jail premises with tears in his eyes. 'I had to be the strong one, for both my father and mother, it is I who had to comfort them as they were so hurt and upset to see me there,' recalls Kanimozhi. At the time Karunanidhi told the media, 'If you have a daughter and if she is punished for no mistake, how will you feel? That's the way I feel.' Throughout her jail term the only face she presented to the outside world was one of stoic calm. There were no tears, no shrill protestations of innocence, no recriminations. Her Singapore-based husband Aravindan and then nine-year-old son were frequent visitors along with MPs cutting across party lines. She admits that her biggest support was her husband. 'Only he knows my tastes in books and brought me all the books that I wanted to read,' she recalls. That helped her pass her time behind bars, for the days would be spent in court, but the evenings were spent in walks around the prison complex where she was particularly upset to see that the branches of all the trees had been cut off. And she read a lot.

The one book she read a lot was the Mahabharata, various versions of it. 'My father was a big fan of the Mahabharata. I always wondered what is so interesting about it. Then I got a chance to read it,' she says. Did she like it? 'It is a masterpiece, a beautiful book on the game of politics. Tells you how low people can stoop,' she explains. What is the one lesson she took away from the 2G episode? 'It hits you. You stop asking "Why me?" You realize anything can happen to anyone. In a way, it was a learning experience; it was also a harrowing experience. Being accused of corruption is not an easy thing, it is very painful. But somewhere it makes you stronger, definitely emotionally stronger.' What wrenched her heart was also the fact that her son had to see her in jail. 'He was very angry,' she said when I asked her about his reaction. Exactly my point, I thought. She clearly believes there was a conspiracy against her, then why wasn't she *angry* instead of all this talk about acceptance? Whom did she blame for all this or did she put it down in a neat box called karma?

'Karma?' she asked surprised. 'Whom are you asking this to? I don't believe in God.' 'Are you a Buddhist?' I persisted, still trying to figure out where this sense of calm acceptance was coming from. 'I am a Periyarist,' she shot back. (Social activist E.V. Ramasamy, better known as Periyar, was one of the pioneers of the Dravidian movement, campaigning against the caste system.) 'I don't believe in superstitions, wearing threads on my wrists and looking for auspicious timings to leave the house.' Looking at her bare wrists I realized that she wasn't even wearing a watch. 'I have a mobile so can see the time on that,' she replied. Clearly a minimalist, both in her accessories and in her answers.

Seven years after being accused, she was acquitted by a trial court that dropped all charges against her in December 2017. Though the case has gone in for an appeal, the acquittal has rejuvenated her politically. DMK cadres celebrated with posters proclaiming, '*Inee Nee Poongodiyalla! Porkodi*' (Henceforth, you are not a flowering plant, but a flag of war). Another stated, '*Agni Paritchaiyai Vendru Varum Agalvilake*' (Welcome our lamp which has passed the acid test). Flags, flowers and lamps aside, the corruption tag was an albatross around her neck. She hated to be bracketed as an ATM politician—a tag given by New Delhi to regional parties who demanded cash-rich ministries.

The acquittal freed her to focus on her politics. Her son, Adithyan, a Singapore citizen, had by then completed his studies and gone to Singapore to do his compulsory stint at the National Service. 'When he was in school I used to run home every weekend to be with him, didn't even take part in any parliamentary delegations that would involve travel away from him. But when I was in prison I learnt that he can survive without me,' she says, a bit regretfully. When I asked her what Adithyan planned to do next she gave the shrug that all mothers give, but added with a smile, 'Not politics for sure. There will be no additions to dynasty from my side.'

Being the sixth child of the third wife cannot make for an easy childhood, yet I wondered how to broach such a sensitive topic. Karunanidhi was once questioned about the new additions to his family on the floor of the assembly in the late '60s/early '70s when Kanimozhi was a little baby; he acknowledged her as his daughter. Ever since her birth Kanimozhi has lived with her mother, first at their house in Oliver Road, from where the family moved to the current CIT Colony residence. Before he fell ill, Karunanidhi used to divide his time between this residence and Dayalu Ammal's bungalow in Gopalapuram. While his nights were spent at CIT colony he used to drive to Gopalapuram in the mornings to do some writing and then go to the party office or the CM's Office as the case may be. Afternoon siesta was back at Gopalapuram after which he went to the office and finally his evening meetings were held at CIT colony. This was a routine all of Chennai knew, and perhaps the rest of India too, for when Pranab Mukherjee began canvassing for the post of president of India, the first call he made was to his old friend Karunanidhi at the CIT colony house. In Tamil Nadu, there was no official CM bungalow allotted by the state government until recently, post Jayalalitha's death, so both his houses were known as CM-House when he was in power. To the public, Dayalu is known as Peri-Amma (older mother) while Rajathi is Chinna-amma (younger mother). For the people of Tamil Nadu, it is as simple as that. However, in the last few years before his death, due to his ill-health, Karunanidhi was based at Gopalapuram where Kanimozhi visited him daily, reading poems or Periyar's works to him.

Adds Radhakrishnan, 'One could say Kanimozhi's political internship began at Karunanidhi's evening durbars at the CIT colony house, for she was often present there. He has always been a man of consensus, who sought opinions from a range of people, and she seems to have learnt that from him.' This was also the room we were sitting in, and looking around the sparsely furnished room with its high-backed arm-chair ringed with sofas I tried to visualize the debates and decisions that must have taken place there. On one of the walls, is a large portrait of Karunanidhi and Rajathi, both of them wearing garlands. 'When was this taken?' I asked, looking for an opening to my next question. 'A while ago,' was the answer. 'Was it easy to share your father with another family?' I asked finally. Her reply was very matter of fact. 'He always had people around him. If you are asking if he came to my Sport's Day or for parent-teacher meetings, then no. But he was as absent and present for me as he was for my brothers.' When I commented that she was seen as his literary heir, she replied, 'I don't think there can be such a thing as a literary heir. Because of my father, I had an opportunity to be exposed to literature, also within the DMK there is always a big romance for words, I think I picked it up from there. But he has written so much, I can't claim to be his heir.' The one thing she didn't have in common with her father was his love for cricket. 'Whenever he was campaigning he used to call home and ask me the score for in those days there was no internet, and I didn't even know there was a match on,' she recalls with a nostalgic smile. Adding, 'I miss him, miss talking to him, he's always been there for me.'

Recently Kanimozhi took up cudgels on behalf of a woman journalist who had complained about a patronizing pat on the cheek by the state governor, Banwarilal Purohit at a press conference. In return, a state BJP leader H. Raja taunted Kanimozhi, asking: 'Would journalists question the leader who made his illegitimate child, from an illegitimate relationship, a Rajya Sabha MP?' The reprehensible attack was condemned by all political parties, but Kanimozhi fought her own battles. She retorted that while it was 'beneath her' to reply to such statements, threats would not stop her from taking up such issues in the future.

This episode was a day old when I met her. It must be tough when people question your parents' relationship, I commented. 'You should ask them, not me,' she replied, pointing to the portrait on the wall. 'I was not part of their decision making. Each person decides how their relationship is structured.'

She has often been asked about her equation with her famous father. During an interaction with school kids she told them that while he may not have been aware if she had a test at school or not, if she had a medical emergency then he was definitely there for it. Her father had certainly taken all the important decisions in her life—he decided that she should major in economics after consulting DMK leader and his confidante Anbazhagan. It was Karunanidhi who chose her first husband Athiban Bose. And needless to add, it was Karunanidhi who decided that she join politics.

But it's always been a two-way communication between father and daughter. Even when he was chief minister she would debate with him or push a certain cause. For instance, it is she who persuaded Karunanidhi to set up a Transgender Welfare Board (in 2008) and issue separate ration cards for transgenders. Being old school, Karunanidhi—and most of his advisors— had a set view of transgenders; she helped him come to a new understanding.

Certainly the poetess-turned-politician is the new-age heir of DMK. At 50, she belongs to a younger generation than Stalin. Hers is also the feisty, progressive face of politics. When I asked her why she had waded into the governor controversy she said what got to her was the 'patronizing attitude' towards a 'professional woman'. Leaning forward in her chair, she said, 'It's highly inappropriate and insulting to answer a question with a pat on the cheek. It's insulting towards the woman and to her profession.' It's interesting to watch her body language. Throughout our hour-long conversation she was seated comfortably on her chair, with her feet curled up underneath her. During the questions related to 2G she spoke, mostly with her hand cupping her chin, but when it came to an issue she was passionate about, such as this, she sat upright and the hand came down firmly on the arm of the chair.

She is fond of quoting Periyar. Describing him as 'one of the few truthful and honest feminists of our country', she quotes him saying: 'In 1928 he had said if we are to be free, we must free our women.' Speaking in the Rajya Sabha on 14 April 2014 during a discussion on the workings of the Women & Children Ministry, she said: 'Many have said India celebrates its women because we have women goddesses ... we are worshipped and put on a pedestal. But I think the time has come that women have to be allowed to get off the pedestal and be treated as equals in society. We have had enough of being patient mothers, of being silent sufferers. I think today women are interested in nation building, in changing society, in fighting for their rights.'

When I wondered how a budding poetess was comfortable majoring in economics she looked surprised and said that logic and reasoning appealed to her. 'Economics is like life, there are no set rules,' she says.

Then, is she pro-reforms or pro-freebies like her father was? Again the question has her straightening up in her chair. 'Our leader when he was CM announced Rs 1 kg rice for Re 1. I would never call that a freebie because it changes a lot of things in society. It is only when you have food to feed your families, then children's education and other reforms become easier. So I wouldn't call that a freebie. We also took out government health insurance schemes for everybody way back in 2009—that's not a freebie. I think that's a basic necessity. One more thing, when our leader announced Rs 10,000 for marriage of girls, which he later increased to Rs 20,000, he brought in one clause that she should be educated till Class 8th. That's a social reform which ensured girls remained in high school, and not a freebie,' she says.

In parliament I have heard her making the case for renewable energy but through inexpensive home-grown technology, for scientific guidance to be given to farmers so they know what crops to grow and fertilizers to use. That tells us about her politics, and her economics. What about her poems?

'My poems are more inward looking. Of late, I have written a lot about ... I won't say physical violence but there are so many other kinds of violence,' she says and trails off.

'Like?' I prompt.

'Like social. I have also addressed issues of capital punishment. A murder is not an answer to a murder, is it? You can't take the right to murder and give it to the government. That is murder too and I don't see it as anything else. I don't think anyone has a right to kill. I'm against war and killing of any kind, even in the name of law. Especially in a country like India it's the Dalits, the minorities, the under-privileged who get the death penalty. People who cannot afford to get the best lawyers. And it's not always the accused who is the person who has committed the crime. Then what do you do? Punishment is to deter people and give them a life to reform but if you take away the life then what is there to reform. Also, has death penalty stopped rape, murder?' She stops for breath and then smiles. 'Social justice is something I am quite passionate about and I think the Dravidian movement is all about social justice.'

In the world of DMK politics, you are given only one chance. If you blow it like Azhagiri, or like Karunanidhi's oldest child M.K. Muthu (a failed actor and son from his first marriage), or even Dayanidhi Maran, then the doors of Karunanidhi's legacy

SACHIN PILOT

Politics in a Grain of Sand

Before he goes to see a movie, Sachin Pilot will first research the film, read the reviews and only then will he sit down to watch it. Moreover, the movie has to be seen in the theatre and not on DVD at home, because, as he says, 'What's a movie without the popcorn?'

That's quintessential Sachin Pilot. When he commits to a project, he throws his heart, soul, taste-buds and planner into it. So when the 37-year-old Congress leader was asked to take over as the state Rajasthan Congress chief in early 2014, he moved bag and baggage to Jaipur, dropping out of sight from the national media, where he was a regular, both on Page One and Page Three. The former because, despite being the youngest minister in UPA-2 he was one of its more credible faces and often fielded to counter charges of corruption that came up during the fag end of the government's term. The very same reasons also made him a must-have at every Lutyens' Delhi bash and hence his presence on Page Three.

There were those who saw Rajasthan as a punishment posting, considering that the Congress had just been decimated in the 2013 state elections, getting its lowest tally ever with only 21 MLAs. Yet Sachin didn't lose his deadpan demeanour when he told the media: 'This is a responsibility that has been given to me and I will do my best to deliver.' At another time, in a more candid mood, he confessed, 'It takes a lot of hard work to revive a recently defeated party [*India Today*, March 2014].'

During the next three years, he toured the entire 33 districts of the state in his Ford Endeavour at least three to four times over, clocking over 3 lakh kms, getting to know every gali and every mohalla of his new portfolio. Also more importantly, he was giving the state a chance to know him for himself and not just another Congress scion (Sachin's father, late Rajesh Pilot, was a popular Congress leader from the state). His calendar was filled with rallies, mundans, weddings and funerals. In the bargain he put on weight from eating all those laddoos. He has, also on occasion been lathi-charged by the state officials. In fact, if you nag him enough he may show you the picture of a baseball-sized purple bruise on his well-toned bicep that went viral on social media; and a copy of which is stored on his cell-phone.

Pilot belongs to the Gurjar caste and he has nurtured this identity along with the many other hats he wears. However, in Rajasthan, the Gurjars are not the dominant caste. Of the total population in the state, 11.93 per cent are Jats, while 11.997 per cent are Scheduled Tribes (STs) of which 6.001 per cent are Meenas and only 4.92 per cent are Gurjars [Source: Congress

Party's internal survey dated 2018 January]. Yet, Jats have traditionally cornered 30–40 seats in the 200-seat Assembly. For Pilot to be made the state party chief without having the right caste combination is a testimony by itself. Sachin, however, is impatient with calculations like these. He says, 'I don't want caste to define what kind of a person I will be as an administrator. You have no choice over which caste or community you will be born into. I am proud and happy to belong to the community I was born into. But it is what you say, what you do, how you act that defines you.' Yet he is by now seasoned enough to tone down his idealism with a touch of pragmatism, for he adds: 'It may play a role in electoral strategy but I don't think it defines anyone.' Interestingly, the same internal Congress survey also states that Sachin has a huge appeal amongst the urban youth from 18–45-year-olds which traditionally voted for the BJP.

What then is his comeback plan for Rajasthan? He replies, 'You are right when you say that the Congress was at its lowest when I took office. But take a look at what's happened since then. During the 2014 Lok Sabha elections, the Congress polled 30 per cent vote and the BJP polled 56 per cent. A year and a half later, during the Panchayat elections—which are the most comprehensive of elections at the grassroot level—the Congress polled 45 per cent and the BJP got 46-and-a-half per cent. The gap went to less than 2 per cent from a 26 per cent gap.'

Interestingly, it is the state of Rajasthan that offered the Congress its first green shoots of hope for the 2019 General Elections. In February 2018, Sachin delivered an impressive morale building win for the Congress when the party won all the three by-polls in his state. Two of these were for the Lok Sabha constituencies of Alwar and Ajmer while the third was for the Mandalgarh assembly seat. Watching the results from the party office in Ajmer, an ecstatic Pilot was carried on the shoulders of his exuberant party workers for he was the face of the Congress offensive. Even amidst celebrations he bid caution telling his supporters that there was still a lot of work to do. 'They should not now rest and think the state elections will be a walk-over,' he told me with a sheepish look. Pilot's rival in state politics, former CM of Rajasthan Ashok Gehlot, was also watching television that day. He later told the media, 'PCC chiefs should not be misled by their followers into thinking they will automatically become chief ministers.' Game on!

By the time the state elections neared Pilot was optimistic enough to dream of a Congress comeback. His four year exile from Delhi was paying dividends. 'I don't think criticizing the BJP is enough. Yes we need to hold them to account but we also need to present to the people of Rajasthan a better alternative. We need to tell the people that if you vote for us this is what we will do in education, labour reforms, employment, sanitation, urban development.'

So, he is not just a dreamer then, but also a man with a plan?

His 'To Do' list has new age, development centric issues not the old lures of reservations and sops. Urban city centres, a water management and conservation policy, incentivizing the Small and Medium Scale Enterprises (SMEs) so they can create jobs. But there is a problem here. For all his drive and charisma, he still lacks a pan-Rajasthan connect. The two time former CM Ashok Gehlot has the edge in that he has a firmer grip on the state organization and has made it clear he is keen on a third term. More importantly, Gehlot is fast emerging as one of the few Congress leaders whose advice Rahul Gandhi seems to heed. Which doesn't bode very well for his young colleague. So, if the Congress does manage to wrest the state from the BJP, will Sachin chalk up the last five years to 'job experience' or will he have something more tangible to show?

For now, as always, Sachin plays it pragmatic. 'It's not important whether they make me CM face or not,' he says, poker-faced. And then, seeing my disbelief, adds: 'I'll tell you why. Most important right now is for us to get a majority. Right now anyone who is thinking about becoming a CM is really not doing a service to the party. I've been given so much. I've just turned 40 but already fought three MP elections, been a minister and now a pradesh adhyaksh (PCC chief). If I can steer the party to victory in Rajasthan, my job is done. Who becomes CM is for the party to decide.' However I don't buy this logic. If there is no assured post then there is nothing to drive the hunger to succeed. 'Working for the party' makes a great Gandhian soundbite, but not practical politics.

Interestingly both Pilot and his Congress colleague, Jyotiraditya Scindia, participated in 'Off the Cuff', a talk show hosted by Shekhar Gupta (Founder, *The Print*) in end-October 2017. At that time Scindia was tipped to be made the Congress party's chief ministerial face in Madhya Pradesh, while Pilot was hopeful of Rajasthan. When asked whether the party should go in for elections with a CM face—since both Madhya Pradesh and Rajashtan are due for polls end 2018—Scindia immediately answered with a yes. Pilot spoke after him and carefully worded his reaction stating: 'In Rajasthan we probably have half a dozen [CM] faces, why just one.' When I asked him later why he had hedged his answer he replied that as PCC chief his job was to take everyone along and not promote himself. One thing I learnt about Pilot is that he always thinks through his reactions rather than go with the instinctive response. 'Yes, I do tend to mull and think things through,' he agrees. Whether he wins Rajasthan or not, whether he is made the chief minister or not, one thing is certain. Both his genes and his name come with a built-in user's manual—you cannot keep a Pilot grounded for too long.

Born 7 September 1977, he was only 21 when his father, Congress leader and former union minister Rajesh Pilot, died in a tragic car accident. An ex-Air Force fighter pilot squadron leader, he was then known as Rajeshwar Prasad and had fought the 1971 Indo-Pak war. Later he joined the Congress under Indira Gandhi. But that's not the entire story. Rajeshwar's father, an army hawaldar, died when he was very young. Soon after, Rajeshwar left his village Baidpura in Uttar Pradesh's Ghaziabad district and came to live with his cousin, a dairy owner, in Delhi. And, in one of politics most celebrated rags to power story, Rajeshwar Prasad delivered milk to the very neighbourhood in Lutyens' Delhi that he would live in three decades later; as Union Minister Rajesh Pilot in the Government of India.

It was only after Pilot Senior's death in June 2000 that his son Sachin entered politics. This was not part of his original plan for he'd slogged for his MBA at Wharton and done a stint at General Motors. 'I was only 21 when he died and at 21 you really don't think long term political careers. While my father was alive we never discussed my political career. I thought maybe I'd start my own business or work in a corporate. Actually, it was four years after his death that I joined the Congress.' It was Sachin's mother Rama Pilot (also a Congress leader) who contested the 2000 by-poll from Dausa after her husband's death. 'I felt that I could contribute most in this field, on this platform. And that is why, despite my education, my degree and working in the business field, I chose to give that up and enter public life.' It's a standard answer that I have heard from most dynasts who join politics.

Has his degree helped him make a difference? The answer is

an unequivocal yes. 'My father used to say no matter what you do, business, engineering or law, a good education will hold you in good stead. It helps you to be open to ideas, to understand critical issues that come your way when you are a policy-maker. And also, it gives you lot more credibility when holding discussions with people from strong backgrounds. I consider myself very lucky that I was able to attend very good colleges, both for my undergrad and master's.' (He completed BA (hons) in English from St Stephen's College, Delhi University.) Clearly education is something he feels strongly about for he goes on to reiterate, 'I think it's very important for political leaders to get a good education. It doesn't have to be a high profile education, but good, sound, qualification is always beneficial.'

I recall my first interview with Sachin, back in 2004, when he entered Parliament for the first time. Even then, young Sachin already had a plan. He had told me: 'I want money raised from disinvestments to be ear-marked for specific projects. For instance, the money raised from a particular PSU could be used for providing water for a specific number of villages. If people can see where their money is going, there won't be such a scare about disinvestment.'

Sachin fought his first election from his father's seat in Dausa. At 26, he was the youngest MP in the 14th Lok Sabha. This was also a time when the Congress party's heir apparent, the then 34-year-old Rahul Gandhi, was making his political debut. Along with Sachin and Rahul, there were a total of 10 young MPs who had won their first election from the Congress, of which 8 were dynasts. Within the Congress they were known as the Cub Class. It was a good year to be young, especially if you were from the Congress for you walked into Parliament as part of the ruling establishment. Sachin soon became a key player in Rahul's youth brigade, along with other public school

young dynasts like Milind Deora and Jitin Prasada. Within the
Congress they were known as Rahul's Camelot as all of them,
except Rahul, went on to become ministers in the Congress-led
UPA-2 in 2009.

Sachin's first portflolio was minister of state (MoS) in the
Ministry of Telecommunications and IT (2010). Looking back,
he recalls, 'Much is being made of Digital India in the Modi
govt but it was under Dr Manmohan Singh that we decided to
connect 2,50,000 panchayats with broadband and optical fibre.'
The National Fibre Optics Network was created in 2011 for this
purpose and as the then MoS Sachin was put in charge of this.
Before then, optical fibre cable connectivity was available in all
state capitals and districts but only at the block level. By targeting
panchayats the aim was last mile digital connectivity.

'Under the BJP government [which came to power in 2014]
it's been given the spin of Digital India, Connect India. But
basically it is the same program that was started by us. Rs 20,000
crores were earmarked for this,' he says. Adding, 'We believed
that India in the 21st Century was always looked down upon
for not having the best physical infrastructure, in terms of ports,
highways etc. So we thought let's leap frog and give India the best
digital connectivity and IT infrastructure that no other country
can boast of. And I can challenge anyone on this—be it Russia,
America, Japan, China. No one will have a better optical fibre
network than the one we started in 2009. The idea is to give the
last mile connectivity of broadband and Wi-Fi.'

He pauses, but only to sip his coffee (which he has with
oodles of milk), and continues. 'I used to tell my officers in the
ministry, IT does not mean that you wear a suit and sit with a
laptop. And if all IT was to be in English, then India would be

left behind. We fought with global agencies such as Google to get a lot of Indian languages on the net. Folks from a country like Cambodia can have a domain name in their language. But a Kannada language person cannot have a domain name. Out of 25 languages, as many as 17 languages were sanctioned in our time so that internet became relevant to those who couldn't speak English or Hindi. Digital literacy doesn't mean that you have to know English. I wanted to democratize IT learning. A common citizen should have access to cheap internet in a local language. Not everyone in a village needs to be on Telegram, WhatsApp or Facebook. But yes, if they want to send emails, resumes, job searches, then they should be able to do this through Common Service Centres. So, we had a lot of ideas that were all put in place long before 2014 came around.'

Despite being the minister for telecom & IT Sachin is not a gadget freak unlike his colleague Milind Deora who also held the same portfolio (both were MoS in the Ministry of Communications and Information Technology during UPA-2). Sachin, however, adds a codicil saying, 'While I am not obsessed with the latest gadgets, I am interested in technology as an enabler, more at the macro level. I know enough not to be called outdated.' When I ask him what phone he uses, he shrugs and says, 'It's an iPhone. But it's not the latest model, perhaps it could be the second-latest!' Guess anyone who wants a peek at the very latest can go to Deora!

Since the Department of Telecom also came under his ministry, Sachin was shocked to discover that soldiers in border areas paid Rs 50 per minute for a satellite phone call. He slashed the rates to Rs 5 per minute. 'My grandfather was a hawaldar in the army ... we have to look out for people who don't ask for very much,' he says. He was also one of the first union ministers to join the Territorial Army in September 2012 as a lieutenant because he wanted to keep his links with the armed forces just as his father and grandfather had done.

During the UPA government, Pilot was one of the few first time ministers to be promoted within two years when he was given independent charge of the controversial Corporate Affairs Ministry in October 2012. His elevation was welcomed by the industry which welcomed the move to promote someone who was in tune with current reality. The need of the hour was modern legislation hence modern leaders who understood globalization were preferred to those who grew up in the '60s and had a controlled mind-set. Pilot was seen as one such face of empowerment.

As soon as Sachin took office, one of the first tasks before him was to pilot the new Companies Bill through Parliament. This was the first time that the act was being replaced since 1956. Though the draft was in place, what was needed was some fancy footwork, and the right optics to see the bill through, to assure both the industry and the consumer that their interests were being taken care of and walk that tight rope between governance and regulation.

Speaking in Parliament when he presented the bill, Sachin said, 'When the act was introduced in 1956 our economy was a command and control one. The 21st century brought along with it multiple challenges. Indian companies are going overseas and making a mark for themselves, foreign companies are investing in India ... I am one of those people who believes it is better to have less regulation but 100 per cent compliance rather than having 1000 regulations and less compliance.' Later he explained further. 'I have always maintained that it's not the severity of punishment that is the deterrent, it's the surety of punishment. There will always be people who will try to evade the law so it's important to make examples of individuals who feel that they are above the law.'

There is a confidence about him that belies his youth. He was only 32 when he became a minister for the first time. 'The bureaucrats in the ministry were used to senior, seasoned politicians. So while I gave utmost respect to senior officials I also kept in mind that ultimately the buck stopped with me. If something were to go wrong, I would be the one taking responsibility, I'd be the one facing Parliament and facing the media. It took a couple of weeks for the bureaucrats to realize that they can't do as they please. Initially there was some ... I wouldn't call it power play, but it took them a few weeks to get used to the fact that I am going to run a very tight ship.'

Even as the corporate affairs minister, Sachin was smart enough not to forget his core constituency—the farmers. His father, Rajesh Pilot, had built a formidable connect with the farming community and was affectionately known as the real Kissan ka Neta, as opposed to other pretenders to the title. Sachin has realized in this era of specialization even politicians need to hone onto a brand identity. And what better than to nurture one that is already associated with his family. 'The party gave me the responsibility for IT & corporate affairs, but the grain of my being is and will always be attached to agrarian issues,' he says firmly. Then why didn't he specialize in agrarian studies instead of an MBA? The answer came with a quizzical look, 'Mahatma Gandhi studied law, but his calling was not that. A good education is important, I learnt about finance which is great but like I said the rooted sense of my being belongs to the agrarian community. That's where I come from, I may not look like a typical farmer but ever since the beginning of my politics, *tab se lekar aajtak* [from then to now], whatever I do, whether in Delhi or Rajasthan, I have tried to raise these issues.'

He's right in that he doesn't look anything like a typical farmer. Dressed in sharp suits and rimless glasses, it's easier to see him in corporate environs than the farming fields. But with equal ease he can blend in with the locals in his constituency, sitting on charpais in villages, sipping tea and discussing monsoon patterns with farmers. He's learnt the art of speed-wearing the colourful safa (a colourful strip of cloth that's usually five to eight metres long and has to be tied manually like a turban) that is an essential part of the welcome at every village gathering. Starched white kurtas and Rajasthani safas are as much a part of his style statements as his Levi's jeans and checked cotton shirts. In fact at a family get together on Diwali when he was quizzed by his sister for turning up in a t-shirt he pointed out that the rest of them wore kurtas when they wanted to dress up, for him it was work-wear. A note about his brand appeal: I have heard customers ask for rimless 'Sachin Pilot glasses' at many opticians.

But fashion talk only has him rolling his eyes. So he gets back to what he really wants to talk about, or to what he feels should be the focus of this conversation. 'Collectively 10 per cent of India is feeding the rest of us. Are we doing justice to them? If we become ministers, it is because of them, they are the ones who actually vote for us. So we have to also raise their issues.'

A late entrant on social media, he was at first wary of the medium, pointing out its pitfalls to his colleague from South Mumbai Milind Deora, and Rahul Gandhi, during an informal chat. However, he has since embraced the new medium to reach out to both his constituency (usually in Hindi) and to the media. He certainly is a media delight for an interview with him gets top-rated TRPs and his is a regular Congress-face at media conclaves to take on the BJP. Some come to listen to him, others to just get a selfie clicked with this earnest bespectacled youth leader.

He is certainly no armchair politician and has been sent to jail on more than one occasion for 'protesting too much'. He says with one of his rare smiles: 'I've courted arrest four or five times. It's not as if we are breaking the law, it's a form of protest.' The first time was in 2007 when he was part of a protest against the Vasundhara Raje-led BJP government in Rajasthan. The Gurjar community in Rajasthan—which Pilot belongs to—was demanding ST status (this would help them reap the benefits of reservation) while the numerically stronger Meena community was opposing their inclusion. Pilot joined the protests on behalf of the Gurjars, was laathi charged (which is when he got the aforementioned bruise on his shoulder) and arrested by the BJP government. Not only was Pilot kept in custody for three days, he was also lodged in a high security cell in Jaipur's Central Jail which is meant for hardened criminals. He laughs when he recalls, 'Everyone else was sent to makeshift jails as is what happens during political protests. But I was singled out for a great honour for the CM made sure that I was sent to Central Jail. Nobody had access to me, I was kept in solitary confinement, not allowed to meet anyone, not even my lawyer. I couldn't talk to anyone, no newspapers, nothing.' He was given a chatai (floor mat) to sleep on, and food was a combination of water and haldi served in a plastic mug with a few pieces of vegetables floating in it, along with some rotis. 'It was a different experience, *par unhone apni saari bhadaas nikali mujh par* [they took out all their anger of the agitation against me],' he says. And adds with a frown, 'I was concerned about what was happening outside, whether the clashes were continuing and the well-being of the others who had been arrested.'

Since then he has courted arrest in other states, agitating for farmers' rights in Haryana (Bhatta Parsaul) and Madhya Pradesh (Mandsaur) as well. Sachin is one of the few Congress leaders of his generation who has built a cross-country appeal in a very short time. There is no state in the country where he has not addressed an election rally. By the time the 2009 election rolled by, his name was topping the charts of leaders in demand to campaign across states, be it the North East or down South.

The legacy of his father is an accessory he values. There are no photographs of himself in his makeshift office in the capital but there are some old black and white ones of his father, including one with former Prime Minister Rajiv Gandhi. 'You ask me what I remember about my father? It's not his ministerial stint but how he remained accessible to everyone regardless of who they were. His biggest asset was his sense of grounded reality because if people can't connect with you then of what use are you?'

I then ask my favourite question that I have asked all professionals who have turned to politics. Do they raise issues based on caste and religion or do they fight a more progressive campaign focusing on development? For in India, elections are won and lost on these two emotive issues rather than the issues of 'bijli-sadak-paani'. He has an answer. 'Just because we are mindful of a social set up in a state and make sure that everyone gets a place in the scheme of things doesn't mean we are doing caste politics. It's called giving representation, being sensitive to the aspirations of people on the fringes,' he says firmly.

Incidentally, he does have a pilot's license. When asked if this was something he wanted to do or was it a pressure of his surname, he admits it was a bit of both. Some of his early memories are of going flying with his father. He's also won medals for shooting at the national level. But of late politics has kept him grounded and away from his hobbies and even the odd movie break. Ask him about his favourite film star and he'll cite you examples from his grandmother's era—Waheeda

Rehman, Nargis, etc. Was he playing it safe by not naming any of the current actresses? He nods a sheepish yes.

Caution seems this commonsensical politician's reaction of choice. To stand out in a party filled with second generation dynasts such as Pilot is not easy; to carve your own identity when your father happens to be a charismatic son of the soil leader with a fantastic back story is even harder. At just 42 years, Sachin Pilot has managed to do just that. He has been able to achieve more than most of his peers, who wasted the five years in opposition by literally taking a 'Time Out'. Instead, he hit the ground running in Rajasthan, down to even shifting bag and baggage to a house in Jaipur right next to the party office.

Back to more serious questions then. When asked about the charge of dynasty over democracy that is often levied against his party leadership, including himself, Sachin gives a calibrated answer. 'I think the word that is used to describe people who have other members of the family in politics is a very cruel one. It's only done in the sub-continent. It shouldn't be a disqualification for if you are not able to perform or deliver, no matter who you are you will not be able to last.' I note how he carefully avoids using the word 'dynasty' during the entire speech, but let it go. This logic may justify family members contesting elections, but what about party leadership that is handed to a novice just on the strength of the family name? Sachin has an answer. 'Our party believes that a certain unifying force is represented by an individual who is keeping the party cohesive and united,' he says, refusing to take my bait.

Interestingly his father had contested an election against former Congress President Sitaram Kesri for the post of the party chief in June 1997. Although Pilot lost, the election was a learning ground for him. As he told the website Rediff On The NeT at the time: 'I am saddened by the dishonesty among many

Congress leaders. It has hurt me deeply. Privately, they would call me up and say: "Rajesh, you have done the right thing. I am with you." But in public and at Congress Working Committee meetings, these leaders keep quiet and behaved as if they have never met me all these years.' This could be one reason why Pilot Junior relies on his own instincts, turning a deaf ear to those who try to instigate him.

Although sycophants rather than outspoken leaders find more favour in the Congress durbar, Rajesh Pilot always had a cordial rapport with the Gandhis. In her biography on Rajesh Pilot, his widow Rama Pilot narrates how when Rajesh had his fatal accident on 11 June 2000, it was Sonia Gandhi who rang the doorbell of her Delhi home to break the bad news. Instead of breaking the news outright, she tried to cushion it by first preparing Rama for the shock. One of the first questions Sonia asked her was, 'Do you believe in God?' She also accompanied Rama to the hospital in Jaipur where Rajesh Pilot had been admitted (Rama Pilot, *Rajesh Pilot: A Biography*, Roli Books, 2017).

As a minister, Sachin was a favourite in Lutyens' Delhi, sought out at parties and media conclaves. Both he and his statuesque wife Sara Abdullah Pilot made an attractive couple amongst the capital's poweratti. Their marriage was the stuff of headlines, for it was the coming together of two political families—and also two different communities. The Abdullahs have held sway over Jammu & Kashmir for decades, and the daughter of the ex-CM, Farooq Abdullah, marrying the late Rajesh Pilot's son was a story that captivated both the political and the social world. Unfortunately, it came with its own baggage. For political reasons the Abdullahs disapproved of the alliance with a Hindu boy. Yet the two went ahead and tied the knot at a very private ceremony at Sachin's mother, Rama Pilot's MP bungalow, in 2004.

Sachin and Sara met while he was still doing his master's and she was at college in England. They courted for three years before getting married. Later when the two appeared together at the television show 'Rendezvous With Simi Garewal', Sara spoke about her family's opposition saying candidly: 'It's not an easy romance story, everyone knows that, there's no point pretending. There was lot of heartache from all sides. But Sachin and I knew we wanted to get married' (15 October 2012). The Abdullahs did not attend the wedding but have since then come around to it. The couple have two sons—Aaran and Vehann—with whom they celebrate Christmas, Diwali, Eid and Holi. As Sachin pointed out in the same show, 'We have a lot more festivals to celebrate.'

It is this vision of India that he celebrates both in his personal life and at a larger level. 'India is a secular country, not because it says so in our constitution but a majority of the 80 per cent of the Hindus in our country are secular minded. We are secular not because we have Muslims, Sikhs and Christians but because a majority of Indians (i.e., the Hindus) have adopted thousands of years of religious co-existence. If the BJP believes majoritarianism is the way to go forward then they are wrong, because if the Hindu vote is one sided then the BJP would rule for thousands of years. India is secular, because majority of Indian Hindus are secular.'

In the Congress there will always be space for a Sachin Pilot. The last five years have shown that regardless of the brief, even if it means moving out of his comfort zone, he is ready to roll up his sleeves and get the job done. Who wouldn't want such a team-player on board, even though there is a 'danger' that he may become Captain one day?

ARVIND KEJRIWAL
The Argumentative Indian

Arvind Kejriwal said a straight 'No' when asked by one his supporters to attend a charity event. The cause he was asked to espouse was a mass marriage ceremony of brides whose families were too poor to host their weddings. This was in the run up to the 2013 Delhi elections, where every supporter had the added heft of a potential voter. Kejriwal's immediate response was a flat-out refusal. He told his well-wisher, 'Let's not depend upon charity. Charity is for the rich, it's the easy way out. No one wants to change the system. Why marry the girls, let's find ways to increase their income instead.'

This scene comes midway through *An Insignificant Man*, a documentary made on the Aam Aadmi Party chief, starting from the formation of the party right up to his first stint as CM. Directed by Khushboo Ranka and Vinay Shukla, and co-produced with film-maker Anand Gandhi, the movie gives an interesting insight into Kejriwal and the kind of thinking that defines his politics of protest. Interestingly, Kejriwal often refers to himself as an insignificant man implying that it's not him but the movement, and the people, who are more significant.

Now here, I think, Kejriwal is indulging in a little bit of political license for the man has a pretty significant sense of self-worth, one that could rival that of Prime Minister Narendra Modi himself, who has one of the most sizeable egos in the country. Not to mention an equally sharp brain, though neither Kejriwal nor Modi will thank me for this comparison. But if there is one man who could have competed with Modi in political smarts it is Kejriwal, only he lacks all the other essentials including national stature, mass base and a strong pan-India organization to match his ambition. Says Rama Lakshmi, editor opinion at *The Print* and former India correspondent of *The Washington Post*: 'Some may say that Arvind Kejriwal has what it takes—charisma, bravado and oratory. But he has frittered his energy in his daily Delhi battles and his party is now struggling to move beyond the capital. He dared to take Modi on much before he had matured. He over-reached and may have peaked too early. Despite a fawning middle class, brute majority of assembly seats and a formidable social media army, he has been unable to develop the mythology of a developed Delhi like Modi crafted one for Gujarat.'

The Aam Aadmi Party was born out of the 2011 anti-corruption movement that was led by the social activist Anna Hazare. Realizing that in order to change the system, he had to first be a part of it, Anna's most able and charismatic lieutenant decided to form his own political party. The Aam Aadmi Party

(AAP) was launched a year later in November 2012 with
Kejriwal as its chief. Not only is he the creator of this six-year-old
political outfit, he is the party itself for without Kejriwal there is
no AAP. It is he who is the star campaigner, chief strategist and
the face on the party posters.

In the age of powerful orators and (mostly) dynastic,
telegenic leaders, Kejriwal is none of the above. Wrapped in a
muffler, hidden behind a very unflattering pair of glasses perched
underneath a cap that looks borrowed from the Congress
party's almost defunct Seva Dal he hardly looks like the kind
of politician that could separate a child from his candy. Yet,
when he speaks, people stop and listen—whether to agree or
disagree; when he asks for a second chance the capital gives him
a sweeping mandate; when he sits on a protest, other state chief
ministers come calling and when he coughs, the prime minister
prescribes yoga therapy.

Rama Lakshmi deconstructs Kejriwal's connect, especially
with the poor, perfectly. 'From a country that has traditionally
looked at wealth with suspicion, India has moved to celebrating
business success stories in the post-1991 era. But in politics,
it still helps if you are seen as poor. If not poor, the next best
option is to claim you used to be poor. In the US, it is called
the "log cabin" narrative [Abraham Lincoln grew up in one].
Modi's chaiwala story is India's version of "log cabin". Kejriwal
comes from a middle class family, but he too must emphasize
his "ordinary man" life. Manmohan Singh would talk about
walking a long distance to school. Deve Gowda was a humble
farmer. Politicians in India like to carefully construct the image
of struggle and "un-wealthiness". However, she adds, 'There is
a big difference between Modi and Kejriwal in this too. Modi
no longer wants to look poor, he has firmly placed it in his
past. He changes his clothes several times a day, wears neatly

starched, colour-coordinated kurtas and an expensive watch. He represents aspiration: I used to be poor, but with my sheer will, I have achieved power. Kejriwal wants to say he has given up the successful life of an IRS officer. He now wants to look like the poor voter.'

Although I tried to meet Kejriwal for this book, I was unable to do so. Various reasons were cited including the fact that he had developed a healthy distrust of the media. I've noticed that of late he prefers to communicate through short video clips on social media rather than give television interviews. Again, the comparison with Modi who prefers a similar one-way mode of communication.

'The problem arises when you try and understand Arvind from a conventional point of view. He is not a traditional politician, he left his IRS job because he had fire and wanted to change things. His DNA is not of that of a typical politician so his responses, actions, strategy will be different. We don't understand him because we try to judge him by our conventional, predictable parameters, not his,' explains Ashutosh, a journalist who left his profession to join the Aam Aadmi Party, and then quit after four years. Though he cited personal reasons, some say he was disillusioned with the way Kejriwal was distributing Rajya Sabha seats to outsiders (and also moneybags), overlooking the claims of party faithful—such as Ashutosh himself.

But for all his idiosyncrasies, there is something about the two term Delhi chief minister that has clicked with the aam admi. When he speaks it is the voice of someone who knows the problems first hand. And while he lacks Modi's rhetorical flourish he knows how to communicate, whether through his words or his theatrics. He became Delhi's chief minister in 2013, within a year of going political. That he took support from the Congress, the very party he had railed against to form the government showed exactly how 'political' he had become. However, 49 days after taking office, he resigned when the Assembly refused to pass his Jan Lokpal Bill (an anti-corruption legislation). He contested the 2014 Lok Sabha elections with disastrous results winning only four of the 432 seats the party contested, losing his own seat as well, in a big ticket fight against the mighty Modi; yet within a year bounced back as Delhi chief minister with an unheard of mandate—winning 67 of the capital's 70 seats. Enthused he repeated an earlier mistake, and over-stretched himself, contesting two other state elections in Goa and Punjab but was unable to win either state. However, the Aam Aadmi Party, in its debut election bagged the second highest number of seats in Punjab and got 6 per cent of the vote share in Goa. But these were consolation prizes for a man whose ambition was as prime ministerial as his party was local.

He is now working to consolidate his position in the capital and from all accounts, a third term for the Aam Aadmi Party seems probable in the next polls due in 2020. One reason for this is, of course, that neither the BJP nor the Congress has got its act together in the capital to put up an effective challenge at the assembly level. Both parties lack a leader who can take on Kejriwal. Also, despite his high profile wrangling with the Lt Governor (LG; first Najeeb Jung and now Anil Baijal), the Delhi chief minister has managed to deliver on some of his promises that matter: bijli, paani and add to that education and healthcare. A 50 per cent subsidy on electricity bill was given when the AAP came to power and prices have not gone up since. Also, 700 litres of free water per day is supplied to households which receive piped water supply, thereby encouraging metered connections. This was part of Aap's election promise. These were mostly freebies. The two areas where Kejriwal has shown governance initiative and delivered is on education and health.

Even Kejriwal's critics will concede that there's been a marked improvement in these two sectors. Government schools are being given a face lift with work being done both on the infrastructure and to improve the quality of teachers by sending them for training to countries like the US, Singapore, Finland, etc. Private schools have been stopped from hiking their fees, inflated fees of the private schools have been rolled back, parent-teacher committees are being set up to look after schools, CCTVs are being installed in government schools and almost 25 per cent of Delhi's 2017–2018 budget has been allocated to the education sector. And, for the first time, government schools have scored over private schools in results.

As for the health sector, the Mohalla clinics that deliver free, basic healthcare have been a big hit, though the government is yet to construct one in every five kms as it had promised. Of the 1000 clinics promised, almost 200 are operational. 'Everyone doesn't need a major surgery, the idea is to take the pressure from the big hospitals and create a three tier healthcare system—Mohalla clinics, polyclinics and the big hospitals,' says Durgesh Pathak, member, Political Affairs Committee, AAP. A main hurdle in setting up the Mohalla clinics is shortage of land for invariably this leads to a tussle between the Delhi government and the Centre. But more on that later.

However, given his rather hostile equation with the Narendra Modi-led central government I was curious to know where he was getting the funds for all his populist schemes from. I was told all this was possible because of the savings made by the government by stopping corruption. A CVC report tabled in Parliament in March 2017 has pointed out that corruption was down by 81 per cent in the year 2016 over the previous year in

Delhi. As for the free water subsidies which cost as much as Rs 260 crore annually, the money for this has come mostly from Delhi Jal Board profits (Rs 234 crore annually).

If there is a comeback plan then it's based essentially on these deliverables. The rest of Kejriwal's intentions, from coming up with a comprehensive anti-pollution plan, buying 10,000 new buses, to the delivery of 40 essential services at your doorstep are caught in politics, both within and outside—wrangling with the central government and inner party strife. The one thing that Kejriwal has been able to achieve more successfully than any other Delhi chief minister is to put the statehood for Delhi debate firmly in the headlines. When I asked why he continued with his dharnas and agitations instead of governing, I was told that this was the only way he could highlight the non-cooperation from what the AAP leadership clearly sees as a 'vindictive BJP government at the Centre'. The cases are too many and too long to go into, and Kejriwal has been given some relief from the Supreme Court which has ruled in his favour in the turf war between him and the LG, but the main question here is: For how long is he going to continue playing the role of a martyr? Will he fight the next election on his governance model or on a continued campaign of victimhood?

Senior AAP leaders whom I spoke to say that their next election campaign will be based on the deliverables, but I suspect it will be a bit of both for where there is Kejriwal, the theatrics can never be far behind. His stunts have found national resonance, particularly after four chief ministers—including West Bengal's Mamata Bannerjee and the CPM's Pinarayi Vijayan—called on Kejriwal during one of his recent protests against the LG. As one of his partymen explained to me—a run-of-the-mill chief minister would have gone to the LG's office after first seeking an appointment, had a cup of tea and then come out, told the media that his demands are not being met, and then gone back to his own office. However, by protesting right there in the LG's waiting room, Kejriwal ensured his non-cooperation got front page newspaper coverage.

It's clear that like both Rahul Gandhi and Akhilesh Yadav, Arvind Kejriwal nurtures prime ministerial ambition. But unlike the Congress, both Akhilesh and Kejriwal lack a pan-Indian organization. 'I won't comment on the first part of your question [PM ambition]. But as far as the issue of pan-India appeal goes, Kejriwal is a name which the whole country knows and respects. He has a pan-India appeal and charisma. We are India's youngest political outfit. We have our organization in most of the states and are growing nationally at a good pace,' says Durgesh. Be that as it may, there remains a huge gap between the deliverability and gumption and much of this has to do with a weak organizational base, as well as the fact that despite Kejriwal's best efforts, the AAP remains a regional outfit.

Yet, Kejriwal is much sought after by the regional parties looking to set up a federal front. He has a special bond with Mamata Banerjee, who plays the same rebel-without-a-pause brand of politics. She refers to him as her younger brother. But whether it is the swearing in of the JD(U)'s Kumaraswamy or an agitation lead by Tejashwi Yadav in Delhi, Kejriwal's presence is sought after. Points out Shiv Visvanathan, 'Kejriwal certainly has the potential more than anyone else, he has a separate thinking of politics. He lacks the conventional machismo of an Indian politician. He is seen as new and therefore is not expected to fit into the standard costume ball of electoral politics.'

However, Kejriwal has announced that he is not interested in any pre-poll coalition for the 2019 elections. When asked by

The Hindu in April 2017 as to whether he would be a part of the grand opposition alliance, Kejriwal had replied: 'There are two things. One is power politics and the other is issue politics. People are important. Snatching power through different means is not important.' In simpler words, Kejriwal has long term ambitions and he knows that any coalition that is cobbled together to take on the BJP will be an unstable venture and one that will do more harm to his own image of a crusader than good. Also, in all probability the Congress will be a part of such a formation and in states like Delhi, Haryana and Punjab (where the AAP is looking to expand its base) it is pitted against both the Congress and the BJP. The AAP will contest the new Lok Sabha polls but will restrict itself to states where the party has a base, like Delhi, Punjab, Haryana, Goa and some metros in the south. The earlier decision to contest more seats than even the Congress in 2014 has been blamed on rebel leader Yogendra Yadav who has since been ousted from the party.

For someone who prides himself as being a People's Person, for having his finger on the pulse of the electorate, Kejriwal is surprisingly short-sighted when it comes to dealing with his own team. No party has seen as many high profile defections from its core team, as has the Aam Aadmi Party. The various reasons cited are Kejriwal's dictatorial attitude and his compromising with the party's core beliefs, such as when he took on the Congress party's help to form the government in 2013 and more recently, when he gave away Rajya Sabha tickets to outsiders. I would add a third. The anarchist nature of his outfit is as much to blame for his inability to hold a team together. The AAP lacks an organized sector and is made up of volunteers rather than disciplined workers, a set-up in which each fancies himself as a leader in the making. The problem is that they are up against one who, for all his talk about democracy, sees himself as the Ultimate Leader.

The soft-spoken Manish Sisodia is clearly the Number 2 man in the party. He is also the deputy chief minister of Delhi and has the department of education under him amongst other charges. A former journalist, Manish has been with Kejriwal since the '90s when Sisodia enrolled in Kerjiwal's NGO Parivartan. The duo have been together ever since, working in the slums of East Delhi, taking on the Delhi Vidyut Board for its inflated bills, using the Right to Information legislation to help ordinary citizens fill applications in the correct manner to elicit the right answers from the government.

Today, in a party with as many drop-outs as drop-ins, Sisodia is clearly the one man Kejriwal trusts. He has been called Sancho Panza to Kejriwal's Don Quixote, but he is much more than that. When Kejriwal loses his cool it is Sisodia who is the calming influence at his side. But when the leader is attacked, it is also Sisodia who is the first to launch a counter-attack in his favour, as he did against Yogendra Yadav when he quit the party accusing Kejriwal of being dictatorial. Although there have been a series of defections after Yadav and lawyer-turned-activist Prashant Bhushan quit the party in 2015, the next big shock for Kejriwal was probably when Ashutosh put in his papers for the two were friends apart from being colleagues. Ashutosh's resignation was followed by that of Ashish Khaitan, another former journalist and a key team player. However, both cited 'personal reasons', and unlike Yogendra, have refrained from attacking Kejriwal. This, however, led many editorials to wonder if Kejriwal was in a 'self-destruct' mode, but I have learnt one thing about this controversial player—he is not yet ready to be written off. How Kejriwal fills the gap between gumption and capability, how he balances personal ego with team building and his inner dictator with some deft delegation of power, is going to make an interesting study in political experimentation. For it's not a question of Kejriwal's ambitions alone, it's also where India is placed at the moment; where an entire generation is stepping into the sunset, vacating space for the NextGen. At a point where Narendra Modi stands unchallenged, where there is a talent hunt for strong leaders, Arvind Kejriwal gets his second—or perhaps third—chance.

Kejriwal's backstory is his best manifesto. We all know how he quit his IRS job as joint commissioner in the Income Tax department to become an activist. He was also the brains behind Anna Hazare's India Against Corruption movement that held the UPA-2 to ransom. Most reporters remember this fidgety young man, always at Anna's side, whispering in the Gandhian's ear and often upstaging the main act by shifting the focus to himself.

The world as Kejriwal sees it, is best explained in *Swaraj*, a book written by Kejriwal which serves as a manifesto of his politics. The very first chapter lays out his mission: 'The root cause of our problem is that in the political system of our country we cast our votes once in five years and for the next five we grovel in front of the same people we voted for ... The people have no say whatsoever in the entire system.' He cites examples from his travels around India's villages. Although only two years older than Rahul Gandhi (born 16 August 1968), it is clear that this young man is much more focused than the dynastic heir. That's the irony of the two, one is a leader without a party to match his ambition, the other has a pan-India organization at his disposal but not the consuming passion to capitalize on it.

Swaraj is Kejriwal's version of his Discovery of India tours where he cites several examples to show the disconnect between the rulers and the 'ruled'. He talks about Sunder Nagri, a slum in East Delhi that had no potable water and no sewer system. Yet the government wasted Rs 60 lakhs installing a fountain in the locality. Writes Kejriwal, 'Can there be anything more hilarious than this? The fountains have not worked a single day and how could they? There is no water in the area'. He also talks about a village in Orissa where as many as 63 families were suffering from cholera. Yet there was no money to transport them to the nearest hospital 25 kms away. The village Panchayat had more than Rs 6 lakhs in its funds but the sum was tied up to some scheme approved by a government authority far removed from the on-ground reality. 'What good is money that we cannot use to save lives?' writes Kejriwal.

There are many such examples. Another talks about a tree planting exercise carried on in the Bhondsi village in Haryana. To achieve a set target of trees, the forest department showered acacia seeds all over the village from a helicopter. Unfortunately, points out Kejriwal, the acacia plant draws a lot of water from the soil and as a result the water table in the village went down 'alarmingly'.

What Kejriwal wants to do with his Panchayat style of participatory democracy is to bring the citizen into the decision-making system. Of course, with a lack of proper systems in place, this creates its share of chaos, but it does help him keep that essential connect with the public. Even though he is yet to achieve his goal, Kejriwal knows all too well the importance of putting systems in place. As he told Mehboob Jeelani who profiled him for *The Caravan* in September 2011: 'If you travel by Indian Railways, you'll see chaos, confusion and corruption everywhere. But if you travel by Delhi Metro, you'll see everything in order. It is not because good people travel by Metro, it is because Metro has a right system in place.'

His parents stay with him in his three bedroom chief ministerial bungalow in Civil Lines, and his mother is an essential monitor for him, bringing him feedback from her trips to the market and conversations with neighbours about rising prices and the impact of his government's policies. Kejriwal's wife Sunita and their two kids also live with him. An IRS officer, Sunita too resigned from the service in 2016. According to media reports, Kejriwal initially made an issue about shifting into the chief ministerial accommodation that had air conditioners in each bedroom, insisting that the PWD take out the ACs. His earlier residence had only one air conditioner in the living room and perhaps Kejriwal was objecting to the non-aam admi image of the said item. However, he was told that it would cost more to fill the gaps caused by their removal, so it would be better if he simply didn't switch the ACs on! But then where would he get the headlines if he simply switched the off button!

In this age of caste and religion-based politics, Kejriwal's appeal transcends both these conventional parameters and rests solely on his connect with the public and his ability to deliver the services essential to them, in a corruption-free atmosphere. If he indulges in a bit of drama while doing so, the people of Delhi seem willing to overlook that, perhaps for a little while more. Though, maybe, to help the optics if nothing else, Kejriwal should dump the biography of Hitler, which he is said to be perusing with great delight.

ASADUDDIN OWAISI

More Mojo than Mosque

He cuts a figure that says retro cool with his immaculately cut striped sherwani and nerdy glasses perched on a parrot sharp nose. But he's not content with just being cool. He would like to be cool for a cause. Asaduddin Owaisi is the leader of the All India Majlis-e-Ittehadul-Muslimeen (AIMIM). The AIMIM is essentially a Hyderabad-based outfit that had earlier been led by his grandfather and father. Founded in 1927, its original aim was to provide a cultural and religious platform to the Muslims living in the principality of the Nizam of Hyderabad. Over time it acquired a political identity and now Owaisi is determined to give it national clout.

Part of the strategy is to showcase himself as a new age,

pan-India poster boy for the Muslims. The rise of the BJP has given him greater play since as the representative of the hardline Muslim thought he gets to be the counter voice every evening, prime time, in TV studios where he is often pitted against the Hindutva brigade. On the floor of the Parliament too, as a third time MP, he has acquired the reputation of making fiery speeches. Clearly his Barrister-at-Law degree from the prestigious Lincoln's Inn comes in handy, for although he calls himself a 'non-practising lawyer' he is often seen citing the Constitution and precedent in a way that only lawyers can to bolster their case.

But he is known to rev up the tempo as well. In the old city of Hyderabad the Owaisi brothers have acquired the aura of being rabble-rousers. Asaduddin (born 13 May 1969) has a younger brother—Akbaruddin—who is a four term MLA from Telengana, while their youngest brother—Burhanuddin—edits the family owned Urdu daily, *Eternaad*. Their father Sultan Salahuddin Owaisi was a six term MP from Hyderabad until he stepped down in 2004 to vacate his seat for Asaduddin. Arguably it is Akbaruddin who seems to have cornered the family market on hate speeches, his most infamous one being in 2007 when he is said to have threatened author Taslima Nasrin allegedly stating, 'We in Hyderabad want to behead this woman with a fatwa.' (*Firstpost*, January 2013) His older brother plays it smart. He is circumspect when speaking to a national audience but within his constituency he transforms into a fiery demagogue.

During a television interview with me for NewsX (8 September 2015) at his MP bungalow in New Delhi I encountered the soft-spoken version of Asaduddin Owaisi. When questioned about his strident alter ego he replied, 'I don't represent deaf and dumb people. I have to speak. And if I speak better than some, why do you blame me for that … I don't agree with the perception about us [Owaisi brothers] being rabble-rousers; come to Hyderabad and judge us by our work. One has to come and see why we are continuously being elected by the people. You cannot win elections by rabble-rousing—one election maybe, but after that your work counts.' He added, 'We have to make speeches. We are politicians. The important thing is that our speech is within the four parameters of law. So far no criminal case has been lodged against me for my speech.'

With time one could say that the Owaisi of 2018 is a matured version of the Owaisi of even four years ago. For one, he has realized he needs to position his politics in such a way that he doesn't end up consigned to the fringes as another rabid fundamentalist. Moreover, in the vacuum left by the likes of Syed Shahabuddin, G.M. Banatwala, there is space for a new age Muslim leader to come up. (There are roughly 180 million Muslims in India, which account for nearly 14 per cent of the 1.3 billion population. This also makes India home to the world's second largest Muslim population, after Indonesia.) T.S. Sudhir, a Hyderabad based political analyst, points out, 'Asad is definitely moderate compared to his brother who is more firebrand. Also being a good orator as well as his ability to use the social media has made him popular with the youth.' Adding, 'He has the potential to take the party national but at this point in time, does not have the organization beyond the old city of Hyderabad to back it.'

The AIMIM is still to expand beyond Hyderabad in Telangana and a few pockets of Maharashtra. Currently it has seven MLAs in the Telangana assembly and one Lok Sabha MP from Hyderabad (Asaduddin himself). The party's area of influence is essentially the Old City area of Hyderabad. During a parliament debate, Rajya Sabha MP and poet-scriptwriter, Javed Akhtar, once referred to Owaisi as a 'mohalla leader from Hyderabad'. That must have hurt, for one could argue that for Owaisi, the fight is not so much for ideology as it is for identity, i.e., bolstering his own identity as a Muslim leader.

His party has contested elections outside Hyderabad—in Maharashtra, Bihar and Uttar Pradesh—with varying degrees of success. Maharashtra was the only state where the AIMIM was able to open its account. Of the 24 seats it contested, it managed two MLAs and got 0.9 per cent of the votes (2014). This spurred Asaduddin to contest Bihar, UP and Karnataka assembly polls in the following years but he failed to win a single MLA seat in any.

However, Owaisi's motives have been questioned with some alleging all he was doing was helping the BJP by dividing the 'secular' vote. For while he doesn't get much of the votes, his shrill campaign does tend to polarize the votes. 'The Muslims vote tactically for a party that is best placed to take on the right wing, so they don't vote for Owaisi's party. But because he polarizes the vote, it is the BJP that benefits with him further pushing the Hindu vote towards it,' explains a Muslim leader from Lucknow. For the record, Owaisi denies any such 'understanding' with the BJP. But he does have an informal understanding with the Telangana Rashtriya Samiti (TRS, which is currently in power in Telangana) and has publicly supported the TRS CM on many issues, such as forming a non-Congress, non-BJP federal front, an idea that the TRS chief first mooted, then abadoned.

Apart from territorial expansion Owaisi is also working towards enhancing his voter base by reaching out to Dalits as well as Muslims. In doing so, he wants to club two disempowered sections together and increase his own brand value. While speaking in Parliament on a debate on B.R. Ambedkar's legacy on 22 July 2017, he argued, 'A Dalit should be Hindustan's Wazir-e-Azam [prime minister]. That will send the right message.' T.S. Sudhir points out, 'Owaisi believes both Muslims and Dalits are discriminated against and, unfortunately, this is what bonds them together. Over the past many years, Asad has been trying to pitch himself and his party to this joint constituency. He was at the forefront of the Rohith Vemula [a Dalit student who committed suicide claiming persecution] issue at the Hyderabad Central University in 2016. More recently, in the cow slaughter issue, the cow vigilantes have targeted both Dalits and Muslims. Asad is positioning himself as a voice of these two segments.' Though Owaisi is trying hard to woo the Dalits, it is with limited success for they have their own caste-icon in Mayawati who already has a Dalit-Muslim alliance in play.

He is leaving no avenue unturned to acquire national resonance, wading into every controversy with communal overtones. Such as the nationalism on demand mood of the day, clashing with RSS chief Mohan Bhagwat on the issue of chanting *Bharat Mata Ki Jai* (praise for India, our motherland). Owaisi retorted stating, 'Nowhere in the Constitution does it say that one should say Bharat Mata ki Jai.' He also vociferously opposed the decision of some BJP state governments to make the singing of Vande Mataram compulsory in all schools, even the madarsas. Owaisi rejected this stating, 'Vande Mataram is our National Song, but there is no act which makes it compulsory to sing it, like there is one for the National Anthem. Just to promote Hindutva, these kinds of decisions are being taken.' He went on to add that rather than promoting Hindutva, the Bharatiya Janata Party should promote "constitutional nationalism", pointing out while he is not against Hindus, he is against Hindutva.

He also took offence at one of the BJP government's more progressive moves—the bill to abolish 'triple talaq'. According to Owaisi, while the law itself would do little to prevent triple talaq (since implementation of most laws is poor in India), it would however be used as a tool against Muslim men as The Muslim Women (Protection of Rights on Marriage) Bill 2017 states that instant triple talaq will provide a three year jail term for the husband. 'The intention of the government behind the Triple Talaq Bill is not right. It is an attempt to do away with the Shariat,' he told the media. This has since been amended and accused husbands can now get bail.

While he is protective of his community's turf he tries to stay within the ambit of what he calls 'constitutional nationalism'. BJP leader Subramanian Swamy, who has often sparred with Owaisi, says that he is a patriot but not a nationalist. Laughs Owaisi, 'I was called anti-national because I refused to say "Bharat Mata ki Jai". I will not accept your slogan of religious nationalism. I feel pride in chanting "Jai Hind". My loyalty is to the Constitution of India.'

Owaisi is critical of those who celebrate Pakistan's victory over India in test matches. 'Those who celebrate Pakistan's victory are stupid. What have we got to do with Pakistan?' he says. He's also made it clear that he does not support the formation of an Islamic State. Denouncing the 2016 ISIS attack on the holy city of Medina when a suicide bomber killed four guards within striking distance of the Prophet Muhammad's tomb, at a protest meeting in Hyderabad, Owaisi called the ISIS 'an army of criminals ... these people are the dogs of hell.' He has been targeted by radicals for opposing the IS, getting regular abuse on social media. But an unperturbed Owaisi told the media, 'It is for the Almighty to decide who goes to heaven or hell. These IS murderers have no right to decide my final destination.'

Yet he sees no contradiction between his stance against ISIS and his offering legal aid to five Muslim youths from Hyderabad who were detained by the NIA in June 2016, for being part of an alleged Islamic State terror module. He claims that he was not asking for the boys to be released, he was merely offering them what they were entitled to—a legal defence. 'Didn't Subramanian Swamy defend Asaram Bapu [a hindu godman] who was accused of rape?' he asked.

Clearly his belief comes with legal loopholes—and yet he calls himself a non-practising lawyer! He has also spoken out against the hanging of Yakub Memon, an accused in the 1993 Mumbai serial blasts, claiming that he was executed only because of his religion.'The government should convict all death row inmates. The killers of Rajiv Gandhi and Beant Singh have the backing of political parties in Tamil Nadu and Punjab,' he said. Comments like these win him a seat in television debates but also blur the lines somewhat.

For some of his Muslim brethren, to see Owaisi hold his own (in English, Hindi and Urdu) against other community leaders, gives them a sense of satisfaction, not unlike the awe Mayawati, a Dalit leader and former chief minister, evokes amongst the Dalits when she flaunts her jewellery, her statues and her power. There is no denying his influence, especially with the Muslim youth in his constituency. In 2014, when the popular actor Salman Khan was seen at a kite festival with the then CM of Gujarat Narendra Modi, Owaisi appealed to the people not to watch his movies, saying one doesn't become a Salman just because his name is Salman, adding with a wry smile: 'Salman toh Rushdie bhi hain' (Rushdie is also a Salman; it may be recalled that Salman Rushdie's Satanic Verses was boycotted by the Muslim clergy). Responding to Owaisi's call, the teens in Aurangabad slums claimed, 'We have stopped going for Sallubhai's movies because Asadbhai told us not to.'

Author Patrick French writes that Owaisi is not your stereotype 'sarkari Muslim leader (hennaed beard, pot-belly, compliance with authority) ... He does not care whether a politician wears a skullcap, hosts an iftar party and he has scant respect for some Islamic scholars.' (*Hindustan Times*, 13 October 2015)

The Lincoln's Inn scholar who is known for his biryani and haleem diplomacy in Lutyens' Delhi is replaced by a much more flamboyant and brash personality in Hyderabad where Owaisi lives with his wife Farheen, their five daughters and one son. In Hyderabad, he is often seen riding a Royal Enfield without the added protection of security guards. There is even a popular video of him doing the rounds amongst the youth in his constituency. Entitled 'Boss', this has pop artiste YoYo Honey Singh's soundtrack playing in the backdrop. The setting is rockstar-ish, beginning with a dramatic entry by Owaisi in slow motion, as the voice-over intones—Make Way for the Boss!

Owaisi's AIMIM was part of the Congress-led UPA Government at the centre. But in November 2012, the AIMIM withdrew support both from the UPA and also from the Congress-led government in Andhra Pradesh. Ostensibly the dispute was against expansion work being done on a temple adjoining the Charminar (the famous 1951 built mosque located in Hyderabad), but there was a larger plan behind this move. He realized he got more traction being on his own rather than being seen as an accessory of the Congress. Says T.S. Sudhir, 'I think he realized that being with the Congress was not helping him, as there was a constituency overlap. As a lone MP, he was being subsumed in the UPA. But going alone helps him carve out his own identity especially at a time when the Muslim community in the country does not have an articulate and aggressive voice.' But even within the Muslim leadership there are those who are wary of promoting any one leader as the voice of the community. 'There are no Muslim leaders in India, after Jinnah. We have leaders who have also been Muslim but not one leader can claim to be the voice of the community. And we don't want that either—for the day a Jinnah will emerge, the worse possible Hindu leadership will rise to counter it,' explains a Muslim intellectual on condition of anonymity.

Certainly he is no 21st century Jinnah. Owaisi has often argued against what he calls the 'ghettoization' of Muslims, telling the media, 'I want Muslims to come together and find their political voice as have Dalits, OBCs and Yadavs. Every community in India has progressed except the Muslims.'

Considering that the AIMIM is a one MP outfit, his bid to be the pan-Indian face of his community certainly is an audacious one. Then again, his individual initiative has taken him as far as the TV studios, maybe smart political alliances and smarter posturing will take him further.

YOGI ADITYANATH

The Not-So-Reluctant Fundamentalist

When Prime Minister Narendra Modi chose Yogi Adityanath as the chief minister of Uttar Pradesh, the questions that everyone asked were: Is Yogi being groomed to play a larger role? Had Modi, in fact, handpicked his successor at the national level? It was around this time that a cartoon began to do the rounds on social media. It showed BJP patriarch L.K. Advani whispering to Modi: 'Don't make the same mistake that I did with you.' For the un-initiated, Advani (in the cartoon) was alluding to the fact that his support helped cement Modi's rise, yet when it came to the leadership battle, Modi showed no qualms in stepping over his mentor's ambitions. Is Yogi another Modi in the making? Are we seeing the grooming of the BJP's next PM face?

No doubt Yogi's elevation—and legitimization—took most by surprise. Until he became chief minister he was the rebel with a cause. Don't be misled by his baby-face and mischievous eyes, for when he speaks, it is to unleash a harsh, anti-minority rhetoric. Even after becoming chief minister, he remains BJP's star campaigner in areas as far flung as Tripura, Kerala and Karnataka; for there can be no better poster boy for the party's Hindutva agenda, a plank that has little space for the minorities.

During the 2017 assembly elections, the BJP had swept the state largely due to the Modi-Amit Shah duo. It won 312 of the state's 403 seats (the number went up to 325 with allies). Yogi Adityanath played the role of a firebrand campaigner, and that was about it. He had no say in campaign strategy and a limited say in ticket selection outside Gorakhpur in eastern UP which is his area of influence. Yet, after Modi and Shah he was the party's star campaigner, addressing six rallies and two roadshows a day. After he took office as chief minister, during the initial months he was given prime time slots on national television, competing with none other than Modi himself for air-time. This lead to some off-the-record briefings by central ministers, who quizzed the media as to why we were so obsessed with someone who was after all a pawn in the hands of the PM. But, was Yogi a pawn or a genie that had been unleashed?

A five term MP from the state, he was the youngest of his batch at age 26 in 1998. Since then he has never lost his seat, only increasing his margin each election ever since (except once in 1999). Yet, when he was catapulted to the CM's chair he had little administrative experience outside that of an MP, having never been a central or state minister, or even a local mayor. More to the point, the saffron-clad Yogi was known more as a rabble-rouser rather than a governance man. This is something that is fast becoming the biggest hole in his CV as CM.

Right from the word go it was clear that propaganda and not administration would be the hallmark of his government. One of his first decisions, after he took over as CM in March 2017, was to implement a ban on illegal slaughter houses; something that had been promised in the BJP's poll manifesto. This resulted in three things: One, since most of the slaughterhouse owners were Muslims, the minority community felt targeted. Two, cow vigilantes had a field day. Three, there was a drastic shortage of meat in the state known for its kebab platters. When asked pointedly if he was targeting the economic clout of the Muslim community, the chief minister told the media with a smile, 'These are not my orders alone but has been ordered by the Supreme Court. If we don't implement it our officials will go to jail. When I took office, I asked my officials why aren't the NGT [National Green Tribunal] and SC guidelines being implemented, and they told me *yeh kabhi nahin ho sakta* [this can never happen]. So I told them, we are here to implement the impossible. Those who will be unemployed as a result can do *mazdoori* under MGNREGA, but they can't break the law.'

Was he serious? Was this his advice to slaughterhouse owners? Close down your source of livelihood and instead enroll in a rural employment guarantee programme? It appeared that he was indeed very serious. However, within a fortnight the Allahabad High Court reprimanded the Yogi government for trying to impose a meat ban through the backdoor (5 April 2017). The government was pulled up for targeting the Right to Livelihood and directed to renew old licenses and issue new ones. But nonetheless a message had been sent by the CM to the vote banks that matter. And in the world of Yogi, that was what *mattered*.

Another controversial decision taken within the first hundred days of his assuming office was the institution of

Anti-Romeo Squads (22 March, 2017). Again, this became a tool for mis-governance. Ostensibly these squads were there to protect women in a state where law and order had fallen to an all-time low. The squads were told to leave couples alone if their behaviour fell within 'traditional' norms but what was traditional was left open to interpretation, so soon anyone walking hand in hand in parks were made to do *uthak-baithak* or worse. But there were some favourable reports as well, for under the Samajwadi Party rule a jungle raj had set in where even girls in the capital city complained of 'eve-teasing'. The courts supported the Yogi government on this, stating that what was criticized as 'moral policing' was actually 'preventive policing' (Allahabad High Court, 30 March 2017). A vindicated Yogi said, 'During the *chunav* [elections] we were told, specially by housewives, that we can't send our daughters to school, things are so bad we either send them to hostels or outside the state to study, so we set up Anti-Romeo Squads to prevent harassment of our daughters and sisters.' He added with a smile, 'Genuine *pyaar and mohabbat* [love] will not be harassed but not fraud.'

What really got the liberals screaming was Yogi's policy of encounters. As part of an aggressive campaign against crime— and to send the right optics—the police was given the go-ahead on an aggressive hot pursuit policy. According to figures released by the UP Police for the period from 20 March 2017 (when Yogi took office) to 31 December 2017, there had been as many as 921 encounters in the state, in which 31 criminals had been shot dead. There had also been 2214 arrests and 196 criminals had been injured. On the side of the enforcement agencies, three policemen lost their lives while 210 were injured. The National Human Rights Commission has taken note of this but the Yogi government remains firm on the message. '*Agar voh bandook chalayenge toh hum chudiyan nahin pehente* [If these criminals use guns then we don't wear bangles either],' he said ominously. When questioned by the media, the state's Deputy CM Keshav Prasad Maurya commented, 'Today criminals are terrified with the thought that either they will have to give up crime or leave UP or maybe even leave this world.' Clearly the entire cabinet was reading from the same '56 inches chest beating' script.

In-Your-Face seems to be his preferred modus operandi. Soon everything government-owned began to be painted saffron—from buses, to school bags (those that were distributed free of cost under government schemes and earlier these had Akhilesh Yadav's face imprinted on them). Saffron was also the colour of government booklets and diaries, and the colour of the towel that is placed on the CM's chair. Sundry state ministers suddenly acquired a PhD in the neuroscience of colour, proclaiming that saffron didn't simply denote Hindutva, but was also a 'bright, vibrant colour that gives off energy'. Yogi, being Yogi, did not bother to explain.

Even his austere lifestyle has been over-hyped. Before moving into the CM's official bungalow on Lucknow's 5 Kalidas Road, he ordered a makeover in which all the ACs were removed. Yogi told the media, 'Is the entire state air-conditioned? Anyway, I feel temperatures should be above 25–26 degrees so when we go out in the heat we don't feel the loo [hot winds]. Those who keep the temperatures 18–20 degrees inside the house cannot take the temperature outside.' Another casualty of the makeover was the fine cuisine at the CM's kitchen. All of Akhilesh's fancy chefs were sent packing and replaced by Yogi's trusted cook from Gorakhpur. Hawans and purifying rituals were done at the bungalow and finally a swastika sign was painted above the CM's name plate, after dipping marigold flowers in haldi and sandalwood paste. The Hindu leader now had a fine Hindu abode. The problem, of course, is that the state of UP doesn't need a mahant, it needs a chief minister.

But to be fair to the UP chief minister, 'administration' was not highlighted in the brief he was given when he was handed charge of India's largest state. His task is to preach, or in political terms, propagate the party's core Hindutva agenda. As mentioned earlier, he is the chief campaigner both within and outside UP—in every state that has held elections since he became CM, from Gujarat, to Tripura, Kerala and Karnataka. It's a neat act where Yogi is used to whip up the required emotion as a sort of campaign foreplay to Modi's own rallies. Take for instance the Gujarat elections in November 2017. The bugle for the hardline rhetoric in Gujarat was sounded in Ayodhya when Yogi performed a grand Ganga Aarti on the banks of the River Saryu, right before Diwali on 19 October 2017. A record number of 1.71 lakh deeyas were lit and Ram and Sita (characters in costume) descended from a helicopter to be greeted by the chief minister in a televised ceremony. The message was not lost in Gujarat which is known as the core laboratory of Hindutva. Soon after Yogi began his Gujarat campaign, talking Love Jihaad, Ram Temple and saffron pride. Lucknow based political analyst Sharat Pradhan commented, 'Starting with the Ayodhya issue, BJP campaigners went about using various ways to light up Hindutva emotions.'

Points out Siddharth Varadarajan, founding editor of *The Wire*, 'There is an impression in Lutyens' Delhi that Modi had no choice but to appoint Yogi. I don't buy that, Modi is the supreme leader of the BJP and everyone would have fallen in line with whomsoever he appointed. Yogi has been put there to polarize and he is performing that task perfectly.'

There is an obvious difference between the young UP CM and Modi's own profile as a chief minister. Unlike Modi, the UP CM is so busy being deployed all over the country that he has little time to focus on his own state and build a Yogi Model of

Governance. To build loyalty with his bureaucrats he has fallen into the community trap and is busy promoting Thakurs over other castes. This has alienated the others, specially the Brahmins in the state who accused him of promoting Thakurwaad. They felt alienated, as Mayawati is known to promote Dalits while the SP patronizes Yadavs. It was the BJP that was traditionally expected to cater to the upper castes. This did not raise any red flags in New Delhi until the Unnao rape case. An 18-year-old girl from Unnao in UP accused BJP MLA Kuldip Singh Sengar of raping her and also blamed Sengar and his brother for her father's death in custody. Although the rape incident happened in June 2017, the case came to light when the victim threatened to immolate herself in front of the CM's residence in March 2018. Still Yogi did nothing—some say it was because the MLA in question was a Thakur—until he was reprimanded by the PMO. The case was transferred to the CBI and the MLA was arrested.

This coming on the heels of the Gorakhpur by-election loss showed that Yogi was spiralling out of New Delhi's control. In March 2018, the BJP lost the high profile Gorakhpur by-poll that took place after Yogi vacated his seat. Since this was Yogi's stronghold he was angry that Amit Shah did not give the ticket to a candidate of his choice and instead nominated a Yogi baiter. One is not quite sure why Amit Shah took this step—did he want to cut Yogi to size? But the BJP lost this seat. The official reason cited by the party was the coming together of the SP and BSP against the BJP. But it was also clear that the influential Gorakhnath Peeth of which Yogi is the high priest did not back the party candidate. Yet this explanation lost steam once Yogi lost another round of by-polls in the state—including the crucial Kairana Lok Sabha seat that was held by the BJP. This was a campaign that both Amit Shah and Modi steered clear from. After the BJP's defeat, party leaders began to speculate as to whether Yogi was the vote catcher he was touted to be.

The state unit of the UP BJP soon became divided between those that were 'for Yogi' and those that were 'against Yogi'. Both Modi and Amit Shah have realized that having unbottled the genie, they will have to deal with it. But they prefer to wait till after the 2019 elections before taking any harsh step. After all, using Yogi as the poster boy for the hardcore Hindu vote was the real reason behind his elevation as the CM of the Hindi heartland. Despite all the by-polls losses, Yogi's stature as the magnet for the hardline vote is intact and he will be one of the star campaigners in the next general elections.

Yogi has an interesting backstory, which is now part of the state's folklore. Born as Ajay Mohan Bisht (5 June 1972) to a forest ranger's family, he completed his BSc in mathematics from Garhwal University, Uttarakhand. During his college years, he came into contact with the Sangh and was drawn to the Ram Mandir agitation, attending RSS shakhas. Somewhere around this time he met Mahant Avaidyanath, the then high priest of Gorakhnath Peeth, named after the 11th century medieval saint, Gorakhnath. Situtated in Gorakhpur in eastern UP, sprawling over 52 acres, the Math runs 44 institutions, which include hospitals, colleges and temples. The Peeth also has cultural influence over the Nath sect. Named after Guru Gorakhnath, the Gorakhbani (his teachings) professes faith in an unseen God that is neither Hindu nor Muslim. It was Mahant Digvijay Nath who preceded Mahant Avaidyanath—who refashioned the community as decidedly Hindu, and also carved a political role for the Peeth.

During a TV interview with Rajat Sharma on his show *Aap Ki Adalat*, Yogi recalled, 'But before taking *sanyaas* I put forward a few questions to my Poojya Gurudev. I wanted to know if sanyaas means *palayaan* [escape], and if it means palayaan then I don't want to adopt *palayaan ka jeevan* [a life of escape]. For me sanyaas meant seva [service]. He told me to first see what Gorakhpeeth is all about. He said see for six months, and after doing that I felt that truly here they follow the true form of sanyaas. So he accepted me as his student and I came to be known as Yogi Adityanath.' This was in 1994.

From being a mathematics graduate the 22-year-old was now a Yogi, complete with the 'splitting of the ears' which is part of the initiation process, and is why Nath Yogis are also known as *Kanphatas*. Large globe-shaped ear-rings are part of the look along with the saffron robes. As a Yogi his day began at 3.30 am with temple rituals, junta durbars and ended late into the night as he helped the Bade Maharaj (Mahant Avaidyanath) in the administrative running of the trust. Those who have attended his junta durbar in Gorakhpur say that the court was open to both Hindus and Muslims, despite his hardline Hindutva image, and on-the-spot solutions were given to problems, with Yogi himself picking up the phone or signing letters to the requisite authorities. Yogi's red SUV was also a familiar sight as he often took off for a tour of troubled areas. Later, after Mahant Avaidyanath's death, Yogi became the high priest in September 2014. But both within Gorakhpur and outside he is still known as Chotte Maharaj.

Equally notorious was his Hindu Yuva Vahini, a militia youth organisation founded by him in 2002 to promote 'Hindutva and nationalism', as well as Yogi's own political aspirations. In fact, in 2002 when the BJP fielded an assembly candidate from Gorakhpur against Yogi's wishes, Yogi fielded an independant candidate. The HYV ensured his candidate won against the BJP's.

When Ajay Bisht left his home in Pauri Garwahal for Gorakhpur he did so without informing his friends and family.

His family was only told that he was pursuing higher studies and a job offer in Gorakhpur. Later on during his media interactions, Yogi recalled how his father read about him joining the order from the newspapers and came to Gorakhpur to meet him. Senior Bisht saw his son in saffron robes, head shaved, supervising the cleaning of a temple. Whenever Yogi is asked if he has any regrets about abandoning his family he explains this as 'leaving a small parivaar for a bigger parivaar'. And if you ask him if he has any regrets on not being married, pat comes the answer: 'I have seen many people who have [started a family] and at least I'm free from this tension!' The monk does have a droll sense of humour. His chubby face is always alight with his eyes sparkling with a zest for life. In fact, with his shaved head and ever smiling eyes, dressed in saffron robes, he reminds one of an impish Buddhist monk. But, that's just the optics.

It is this same Yogi who has made the most vitriolic of hate speeches targeting the Muslim community—before he became CM, of course. At a 2007 rally in Azamgarh he allegedly stated, 'If they [read Muslims] kill one Hindu girl we will kill 100 of them.' Later when he became CM and was quizzed by the media about these hate speeches, he smiled and brushed these aside as 'conditional statements'. On the *Aap Ki Adalaat* show he claimed, 'In places where there are 10 to 20 per cent minorities, stray communal incidents take place. Where there are 20 to 35 per cent of them, serious communal riots take place and where they are more than 35 per cent of Muslims, there is no place for non-Muslims.' How does he balance his image of being a Muslim basher with his role of a temple priest whose junta durbar both Muslims and Hindus were known to attend? Points out Pravin Kumar, author of *The Rise of a Saffron Socialist*, 'His hardline is from the dais, when he retires to his role as a temple priest, he's a completely changed man. As the Hindutva face he knows he has to raise his talk a couple of notches higher than other BJP leaders.'

Not surprisingly then he has also taken a stand against homosexuality and reservations for women. A citizen journalist website, *Youth Ki Awaaz*, pointed this out, commenting wryly: 'This is the man who will call the shots in Uttar Pradesh for the next 5 years, a state with 38,483,967 Muslims, 95,331,831 women, and an uncounted population of trans and queer people!'

But what citizen journalists miss is the fact that while these issues may matter in Lutyens' Delhi's drawing rooms, within the RSS this is a mind-set that finds favour. Most of the Sangh Parivar is against both the women reservation bill and legitimizing homosexuality.

To sum it up, I spoke to Radhika Ramaseshan, consulting editor, *Business Standard*, and also someone who predicted the BJP sweep in UP before the results came out. I asked her two things: How does Yogi stack up against Modi and can he be seen as his successor? 'The first point to remember is that Narendra Modi is a die-hard RSS pracharak. While he might have had bad moments with individual RSS seniors, he will never veer away from the Sangh's cast-iron disciplinary framework and commitment to a core ideology. Yogi continues to remain an outlander in the "parivar", he is not even a primary BJP member; he has not made a single statement to the effect that he has merged his Hindu Yuva Vahini with the BJP. Therefore, the Sangh's writ will never run on him. Of course, he has expediently reined in the Vahini hotheads and will be on his best behaviour so long as he remains the CM,' she said. And added, 'I personally never bought into the theory that the RSS is grooming him as Modi's successor. Modi was more than Hindutva and a deep shade of saffron. His plus size before 2014 had elements of a strong leadership, the promise of decisive governance and of course the OBC factor. In his stint as UP CM so far, the only feature that has stood out for Yogi is "Thakurwaad", because he has pandered no end to a community that had ruled the roost under the Congress and briefly under Rajnath Singh when Singh was the CM.'

Just as Modi has his Gujarat Model to back him, Yogi has his track record as a five term parliamentarian and the leader of the influential Goraknath Peeth. Interestingly, ever since he became CM, the Congress began to refer to him as plain Ajay Bisht to undercut his Yogi aura. The parallels between Yogi and Modi may be superficial but they strike a chord just the same. Both Yogi and Modi were labelled as Heroes of Hatred in their initial days. Both then graduated to being the Hindu Hriday Samrats. And if anyone can parallel Modi in his oratory and mass appeal it is his saffron-clad protégé. Pravin Kumar told me, there is a story that when the RSS was asked about its choice as UP CM, Mohan Bhagwat is said to have told Amit Shah: 'Choose someone who matches the mandate.' Who knows what else is mandated for the monk who walked away with the chief minister-ship of India's largest state.

MILIND DEORA

The Urbanator

Milind Murli Deora is probably the only Indian politician whose Wikipedia page has a section called 'Independent Stands' [as of September 2018]. Usually politicians—especially those belonging to a national party—follow the beat. Some may drum louder than the others but very rarely does an individual strike a different note and still remain a vital part of the band. Being a musician Milind Deora would appreciate the analogy, though his instrument of choice is the guitar more than the drum.

'The Wikipedia page is not done by me, it's more by the public,' he says. Then that's the way the public sees him. 'I personally believe in what Lyndon Johnson [36th President of the United States] said. He said, "I am a free man, an American, a

United States Senator, and a Democrat, in that order." That's the kind of philosophy I have applied in my political life,' says Deora. 'No one has the right to take control of my own views. And that coupled with the fact that I am an Indian means what I believe is right for my country has to precede what any organization believes or what any other role believes. My first duty is to my constituency, and to my job as an elected representative, when I was one.'

That pretty much sums up this 42-year-old's (born 4 December 1976) political ideology. He is quick to add, 'Party affiliation is very important but for me that is secondary to the fact that you are an elected representative or that you are a free thinker and an Indian; and in our system of politics, perhaps in the rest of the world as well, people often do it the other way round—where they attribute their identity to their party affiliation and less to their own beliefs. There are also some who do this deliberately to rock the boat and to show that they are mavericks. However, I have no such qualms. 90 per cent of the time I agree with my political party. But 10 per cent of the time when one does differ, one has every right to criticize constructively. That's the kind of approach I have always had to politics and public life.'

Evidently this is something he's been thinking about. His approach to career politics was more incidental than planned. Milind's father, the late Murli Deora, was a former petroleum minister in UPA-1 but he'd been with the Congress party for nearly four decades (joined in 1968), becoming an MP at 47. He was also the youngest mayor of Mumbai. More important than what his curriculum vitae reflects, Deora Senior's real legacy was in the goodwill he had, cutting across political lines, across industrial houses and across continents. According to his son, he would rather be remembered as a social worker, than a politician.

For Milind, his first choice of career was social work, with the family business providing a comfortable cushion—this being plastics packaging. After his initial schooling at South Mumbai's prestigious Cathedral and John Connon School (which boasts of an alumni list comprising the Tatas, the Godrejs and the Ambanis) he went on to graduate from Sydenham College of Commerce and Economics. Later he completed a BA in Business Administration from Boston University. After college he also worked with his NGO SPARSH that organized digital literacy (including the hardware) for government-aided schools.

'Ask my close friends, even now we joke that there was no way anyone saw it [politics] coming for many reasons. For one I had zero interest in it. I grew up in a family where public service was important. My father was more of a social worker than a politician. He loved getting Bill Gates to give five million dollars to eradicate digital illiteracy in India. But if you asked him "What about getting a legislation passed to do that?" Well, he would like the idea, but he would be far more excited by "Can I build a public-private partnership to do this?"' explains Milind. Adding, 'We were brought up on a platform of social service, not really politics. Guests at home were never politicians, it was kind of a rule that my mother had—don't invite politicians home for dinner.'

Rules are meant to be circumvented and even though Chez Deora is yet to host political guests at its dining table, the number of politicians at the said table did double (from one to two) when Milind contested his first election in 2004 from his father's erstwhile Lok Sabha seat—South Mumbai. By then, Senior Deora had moved on to the Upper House. It was then that the party turned to Deora Junior. 'I was 27 years old at the time, had zero political aspirations,' recalls Deora with a smile. But, of course, that did not come in the way of his ticket.

❦

It's a telling commentary on the way the Congress party functions, where a novice dynast gets preference over veteran party workers. Deora Junior was not the first nor the only dynast who has been recruited on the strength of his family name alone. The very same year also saw the current Congress heir apparent and now party president, Rahul Gandhi, contest his first election. In fact, including Gandhi, Deora and Sachin Pilot there were nearly a dozen first time dynasts, from the Congress itself, who entered the Lok Sabha for the first time. I remember dubbing the group as the 'Cub Class of 2004' for a cover story I wrote for *India Today* at the time. Milind points out, 'Some of my colleagues were contesting elections either because their father had died [and they stepped in to represent the constituency], or they were representatives of their caste. I didn't have any of these issues. [His father was alive and very influential within the Congress at the time of his debut.] My entry into politics was natural and happened very organically in a sense.' Yet, he adds, 'It took me a long while to get used to it. I liked social service, I was interested in the legislative process but definitely not interested in politics. If you are a caste leader, then politics is a natural progression. I was more about helping people and finding a solution to problems. In fact, politics came in the way of that. It was often not an enabler; it was more of an obstacle.'

'Obstacle in what way?' I ask.

'You wish things can be done faster, but that's also what democracy is about. You have to take people along,' is the answer accompanied by a sigh. If Murli Deora was around today this would raise a smile. On his very first day as an MP, as Milind was leaving for the Parliament he had surprised his father by asking, 'Oh, you're coming along too?' This got a wry rebuttal from Murli who grumbled, 'Now he thinks he is the only MP in the family.' Not only did Murli accompany his son on his first day to the Parliament but he also introduced him to most of his colleagues, even those from Milind's generation like Sachin Pilot and Jitin Prasada, because Deora Senior had known their fathers.

Milind caught a break sooner than some of the other first-timers for he was picked by the party in May 2005 to initiate the debate on one of UPA's trophy legislations—the Right to Information (RTI) Bill. First-time MPs don't get to initiate debates on flagship schemes, that too barely a year since they've been in the parliament. But prior to becoming an MP this was a subject that Milind had been interested in since the previous government had been toying with the same idea. Added to that, he had access. 'At that time I met Mrs [Sonia] Gandhi who was very keen that we do some variation of this act.'

The legislation empowers citizens to directly question the government, mandating a time-bound response to its queries. 'In SoBo [as South Mumbai is popularly known from the time it was called Bombay] many constituents would come up to me and say Mr Deora can you raise this issue in the parliament. It could be a doctor concerned about harassment by the Medical Council of India, or an exporter wanting clarity on some policy. I do remember thinking to myself that right now, the questioner has to really struggle to be heard. He has to approach his elected representative which is not always easy; the elected representative has to be open to asking that question, then that question has to be allotted time in Parliament, the government has to be willing to answer that question, and only then does the person get his response.'

In July 2011 Milind was made minister of state for communications and IT at a time when India was just about discovering social media and the world according to hashtags. Even at that time he foresaw the pitfalls of an unregulated online world and since then has maintained that 'the rules that apply to the offline world should also apply to the online world.' It wasn't a very popular stand to take for at the time the UPA government got flak for trying to police the Internet but Deora has remained consistent for the need for 'some regulation' that is not draconian but definitely not laissez-faire either.

Apart from his official role, I do feel that Milind has an unofficial role as a sort of 'new age conscience' for the party. He is quick to tune in to the mood of middle class India and doesn't hesitate to speak his mind. For instance, in 2013, at a time when the Congress was pulling out all the stops to woo rural India with sops and freebies, Deora was worried that the party was not doing enough to reassure aspirational India—job seekers, students and the middle class. He voiced this concern on more than one occasion. But four years later, on a rainy October Mumbai evening, with the benefit of hindsight, he does a rethink: 'We were actually pioneers for the middle class. Through RTI we took accountability and public scrutiny from an NGO and wholesale level to the retail level where it could be accessed by each individual. Opening up FDI in retail struck a chord with middle class India. In hindsight, when I look at it now I think we actually struck a healthy balance in UPA 1 and 2.' Perhaps the UPA was doing all that but one of the reasons why it lost to Narendra Modi in 2014 was that the middle classes felt alienated by the NGO driven outlook of both Sonia and her son Rahul.

One reason why Milind can afford to be outspoken is the unique equation he shares with the Gandhis who monopolize the party leadership. There is a backstory of trust and friendship that he inherited from his father, and thereafter built upon. Murli Deora had worked closely with three generations of the Gandhis—from Indira Gandhi to her son Rajiv Gandhi and his wife Sonia Gandhi, and thereafter, their son and current party president Rahul Gandhi.

When quizzed about his proximity to the Gandhis, Milind is candid but not forthcoming. 'You know my family has been associated with them for a long time, so it's but natural that the relationship continues. However, I have never taken my proximity to that family for granted. My politics has never been based on my proximity to them and neither do I think that's anyone's business.' He adds, 'I like to be judged on [the basis of] whether I am capable, do I have good ideas, am I trustworthy and ultimately am I reliable—because in politics reliability is very important. So, if someone comes up to me and thinks that by being nice to me they can get close to this family, then I'm quite candid about telling them that they are not going to gain anything from there. That's because I firmly believe that proximity to anyone shouldn't determine who you are or the efficacy of your politics.' He goes on to say, 'People often cement their politics based on their proximity to someone, not on their ability and to me that's really selling yourself very short. That's a good method if you don't have any talent but I have a lot of confidence in my talent and ability. So I would never want to be treated that way.'

Yet, for whatever reasons, be it proximity or a shared set of values, he and Rahul Gandhi see eye to eye on a host of issues. For instance, in the run-up to the 2014 elections, the Congress-led UPA government had passed a controversial ordinance which allowed a convicted MP to continue in office if he'd appealed the conviction. The first to protest was Deora who made his displeasure known via a tweet. A day later, Rahul Gandhi walked into a press conference and commented that the ordinance 'should be torn up and thrown away'. Although it embarrassed the rest of the party, particularly the prime minister, the move against tainted lawmakers was appreciated by the middle classes. Later when Deora took on Prithviraj Chavan, then chief minister of Maharashtra, for rejecting a report on the Adarsh Housing scam that indicted another Congressman, former CM Ashok Chavan, for allotting flats out of turn, Rahul took a similar stand against the Congress CM.

Therefore, it is interesting that though Milind claims that he is in tandem with the rest of the party 90 per cent of the time, the 10 per cent when he has differed, his party's leader has taken note—even agreed with him. Milind is quick to rubbish the 'Dual Act' script. 'First, as to whether there was some coordination between him [Rahul Gandhi] and I on the ordinance issue, there was none whatsoever. It was a mere fluke that I said something on Day One and on Day Two he echoed something similar. Speaking for myself, why a large part of my philosophy is similar to that of Lyndon Johnson, is also the nature of a constituency like South Mumbai. You can't have it any other way. The constituency respects you for your opinions and philosophies, as much as it respects you for your party's opinions and philosophies.' Explaining his stand against the controversial Ordinance, he says, 'People were tired of scandals that were appearing in the news media every day, whether or not they were true is a separate issue. But the optics of saying that we are allowing an elected representative a chance to clear their names before they lose their positions was not something that was going to be digested by the public.'

So does the constituency maketh the man? Does the fact that his constituency is predominantly an urban middle class one make Milind more sensitive to middle class India than some of his other colleagues? SoBo covers an influential acreage for its houses the Reserve Bank of India, the Bombay Stock Exchange and Antilla—residence of India's richest man, Mukesh Ambani. Naturally, corporate India, middle class issues and entrepreneurial concerns are much more on Milind's radar than your average parliamentarian.

Milind nods his head in agreement. 'Yes, it [the constituency] totally does make a difference [to one's politics]. I've been telling all my colleagues across political parties that South Mumbai is the epicentre of all aspirational politics.' Unlike the to-the-point Sachin Pilot, this Congressman gives his answers in paragraphs. So I'm not surprised when with the briefest of pauses, he goes on to explain, 'When I say aspirational, I don't just mean economic aspirations in terms of job seekers. But the trends that you see happening in South Mumbai, in terms of accountability, in terms of public scrutiny those are the trends which five or ten years later, we will see happening in the most far-flung districts of India. During the 2004 elections, I was quizzed on my entire affidavit—by constituents and by NGOs. I didn't meet a single MP in 2004 from the other 544 constituencies who had faced public scrutiny on their affidavit, not even in neighbouring constituencies within Mumbai.' He adds with a smile, 'I welcome that. SoBo is a harbinger of what's going to happen and gives a sense in which direction that wind will be blowing.'

After the 2014 Lok Sabha debacle, he was one of the first to point out that the Congress needed to find a credible narrative of its own. In the elections, the Congress party had been reduced to its lowest ever tally and even Milind had lost his seat. Soon after the defeat, he was one of the first to speak up, pointing out that the then Congress vice president needed to change his advisors. Speaking to *The Indian Express* he said, 'The question is whether the set of advisors had their ear to the ground. There were strong murmurs in the party that the people who were

calling the shots were people with no electoral experience ...
no stature, standing, respect and credibility in the party.' He was
voicing what everyone else was whispering for Rahul Gandhi
had surrounded himself with a set of laptop-toting professionals
instead of taking advice from his own party colleagues.

For the first three years after the Lok Sabha drubbing, it
seemed as if the Congress was floundering to find a way to
counter the BJP juggernaut that kept gaining strength as Modi
kept winning one state election after the other. On the eve of
a crucial Uttar Pradesh election in March 2017, I interviewed
Milind at his office in South Mumbai for NewsX. My camera
team chose the M.F. Hussain painting hanging on his office
wall as the backdrop. Dressed in a bright red shirt, Milind
matched the colours on the artwork but his words were grim.
Citing the example of the Hillary vs Trump election in the US
(2017) he said: 'The Congress does need to come up with a
credible narrative which has to go beyond criticizing the BJP
and Modi. Simply expecting people to vote for a party because
they are disillusioned with an incumbent is not a strong enough
strategy for any political party to deploy.' A fortnight later when
the BJP swept the 'cow belt' with a decisive win that decimated
the opposition, I noticed many Congress leaders were echoing
Deora.

When Rahul Gandhi undertook his nth but final image
makeover before taking over as the Congress president during
a US tour where he interacted with university students, think
tanks and professionals, he was accompanied by Deora. Deora,
who put the trip together when on a visit to Berkeley he was told
that Rahul's great grandfather had addressed the University in
1949, two years after India's independence. In fact, whenever the
Gandhi scion travels abroad for such interactions, he is usually
accompanied by Milind, whether it is to attend the Weekend

with Charlie Rose conference in Aspen (September 2015) or to Brazil and Cuba to study their healthcare system. This is only fitting for earlier it was Murli Deora who organized such events for the Gandhi family. I have a feeling that if Rahul ever becomes the prime minister he will appoint Milind as his foreign minister, in the spirit of continuity. During Rahul's 2017 visit, a US Senator told him that he was not just a friend of the Congress but also a friend of the Deoras! Interestingly, in Parliament, Milind is also known as the 'MP from Manhattan'—a name that was given to him by the BJP's Manvendra Singh.

Initially, during the party's stint in the Opposition, Milind preferred to remain on the side-lines, carrying on with his NGO work, venting his angst in newspaper columns and touring the lecture circuit, both at home and abroad. There was a lot of pressure on him to join the party's team of spokespersons because when out of power that is one way of retaining relevance and visibility. But he has consistently refused to do so, although he appears in studio debates on areas that interest him such as geo-politics, social media, the economy and Mumbai's civic issues. When I asked him whether he was deliberately keeping a low profile, he offered a logical rationale for what most others had passed off as a quirk. He said, 'I was not very interested in becoming a spokesperson of the party for many reasons. But the main reason is that a spokesperson's job is really to echo [the party line]. Let me put it this way: The nature of a spokesperson is really to drown your own opinions in favour of the party's and I find that very difficult to do. It doesn't come naturally to me, so for me the job of a spokesperson is really the toughest job to do.'

He explained further, 'If you have a strong personality and strong views then it's very tough to tell yourself that those views don't matter. Therefore, I can never be a spokesperson. At the same time, I am not denying that I am some sort of an informal spokesperson of the party—I do echo the party line when necessary and am definitely involved closely with the party.' This effectively sums up the quintessential Milind—relaxed outside, conflicted inside.

There are times when the party has had to issue a statutory warning in response to some of Milind's statements, declaring that the views expressed by the individual are his own and not necessarily the party line. For instance, when the Congress lost the Mumbai civic polls to the incumbent Shiv Sena-BJP alliance, he tweeted in frustration: 'Conclusion one can draw from BMC election results is that Mumbaikars seem content living with potholes, flooding and malaria.' When criticized for being a sore loser, he shot back: 'I'd take potshots over potholes anytime.' Not quite politically correct but there it was.

After Rahul Gandhi's elevation as Congress president in December 2017, most were puzzled when he didn't include Milind in the newly constituted Congress Working Committee. Certainly he is no mass leader, nor is he an organizational man, although he certainly fancies himself as a thought leader, and an unofficial link between the party and middle class morality. To reiterate what I said earlier, there is an equation of trust between Milind and Rahul, a rapport which doesn't come with a party post but over a shared set of values. Which is why, regardless of any party post, Milind will remain an influential sounding board in a Rahul Gandhi led Congress.

One cannot deny that Deora brings a certain freshness to the political narrative. He's certainly not one to confine himself to a stereotypical political silo but weaves his many interests into his political life, whether it's his love for gadgets (always seen with the latest iPhone), or his fondness for blues music and biopics.

During the Justin Bieber concert in Mumbai (held in May 2017) he tweeted: 'Apparently, I'm too old to be called a Belieber.' He immediately got a response from his then 39-year-old friend and colleague Sachin Pilot, who took a dig at him by tweeting back: 'Alas Milind. It seems just about everyone is younger than you, even me.'

Who says all politicians are staid and boring?

Before he became a minister in the UPA, Milind was often seen in both Delhi and Mumbai's nightclubs strumming the guitar with his band called Tightrope. He often joked with the media, 'I used to play the guitar, but now I only play the fool.' Speaking to Aditi Phadnis (25 October 2013), political editor at the *Business Standard*, he said that he quit the band once he became a minister. She pointed out that it made sense as he couldn't keep his ministerial work pending just because he had to run off to a 'gig in some corner of India'. Milind's reply was a statement only he could have made. He replied: 'Yes, it would have been disrespectful to the musicians. Music is serious business.' From anyone else the answer would be tongue-in-cheek but being Milind he was dead serious.

There is no denying that music is his foremost passion. During that conversation with Phadnis he also pointed out that there is no better place to learn about politics than through music; because for him music is not just about the lyrics, the tunes, but also its context with the times. 'When I sing a song I know how it was born, and what it went on to do. Robert Johnson is not just a blues musician. When I play a song he sang, I am channelling the black empowerment movement of the Mississippi Delta. I am a great admirer of Ravi Shankar, for what he did for the music of India, turning it into soft power for our country.'

When he went to Mali as part of a United Nations conference, he met Toumani Diabaté—the country's best-known musician. 'He played an instrument called the kora. I learnt how slaves were taken from Mali to Ghana, the songs they sang of liberation became anthems along the Mississippi. From the Rolling Stones, we learn the importance of decadence, which highlights fluidity and flexibility, allows you to be timeless,' recalls Deora.

Milind married Pooja Shetty Deora in 2007 just before the 2009 elections. Pooja is a film producer (her father is the famous Manmohan Shetty of Adlabs) but even that didn't prepare her for the drama of the campaign trail. 'I was seeing a whole new side of Milind that I didn't see earlier,' she said during one of his election campaigns. Traveling to slums and shanties that are as much a part of his constituency as the posh locales, Deora was at ease talking to traders and shopkeepers about issues that really concerned them—storm drains to market trends. 'Whether you win or lose, you sign an informal contract with your constituency,' he says, speaking as an ex-MP who is keen to win back his constituency. Through Pooja, Milind is also now familiar with the world of Bollywood and often ropes in film stars to further his cause. He got Salman Khan to attend a soccer camp that he organizes for municipal school kids, the winners of which get to go to London for a training camp with the Queen's Park Rangers. Though both deny he had a role to play in it, I do see some of Milind's wry humour in Pooja's satirical film, *Tere Bin Laden*.

In January 2018, the couple had a baby girl. Announcing her birth, Milind tweeted that he and his wife had been able to fulfill their dream, thanks to a surrogate mother towards whom they will always remain grateful. A month later when I asked him how he was handling fatherhood, he replied that he was still trying to figure it out. Sooner or later he will find out what all experienced dads know—this is one constituent he will never quite 'figure out'.

An interesting side story is that Milind and Pooja met during a cover shoot for an issue of the *India Today* magazine which featured successful young professionals. At that time I was with *India Today* and bullied Milind to pose for the cover (not an easy task for he cancelled many times, once even complaining—of all things—a bad hair day), while my colleague, Kaveree Bamzai, roped in Pooja. As a wedding gift, the *India Today* team gifted them a copy of the cover with 'Jab They Met' captioned on top (a take-off from the popular Bollywood film *Jab We Met*).

One hopes that Milind has been having 'good hair days' ever since!

JAYANT CHAUDHARY

The Renaissance Jat

In another life he'd have made a great copywriter, though one can argue that there's no bigger selling space than the political stage. Jayant Singh Chaudhary, is the vice president of the Rashtriya Lok Dal (RLD), the western Uttar Pradesh-based regional party. More importantly, he is also the grandson of India's former prime minister and Jat leader, Chaudhary Charan Singh.

Although he has been in politics for the last 15 years, it was only during the Kairana by-poll held in May 2018 that he shot to national fame, for, despite being a Lok Sabha by-poll this was one election that the entire country was watching. Kairana was a test case where the Opposition came together to support an RLD candidate against the BJP. As the man leading the Opposition's charge, a lot rested on Jayant to ensure a win because the successful outcome of this election played an important role in the Opposition strategy for 2019, but more on that later.

Kairana was also in the national eye because of its many layered caste politics. It had seen Hindu-Muslim face-offs with the former BJP MP Hukum Singh (his death necessitated the said by-poll) claiming a mass exodus of Hindus—mostly Jats—from the area. Later, this claim did not survive the test of scrutiny but it does indicate the lay of the land. The Jats and Muslims were two communities that Charan Singh had united in his rainbow coalition of MAJGAR (Muslims, Ahirs, Jats, Gujjars and Rajputs) against the upper caste hegemony. Whoever controlled this combination controlled Western UP—an area that has roughly 77 assembly and 10 Lok Sabha seats, geographically larger than the entire neighbouring state of Haryana which has 90 assembly and 10 Lok Sabha seats.

Over time, the Muslims migrated towards the SP, the Rajputs towards the BJP and the RLD was seen predominantly as a Jat party that still retained its goodwill amongst the farmers. Chaudhary Charan Singh was also known as the farmers' neta and his *samadhi* (memorial) in New Delhi is called the Kisan Ghat. However, in face of the 2014 Modi wave the RLD's account had hit ground zero—with not a single MP winning a seat. Jayant too lost from Mathura. It was time to craft a comeback and he used both the traditional and the modern methods of campaigning to do this.

First, he sent a text message to the SP leader, Akhilesh Yadav, suggesting they combine forces and fight the two by-polls due in May 2018 together instead of dividing the anti-BJP vote. Akhilesh, fresh from winning two by-polls with BSP support (March 2018), agreed immediately. The duo not only got the Congress and the BSP on board but also came up with an ingenious plan to field a SP candidate on a RLD ticket. That the candidate in question, Tabassum Hasan, was a Muslim helped unite the Jat-Muslim vote. This was important because in the 2017 state polls the SP and the RLD did not form an alliance as they were worried about antagonizing their individual vote banks (SP's Muslim base and RLD's Jat support), especially after the 2013 Muzaffarnagar clashes between the two communities.

Predictably the BJP tried to stoke this divide between the Muslims and the Hindu Jats by playing up a controversy created by the hanging of Pakistan founder Muhammad Ali Jinnah's portrait at the Aligarh Muslim University. It is here that Jayant's aspirational copywriting skills came in handy for he turned the BJP's game with a catchy slogan of his own: 'Gannah not Jinnah'. Gannah means sugarcane and this was a belt where the sugarcane farmers had been badly hit due to unpaid dues by cash-crunch-hit sugar mill owners. The slogan hit a chord. Very cleverly, and with the 'right' candidate in place, Jayant managed to turn the narrative from a caste/religion based one to one on farmers' rights. 'Let's talk about the real issues, let's talk about the farmer. That's the message we sent with that slogan,' he explains.

When I met Jayant, it was in the aftermath of the Kairana win (the RLD won with a margin of 44,618 votes). Dressed in jeans, cotton shirt and kolhapuris he made for a very new age kisaan neta. This was clearly his coming-of-age election and his Twitter timeline was flooded with congratulatory messages. The media was camped outside with interview requests and his wife, Charu, was on the phone wondering if he'd make the time for a much-needed family vacation. 'Kairana was a watershed moment,' agrees Jayant. Adding, 'Until then, I was known as the one who lost elections to Hema Malini [the Hindi film actress on a BJP ticket beat him in 2014]. Or else, as Chaudhary Charan Singh's grandson. Now I am introduced as the one who won Kairana.'

A BCom graduate from Delhi University, he completed his MSc (accounts and finance) at the London School of Economics followed by a stint with the asset management company, Lazard, before he joined politics. To my surprise, he immediately said 'Not much', when I asked him if his education helped in any way with his politics. He explained with a laugh, 'This political system is about relationships and your social skills. You have to have depth on certain issues but you also have to be an all-rounder. The leader is not expected to have domain knowledge but he should be able to build a team around him, he should be able to sustain and bring up other leaders. For me that's leadership and for that I don't need a degree.' He then added as an afterthought, 'It was good to go there and to have a stint in the private sector, it gives you perspective.'

Global perspective to play politics of caste in the Jatland, I wondered?

'I don't do politics of caste but that story has to be told. Pretending that caste does not exist is an elitist argument. Even Bar Association elections are fought on caste lines,' he said. And quickly added, 'Our demography is Muslim-Jats [Western UP]. This fabric got badly affected by the trauma around the 2013 Muzaffarnagar riots between the two communities; and the event was used by the BJP in the last elections to ensure that we don't get their votes. To counter that I do speak against "dange ki rajneeti" [politics of riots].'

How does he make his legacy relevant to today's youth that needs an immediate connect to stay interested? He admits, 'It's a challenge to get the young people to connect to the past because the attitude today is *chalo bhai* what I've got is in my pocket, now what more can you do for me. The youth vote is dynamic and no one can take it for granted. Neither can you simply hope to appeal to them because you are also young, because tomorrow some other 30-year-old will come and stand against me.'

Young Jayant is known for his one-liners which he delivers with a dead-pan face. For instance, while campaigning in the sugar belt during the 2009 polls, at a time when the BJP was busy marketing its 'Feel Good' factor, Jayant had quipped: 'It's not so much about Feel-Good, as about Feel-Gud [jaggery].' Though he had to repeat it a couple of times before the television reporter caught the joke!

Over time he's made his jokes more colloquial. During the Kairana by-poll, which became a face-off between him and UP CM Yogi Adityanath, he was accused of going door-to-door 'begging' for votes. Jayant retorted, asking, '*Inko kya khujli ho rahi hain?*' (What is tickling him?) During rallies, he carried an anti-itching ointment which he waved to the crowds, claiming that it was a gift for Yogi.

The vision of him waving Itch Guard at Yogi reminded me of an impish school boy and I told him that the idea behind this piece was that the readers could get to know the real Jayant. 'Maybe they should not get to know too much of the real Jayant,' he replied with a wry laugh.

What made him give up his corporate job and join politics right before the 2004 polls? Was it family pressure? He shakes his head at that, saying, 'My father never pushed me in this direction.' Adding with a rueful smile, 'When I quit my job, he [his father] got very angry and said *mujh se poocha bhi nahin aur naukri chod di?* [you quit without asking me?] He called Charu and spoke through Charu to me, as fathers do sometimes.' What is equally important is that Jayant had his wife's support.

His father Ajit Singh's career had followed a similar trajectory. After completing his MS from the Illinois Institute of Technology, USA, he was one of the first Indians to work with IBM. But he soon quit the private sector and joined his father's party. Jayant explains, 'I thought it would be difficult for me if I lead a normal urban life till my 40s and then quit to join politics. It's not easy to make the transition so I knew, if I have to do it, then I should do the learning curve—and the tripping, while I was still young.'

What he is still getting used to is the varying demands of his constituents. Smiling at the memory he says, 'My secretary once got a call complaining that the rains have plugged all the storm drains in a constituent's area. The exasperated secretary asked in jest, should I send the MP across to unplug it. The answer was, Yes, what time will he reach?' Jayant then remembers another anecdote that has him shaking his head. 'With cricket boards having politicians on them, there is a huge demand from the youth to get a place on the Indian cricket team. When I say I can't do that they say, *IPL toh khila sakte ho* [at least get us to play in IPL].'

At age 39 (born 27 December 1978), Jayant certainly doesn't look anything like the world-weary man of experience this statement seems to indicate. But, you can see the ease with which he straddles his two worlds with the way most of his sentences are a mix of English and colloquial Hindi. While he was eligible to fight the 2004 polls (he'd just turned 25), he waited for the next elections before contesting from Mathura in 2009. As a first time MP he spoke in favour of a pro-farmer Land Acquisition Bill and batted for FDI in multi-brand retail, arguing that it could provide an alternate avenue of employment for the aspirational GenNext from farmer families.

To me, a part of his political relevance is the way he meshes new age concerns with the politics of old. Apart from loan waivers and sugar cane dues, even environment concerns find mention in his conversations in the Jatland. He has banned the use of plastic flags and banners in his party. But can your average farmer afford the luxury to be environmentally correct? 'The environment is a concern, even with the farmers, for don't forget cancer is a big issue in Western UP as is pollution and water shortage, so even the farmers have come around to this, it's ok to be talking about environment to them. I'm not saying this is Germany where you set up a green party, we are not ready for that but if you talk about renewable energy—we spoke about it in our manifesto as well—they do relate to it. I think people are aware that our current model of growth is unsustainable.'

What about religion as a political tool? 'We are Arya Samajis, we don't follow the rituals of religion but I believe in fate, that some things work for you and some things don't. The miracle of life is beyond humans so why should god be just human centric. For me, sustaining our environment is a religious practice.' He, however, doesn't believe in the competitive Hinduism that has gripped the Opposition in an attempt to steer the majority vote away from the BJP. 'This is playing the BJP's game,' he says.

His father, Ajit Singh, has done business with the BJP—in fact, he's acquired the reputation of being an itinerant politician who will work with whichever party is in power, whether it is the BJP, Congress or the Janata Dal. He was a minister in V.P. Singh's government (1989), and when that was replaced by a Congress government, he was back again in then PM Narasimha Rao's cabinet (1991). Later Ajit Singh joined A.B. Vajpayee's government (2001) and once the Congress came back to power with the UPA, he too made a comeback as a minister (2011).

The charitable explanation for this opportunism is that a small regional party needs the perks of office to stay relevant. 'My dad did what he had to survive,' is all that Jayant would say when asked about his father's somewhat promiscuous brand of politics. But, unlike his father, Jayant is certain of one thing. He will never do business with the BJP, at least not the hardline version of the party under PM Modi. 'For me the turning point was the Muzaffarnagar riots [between Muslims and Jats]. I think what happened in 2013 affected my mental makeup and the way I judge the BJP.'

Not the 2002 Gujarat riots, I ask?

His answer is simple and to the point. '2002 is also a part of Modi, but I'm closer to Muzaffarnagar and saw what happened then. For me, there is a lot of negativity around the naked ambition that I saw then and how the BJP used that event for their political gain. My basic make-up is that I am a liberal person at heart,' he says. Clearly he has singled out the BJP for censure and not the SP that was in power in the state or the Congress that was in power at the Centre.

How does he see the churn in the opposition politics which has made an anti-Modi stand its cornerstone? 'Earlier there used to be some middle ground amongst most parties because your genesis was the same, or you agreed on certain issues but now it's *bilkul black and white ki kahani* [totally a story of either black or white], either you are with us or you are anti-national! The political environment has become very polarized, so I don't see the atmosphere as flexible anymore.' Adding, 'My father has worked with Vajpayee. There used to be more dialogue in Vajpayee's BJP with their alliance partners. Now the BJP leaders are like Voldemort, no one must mention their names. There is great fear in their own ranks.' Jayant has also penned a tongue-in-cheek limerick which is posted on his Twitter page: 'Globe trotting, Clothes strutting, Maximum gloating, Economy shutting, Liberals fretting. GUESS WHO!!' Clearly it's a thinly disguised attack against He Who Must Not Be Named.

Jayant has chosen his side in today's rather polarized political narrative. Yet, I wonder, how confident is he of the Opposition game plan which has basically come together on an anti-Modi platform. 'There is this very virulent campaign to show Modi as a demi-god sort of figure, who doesn't sleep, works 23 hours in a day, is absolutely incorruptible, has a moral fiber made of steel— this sort of super-human deification. I'd rather have someone more human as a leader rather than have someone with a god complex. Our political system and structure cannot support a god complex,' he replies. About Rahul Gandhi he says, 'He is a liberal person, has a well-rounded world view. You know where he is coming from, what he is thinking.'

Does he seriously think Rahul has a chance in a Rahul vs Modi battle? He hedges his bets on that one. 'I don't think you have to have one person as a leader. Why should we allow the BJP to set the narrative? The BJP is also not fighting alone. They are running a coalition of 46-47 parties yet it's very convenient for them to feed into the personality cult of Modi as this lone fighter, *jungle mein sher dahaad raha hai* [like a lone lion roaring in the jungle]. We will not talk personalities, we will talk about issues. We will talk about the BJP MP in my area and why he did not perform in the last five years, *tabhi toh gheroge* [that's how we will ambush them]. See, it's not one personality taking them on. In UP you have me and Akhilesh and Mayawati, if all of us can come together and we all say the same thing, then it's a strategy of encirclement.'

He met his wife Charu when they were both studying in Delhi's Sri Venkateswara College. Although politics wasn't on his agenda when they met, she supported him when he quit his job. Charu runs a multi-brand store, Zooki, in Delhi's Meherchand Market and is quite happy with her work despite Jayant routinely 'scaring' her that she may have to fight an election one day! It's easy to see he enjoys his time off with his family, having given up on his guitar as a casualty of the pressures of his political life.

Jayant's connect with the stage goes back to his school days at Delhi's Modern School where he took part in several plays, including the *Mahabharat* (where he played Duryodhan) and *Jesus Christ Superstar*. For the latter, his school awarded him a certificate for 'Creative Dancing' which was to be presented to him by the then Union Minister Madhavrao Scindia. 'But I never went to collect it. Who wants a certificate for creative dancing of all things!' He says with a boyish grimace.

What about movies, I asked and wondered if he's seen the latest Hindi blockbuster *Veere Di Wedding*. He's seen it, though he shrugged and said, 'You know there is a scene where the girls are looking through some old trunks to find an old lehenga and they find it in the very first box that they search! That strains credibility, at least they should look in a couple of trunks before they find it.'

So he is pragmatic, in a way that wouldn't quite work in Bollywood. But he is fond of art and the walls of his drawing room display works chosen by both him and his wife Charu, the centre piece being a painting by Bengali artist Subhaprasanna. Their South Delhi house with its manicured lawns and makeshift basketball court is very different from his grandfather's crowded Tughlaq Road bungalow where Jayant grew up, with cows and goats in the outhouse. 'I was very young when he died but I remember every evening the family would gather around him and we would play *tuk-tuk* [backgammon].'

Do his voters see his grandfather in this modern day

Chaudhary? 'The legacy is enormous but it's not a burden, it's more of an *ashirwaad* [blessing]. People do make comparisons, but they are the people who belong to that generation, who have seen Chaudhary sahib, *aur voh mere Dada ki umar ke hain so pyaar dete hain* [they are my grandfather's age so they are indulgent]. They do not make harsh comparisons. My father had to face the harsh comparisons because it was an immediate comparison, mine is removed one generation,' he analyses.

Jayant and Charu have two daughters, Sahira and Ilesha. He laughs and says, 'A lot of my constituents are worried that I don't have a son. They don't understand that I am happy with my daughters and don't want a son. But the older women keep giving my wife "advice" on how to have a son and once I got a call from an old man who had gone to Vaishno Devi and had the head priest on the line to give me blessings for a son!'

There is something appealing about the frank, still boyish nature of his politics, where he talks new age environment concerns in the hinterland, presents his political opponents with a tube of an anti-itching cream, and agitates against unpaid sugarcane dues. The nature of his party is such that the RLD today is relevant only in one region of Uttar Pradesh; so the best he can hope for is to be a coalition partner in a government, be it at the state or the centre. Yet, Jayant still retains enough idealism not to compromise his beliefs for the sake of a cabinet post. That is also one of the reasons why, when we are counting the leaders of tomorrow, Jayant is One Who Must Be Named!

ANURAG THAKUR

Down but Not Out

The Indian imagination is essentially ruled by three categories: cricket, politics and Bollywood. Anurag Thakur checks two of these three boxes—cricket and politics. Success came to him very early in his life, and after a tempestuous flirtation, left him as suddenly. At the time of writing this, Anurag had begun his fight back for relevance. And as we all know from Bollywood, comebacks make the most interesting tales which is why I decided to include this flamboyant, young politician in this anthology. At age 44, he is too young and too resourceful to retire hurt (born 24 October 1974).

Three years ago, this young politician from one of North India's hill states, hit an all-time high on his biodata when he became the youngest president of the Board of Indian Cricket Control of India (BCCI, the all-powerful body that administers cricket in India). This was in 2015. With his rakish looks and a stylishly trimmed French beard he added to the style quotient in the cricket stadia, and soon became a regular fixture in Lutyens' Delhi's circuit.

At the time Anurag was also the BJP's Yuva Morcha (youth wing) Chief. A fiery orator, with a flair for theatrical punchlines, he was often fielded to take on the Congress Party's heir apparent—Rahul Gandhi—during Parliamentary debates. I still recall, once when Rahul walked out halfway during one of Anurag's speeches, he made it a point to stop speaking and asked loudly, 'Arre, kahan gai voh' to highlight his opponent's absence.

Then suddenly it all went wrong. In a regime change, he saw himself relinquishing the post of the youth wing chief in January 2017. Some say this was due to his preoccupation with cricket, others pointed out that after approximately seven years Anurag had served one of the longest stints as the Yuva Morcha chief.

However, the next month dealt a harsher blow. The Supreme Court asked him to step down as the BCCI Chief in January 2017. This came after a high stakes battle between the BCCI and the courts over cricket control.

'Yes the timing is such that both the decisions came at the same time. I never expected that kind of a decision from the Supreme Court. As for being the youth wing president, I have served the longest term with three BJP presidents. Not only me, but other Morcha presidents too were also relieved,' says Anurag. And then adds, 'In a way it turned out to be a blessing in disguise. I got more time on my hand to spend in Himachal Pradesh and work on ground, amongst my people.'

I was then meeting him right after the Himachal Pradesh assembly election in November 2017. The votes had been cast but the results were not out. Anurag's house was buzzing with visitors dropping in with sundry invitations for weddings and birthdays, followed by requests for taking selfies with the young leader. Apologizing for keeping me waiting, Anurag obliged his visitors and it was a while before we could sit down for a chat.

Anurag's father, Prem Kumar Dhumal, had been a two term CM from the state and was tipped for a third term in office. The BJP, which was expected to win the state had declared Dhumal as its CM face. Yet, in a bizarre twist of fate, while the BJP won the state, Dhumal lost his seat, and hence the chief ministership. This was the third strike against Anurag. A three term MP from Hamirpur in Himachal, he had indeed worked hard, spending the last few months travelling all over the state in trains and buses.

The result, when it came a week after our meeting, robbed him of some of his swagger and I must confess, made me do a rethink as to whether he was indeed a leader of tomorrow. Yet, there is something of a fighter in this young MP, for despite his penchant for flamboyance, he is not averse to rolling up his sleeves and finishing the fight. And as he often tells me, 'Don't go by what people tell you about me. Because if there is one thing that I have learnt, it's that in politics few know what you are, rather it is the perception about you that makes you a different creature than what you really are. So many people who interact with me say, *Arre aap ke bare mein jhoot bahut bolte hain* [A lot of lies are spread about you].' He adds, 'I have been told I am arrogant and high-flying. I have paid a heavy price for this perceived image and am trying to do what I can to change that.' He stressed on the word 'perceived' making it clear that he didn't agree with said perception.

According to my sources, it wasn't just a twist of fate that defeated Dhumal, but rather the machinations within his own party. Not only did the BJP wait till the last minute before declaring Dhumal as the CM face, he was also made to shift his seat from a secure Hamirpur to the neighbouring Sujanpur. However, as Sujanpur falls within his son's Lok Sabha constituency, the loss was an even more telling commentary on the son as it was on the father.

'One cannot blame the party for this. Every election has its own dynamics and it would be unfair to blame the party leadership. My father is a committed worker of the party and dedicated his life for the betterment of Himachal. He has been an MP three times, the chief minister two times and the leader of the Opposition twice. There are no complaints and no grudges as certain events in life are beyond expectations and explanations. They have to be taken in stride and one must keep moving on,' replied a poker-faced Anurag, when I ran this theory by him at a later meeting.

But with the BJP appointing a relatively young (then 52 years old) Jairam Thakur as the CM, it does seem as if the Dhumal legacy in the state has hit a pause button. Jairam is a popular face and has been a five time MLA and most importantly has the party chief Amit Shah's trust. With the BJP leadership becoming more and more centralized it is the duo at the top— Prime Minister Narendra Modi and his deputy Amit Shah—who hold all the strings.

This is also going to be Anurag's biggest challenge. How does he retain his family's grassroots legacy and still remain relevant in this new BJP? 'Creativity and hunger to do something doesn't hinge on any post. Why work with a small heart in politics? Without being on any key post or being the chief minister, you can still do wonders,' says Anurag with a smile. Six months after the Himachal loss, Anurag was made the party's Chief Whip in the Lok Sabha. The role of the Chief Whip is to ensure discipline on the floor of the Parliament, to keep the flock together and use his cross party network to pass government legislation. This was the first sign of a comeback for the young MP as the party faced a crucial No Confidence motion on his first day on the job. The new post may not live up to his past honours but it did signify a direction change in his fortunes. It was with a defiant look, he dismissed speculation about his falling out of favour as 'rumours'. This is not a leader who is going to accept a certain turn of events but someone keen to grasp at whatever chance he's given, to make a comeback.

The state of Himachal nestles at the foothills of the Dhauladhar Range in Western Himalayas. It's largely a mountainous state with twelve districts and sends four MPs to Parliament.

A three term MP from Hamirpur in Western Himachal, Anurag won his first election in a by-poll in August 2008 with a record margin of nearly 1.75 lakh votes. His first day of Parliament was not without incident, for when he reached the legislative building he met a senior BJP leader Arun Jaitely (at that time the Congress-led UPA was in power). 'You will probably go down in the record books,' said Jaitley. Relating the story with some relish, Anurag added with a smile, 'I thought he was referring to my record margin, but to my horror he hinted that I may be an MP for just a day as the Opposition had planned to expose a Cash-for-Votes scandal against the government that afternoon.' Luckily for Anurag the government survived, otherwise it would have been back to the hustings for him.

Interestingly, he does not take his father's surname Dhumal but goes by the more generic surname of Thakur. 'I dropped Dhumal from my name in school, during cricket playing days because I wanted my own identity in life,' he explains. This led to a very interesting interaction between him and a senior Congress MP on his first day at BCCI in 2000, for when the MP heard that the young lad was from Himachal he commented that the CM was a very good friend of his and in case he needs any help in the state government, he would be happy to ensure an introduction between Anurag and the then CM—Dhumal Sa'ab!

His game plan is not new but it is agenda setting. 'We need to change both systems and mindsets,' he says. And adds, 'Why should the common man have to go to his MP for getting water, electricity connections or even health care? We are still depending on individuals, not systems. It is ironic that India has the best IT (information technology) brains in the world, yet we couldn't get access to these basic facilities online. This should be the corner-stone for our Digital India project. People should be able to access these services by right, and not as a favour done by their local MLA/MP.'

However, a favourite story of Anurag's—and one that he repeats often—is the fable of how when Napolean was told by an astrologer that he didn't have a fate line, he took out a knife and carved a long line on his own hand saying, 'Now tell me that I don't have a fate line!' Anurag enacts this tale with a flourish, telling his young audience, 'I am standing before the youth of today who will not only carve out their own future but also that of the country.'

Maybe he sees a message here for himself as well, because in Modi's BJP 'dynasty' is a bad word and his family legacy has taken him as far as it could. Now it's up to him to carve his own fate-line. A fiery speaker with a grassroot connect he has built a network of his own, both amongst the older lot and the youth brigade, and is certainly one of the more recognizable faces of the party amongst the public even more than some of his older party leaders.

❖

He has also learnt some of the catchwords that work in Modi's BJP. Anurag was the lead speaker during a parliamentary debate around nationalism in Febuary 2016, that followed after students at Delhi's JNU campus were arrested on sedition charges. Speaking passionately, Anurag made the government's case that there was a difference between being patriotic and the freedom of speech. 'This is not freedom of expression. There is a difference between the government and nation. You criticize the government, the ministers, policies and programmes. But don't criticize our country. We will not tolerate that.' The speech got him prime time ratings, and I am sure his leadership's approval.

Even before Modi made it de rigueur, Anurag used to begin and end his speeches with either a Vande Mataram or a Bharat Mata Ki Jai. He has also always been attuned to the needs of the armed forces—one reason being that for the hilly state of Himachal, the army is a major source of employment. The state lost as many as 53 of its men in the Kargil war. Dhumal was amongst the first to raise their demand for One Rank One Pension. Visiting a martyr's home and camaraderie with the soldiers have been an essential part of Anurag's political life. It's also a part of his family legacy for his grandfather and great grandfather have served in the army. 'I think it's a combination of my background and my party's ideology,' he said when I asked him about his hyped-up sense of nationalism. 'I think most Indians are patriotic at heart. It's just that I got a platform to voice my feelings.'

He points out that as the youth wing chief he had organized the 'India First' programme. In response to the stone pelting incidents that took place in the Valley in 2010, Anurag got some MPs to sign a resolution against stone pelting. They also met with some of the disgruntled Kashmiri youth. They all talked about Azaadi—but were vague about the specifics. Azaadi from what? They had no clue. They said, *Bas azaadi chahiye* [We want freedom that's all]. It sounded like a mugged-up line and got me thinking. I wanted to find out what were the sentiments about Kashmir in the rest of India. So we travelled to more than 20 states and everywhere we went we heard that Kashmir is an integral part of India. We heard slogans like *Doodh Maangoge Toh Kheer Denge, Kashmir Maangoge Toh Cheer Denge* [If you ask for milk we will give you dessert but if you ask for Kashmir we will kill you].' At the time, Anurag reached out to his party president, Nitin Gadkari, and organized a 'Rashtriya Ekta' yatra (National Unity March) from Kolkata to Kashmir in 2011. During the yatra, Anurag was arrested on the way to Kashmir to hoist the national flag, along with his party seniors like Arun Jaitley and Sushma Swaraj.

Being the head of the youth wing at a time when the party was in Opposition saw him courting arrest and being laathi-charged frequently since he spearheaded many agitations against corruption in the then UPA government. Now, of course, the bruises have faded and these are stories to be recalled over a cup of tea with friends.

On 29 July 2016, he joined the Territorial Army (TA) as a lieutenant. The TA assists the civil administration during natural calamities and can be called upon to provide units for the regular army whenever the security of the country is threatened. He created quite a stir when he walked into Parliament wearing a uniform. Speaking to the media Anurag said, 'I didn't want to be one of those who just talks. If the need arises I also want to go and fight along with our men.' A line in sync with the 56 inches chest thumping rhetoric of the PM? However, Thakur simply said, *'Dil mein jazbaa hona chahiye aur junoon'* (You have to have both the passion and the will). The flair for theatrics only adds to a political statement!

This is the kind of talk that goes down well with the populace. As mentioned earlier, the many sightings at cricket stadia ruffled some feathers back home. 'Yes cricket has its share of glamour but no one can complain that I was neglecting my duties in parliament. I have more than 95 per cent attendance there, and at the same time I was contributing to the youth wing, heading the Parliamentary Standing Committee of IT and looking after my constituency. I can multitask. The only ones who can complain that I am not giving them enough time, are my wife and kids. No one else,' he says firmly.

Anurag is married to Shefali, whose father Ghulab Singh Thakur had been a senior BJP state minister, so she is attuned to being part of a political household. Incidentally, Gulab Singh also lost his seat in the 2017 state polls. But what very few know is that the first time Anurag met his wife was on their wedding day. The then 28-year-old Anurag had gone to the US on a business trip when his mother informed him that the family had picked a bride for him and he needed to come back to meet her. 'I told my mother that if she likes her how could I then say no. So she should go ahead and fix the marriage', said Anurag. He added, 'I find such formal match-making meetings very awkward and rather find it very difficult to say no to anyone.' But instead of coming back to India he decided to first take off to London for a week's holiday, and then came back to get married.

Ironically, the only complaint in their marriage today is that Anurag just doesn't know how to say no. According to his wife he has time for everyone but his own family. Being an avid batsman, Anurag knows that there are some balls that you hit and some you duck so that comment goes without being contradicted.

There are some who would say his political career got interrupted by his cricketing one. Anurag Thakur had become the joint secretary in the BCCI in 2011. By then he had already spent time as the president of the Himachal Pradesh Cricket Association (HPCA). His first love was probably cricket not politics for he'd played for India's Under-16 cricket team, as well as the Under-19 team.

He traces his love for cricket to the time when he went to watch an Indo-Pak test match at Jalandhar's Burlton Park. The match took place a few months after India's historic 1983 World Cup win, and ended in a draw. But the sheer exuberance of being part of the atmospherics of an India–Pakistan match stayed with him. 'There was a lot of buzz about Reena Roy and the Pakistan opener [Mohsin Khan]. People bunked work and school to watch that match. The atmosphere around it was incredible,' he recalled with an excited smile. What added to the lure of cricket was how the cricket team in his school was always singled out for honours in front of everyone during the morning assembly. 'The principal used to praise them if they did well and that kind of recognition inspired me,' he admits frankly.

Many important lessons were learnt on the cricketing pitch. He remembers all too well when he was captaining the Under-16 team he got out scoring 94 and at another instance, 76 runs. 'One of the selectors told me that both the scores were treated as two half-centuries, no more. If I wanted to be noticed I had to score the entire century in one match,' he said. That's when Anurag learned that while both politics and cricket are exhibitionist sports, you also have to score to survive. In the All India Under-19 tournament that followed, he ensured that he scored 100 not out against J&K, 163 not out against Haryana, 196 against Karnataka in the semi-finals, and 128 in the finals against Baroda. (These are figures he can reel out at a moment's notice which shows how much he treasures his score card as a player.)

Thakur then quit the game in 1995 to 'handle family business in Jalandhar'; politics only happened in 2008. Around that time a Congress leader from Hamirpur asked his help to become the president of the HPCA. 'So,' recalls Anurag, 'I drove down four hours from Jalandhar to help this person but after waiting for a few hours he still hadn't shown up at the venue. We then went to his house and woke him up. He asked his wife to make him some tea. She, however, shouted back: *Jahan se roz peete ho wahin se mangwa lo* [Get it from where you order it every morning].' Shaking his head with a smile Anurag said, 'I told him to come to the hotel and I'd organize the tea.'

So while Thakur agreed to 'ensure' that the candidate from Hamirpur won the state cricket board polls, he made one request to his beneficiary—to make him a member of the Hamirpur district cricket association. 'This would help me do some work for my district,' he explained. To his total surprise, the request was declined. Anurag says the candidate's own supporters 'felt bad' that here he was trying to help him and he refused to do this in return. Thus, they insisted he should become HPCA's president. And this is how he plunged into cricket administration.

He was unanimously voted as the president of HPCA in June 2000. 'Back then, there was one typewriter, seven chairs and one *almaari* [cupboard] and not even a proper ground,' he recalls. Of course all that changed once Anurag took over for it was during his tenure that Himachal cricket—indeed Indian cricket—got its most picturesque stadium in Dharamshala. The stadium cost Rs 50 crore to build but it is the crowning glory in the BCCI stable. Later when the Congress-led government in the state tried to take control of HPCA by passing the Sports Bill, an angry Anurag retorted, 'The state which should honour us has hurt us by putting cases on us. I gave 16 years of my life to cricket. I wanted to give something back to the game as well as put my state on the map of cricket,' he says.

He was only 25 when he became the youngest president of any state cricket association in the country. To become a junior national selector, he needed to have been a Ranji Trophy player. And so, as the story goes, one fine November morning in the year 2000, Anurag walked into the dressing room of the Himachal Ranji team and announced himself as the captain for that match against Jammu & Kashmir. Although he got out for a duck he took two wickets and more importantly, got onto the board of junior selectors. Anurag naturally denies that this was the reason he played that particular match. 'If I wanted to play I could have played many times since I had age on my side. I played the last match just to motivate the team, to tell them that you are playing not just to participate but also to win,' he says indignantly. But, if this story is true, it just shows that once he sets his mind on something, he has the chutzpah to pull it off.

Chutzpah has helped his remarkable rise within the BCCI. He rose to the ranks of joint secretary in 2011. It was when the match-fixing scandal hit the Indian Premier League (IPL) that Thakur emerged from the sidelines. Since the BCCI is responsible for administering the IPL (a professional Twenty20 League), most of the officials quit after the scandal broke, but not the then BCCI president, N. Srinivasan. This, despite allegations that his son-in-law Gurunath Meiyappan, was involved in the betting. Thakur was the first board member to publicly demand Srinivasan's resignation. He says he did this purely in 'the interest of Indian cricket'. Of the four member board, two of the officials had already resigned which left only Thakur and Srinivasan on the board. Srinivasan paid no heed to his demands but it brought Anurag to the centre-stage of cricket politics. In the 2014 elections he was elected secretary, and a Srinivasan bête noire, Jagmohan Dalmiya, was elected president.

Later, after Dalmiya's death, Anurag Thakur was elected

unopposed as the BCCI president in 2015. But by then the Board was already on a collision course with the courts which were advocating transparency and reforms in the BCCI. The courts wanted the BCCI to implement the recommendations of the Lodha Committee report (headed by a former chief justice of India, R.M. Lodha). The report asked for an overhaul of cricket administration and put the onus on BCCI. But the BCCI took on a path of confrontation with the courts. The end result of this was that Thakur and a majority of the BCCI office bearers were asked to step down by the Supreme Court.

Speaking about the face-off between the courts and the BCCI, Thakur says, 'I think it was more of a media trial. Look at how it all began—it started with a betting allegation against one of the team owners [Gurunath Meiyappan of Chennai Super Kings]. He has since been cleared by the courts. The names of the suspected players who were supposed to be involved in match-fixing were given to the courts but they've never been disclosed. So, the allegations on the basis of which the court admitted the case did not go anywhere, but the courts have got involved in everything else. The overhauling of BCCI was never required, yet crores of money was spent on the Lodha Commission for this objective.' The Lodha Committee has suggested a host of reforms to curb what it refers to as 'powerful individuals' and 'coteries' which ran cricket. In the meanwhile, Anurag has moved a petition in the Supreme Court, challenging his ouster.

Does Anurag see a comeback for himself in the BCCI? Cricket administrators like former Captain Saurav Ganguly have been asking for his return. 'I have not thought about it but I am not averse to it,' says Anurag. And then asks, 'The country has to judge whether the Court's decision was right or wrong. What have they achieved and what has the BCCI lost?' He adds, 'Now retired people are running the [cricket] board. We had accepted

90 per cent of the Lodha Committee's recommendations. But the court-appointed committee could not even implement one of these suggestions though it has been in place for more than a year.'

It is easy to guess what his views would be on the debate around the issue of allowing politicians to head sports' associations. 'Why not?' he asks. 'If politicians can run the country why not the sports bodies? Can you restrict Ratan Tata or Mukesh Ambani and tell them they can't run 12 companies, please run only one? It depends on one's potential. Not all politicians do extremely well, and not all fail. Mr Jaitley and Mr Pawar have built world class stadia in Delhi and Mumbai. I welcome politicians in sports but not politics in sports.'

Certainly, if the Game of Life is about *jazbaa* and *junoon* then Anurag Thakur hasn't run out of either. Almost as if he's read my thoughts he tells me as a parting shot, his love for the dramatic all too apparent: 'Life is full of challenges. We have to accept that and live up to it. I've been a fighter from Day One even before I became an MP when the Congress targeted me over Himachal Pradesh cricket politics. I did not run away then either. Whichever field I am in, I always give my best.' He may have begun playing politics like a T20 match, but over time I think he's realized that it's more a game of Test cricket. It's not your first few flamboyant shots that count as much as your long term sustaining power.

ACKNOWLEDGEMENTS

My first words are for Samir Singh, who always manages to have the last word. He was my chief sounding board, and helped conceptualize this book from cover to content; his matter of fact observations bringing perspective when the journalist in me got carried away. There's a reason why he takes my calls with a 'How May You Be Helped Today?' Thank you, Sam, for answering every call of mine.

My mother, who read every chapter, cigarette in hand, stopping in between puffs to make an editorial point—'Darling why begin the profile with "Sachin Pilot never smiles? Is he some version of the Mona Lisa?"' That chapter has since been amended. I suspect Akhilesh and Omar will soon be invited home for tea, for both became favorites along with Rahul who gets a legacy pass because she firmly believes in the Gandhis, even in the age of Modi.

My favorites however are my brother Shiv and sister-in-law Nasim who discovered their inner 'editor' to give some surprisingly perceptive feedback. As did my nephews: Armaan who looked at a Red Porsche and said—'That's your color, Bua, but not your style'. We have taken his advice on red for cover. Kabir's version of Snakes & Ladders, where the snakes only bit Bua since they'd all become his 'friends' was a leadership lesson on how to defang the opposition.

The team at Simon & Schuster—Himanjali Sankar, who fine tuned my style with some rather astute comments in the margins. Sayantan Ghosh who has clearly finessed the cut and thrust of a deft edit. I enjoyed our brainstorming sessions where Sayantan debated with Zen-like calm, and Himanjali with a writer's passion. Also, Dharini Bhaskar who first pitched this book to me. A special thanks to the reassuring Rahul Srivastava, Managing Director S&S—who indulged every query of mine. Thanks to all of you, my fears proved unfounded. Here's to a team that also reads between the lines.

Vir Sanghvi, who not only gave me my first job but has been my Go-To (more of a Save-Me) person for every quandary I've been in ever since, which naturally included various stages of this book. (For example—Can you read a chapter to see if I'm on the right track? Also, could you write the foreword please? And er, will you also moderate the book launch?). Here's to you, Vir for being cool with a K.

Aditi Phadnis, who suggested I do this book when Simon & Schuster reached out to her. Thank you Aditi for always having my back, along with spur-of-the-moment edits. As did Rama Lakshmi and Anuja Joshi, for when you are writing a book it's only natural your friends become consulting editors and existential counsellors. Rama, who knows just how to convert a complex thought into that definitive line, which always gets me wondering 'Why didn't I think of it first?' Anuja, for teaching me a simple rule both about writing and life—Don't Over Explain. And, Seema Goswami who beat me to it, shared writer's tips.

Kartikeya Sharma, founder and promoter, ITV Network, for creating a work environment that encourages both individual creativity and institutional talent. To him and Aishwarya, for so ably differentiating between contenders and pretenders.

Colleagues from the fraternity delved into the notebooks of their minds for insights—Radhika Ramaseshan, Siddharth Varadarajan, Rohini Singh, Kaushik Deka, Sanjeev Acharya and Rasheed Kidwai. While Geeta Datta helped me sort the Introduction, for mission (and style) statements are her forte; Pankaj Sharma & Uttkarsh did some fancy camera work for my author picture. Ujjwal remains my best resource. Deepak Suryavanshi did some pretty neat sketches.

On call were Shankkar Aiyar, Pranjal Sharma, Shahana Basu, Sandeep Unnithan and Abinash Chaudhary taking snap polls on book titles and other dilemmas. As did my resourceful (Dha)BA Hons friends from Stephen's—Varsha, Nikhat, Anshu, Deep, Arjun, Ruma, Gauri, TP, Viraat—who surprised me with some neat nuggets, not to mention neater political contacts. The honours go to the group mascot, Varsha Hoon, who may not read the book but will buy the first copy that's out (It is Indi Hoon who will read it). Also, Welham '87 batch, specially the 'Divas' (Divya, Pratima, Aradhana, Sunanda, Mayuri, Anjul, Jolly and Ritu).

It sure takes a village to write a book.